Civil Life, Globalization, and Political Change in Asia

I0104684

Academics and policy-makers have grown increasingly interested in the ways that nongovernmental organizations (NGOs) may encourage better governance, democratic politics, and perhaps ultimately a global civil society. However, critics of these organizations have pointed out that NGOs tend to be undemocratic in their internal politics, speak for groups of people to whom they are not accountable through elections or financial support, and often represent the interests of people in wealthy countries at the expense of indigenous people. The main questions revolve around whether, and how NGOs actually lead to democratization, and the ways in which NGOs relate to broader global forces.

In *Civil Life, Globalization, and Political Change in Asia*, Robert Weller has brought together an international group of experts on the subject whose chapters address these questions through a series of extensive case studies from East and Southeast Asia including Japan, China, South Korea, Taiwan, Hong Kong, Singapore, Indonesia and Vietnam.

Robert P. Weller is Professor of Anthropology at Boston University, USA.

Politics in Asia series
Formerly edited by Michael Leifer
London School of Economics

ASEAN and the Security of South-East Asia
Michael Leifer

China's Policy towards Territorial Disputes
The case of the South China Sea Islands
Chi-kin Lo

India and Southeast Asia
Indian perceptions and policies
Mohammed Ayoob

Gorbachev and Southeast Asia
Leszek Buszynski

Indonesian Politics under Suharto
Order, development and pressure for change
Michael R.J. Vatikiotis

The State and Ethnic Politics in Southeast Asia
David Brown

The Politics of Nation Building and Citizenship in Singapore
Michael Hill and Lian Kwen Fee

Politics in Indonesia
Democracy, Islam and the ideology of tolerance
Douglas E. Ramage

Communitarian Ideology and Democracy in Singapore
Beng-Huat Chua

The Challenge of Democracy in Nepal
Louise Brown

Japan's Asia Policy
Wolf Mendl

The International Politics of the Asia-Pacific, 1945–1995
Michael Yahuda

Political Change in Southeast Asia
Trimming the Banyan Tree
Michael R.J. Vatikiotis

Hong Kong
China's challenge
Michael Yahuda

Korea versus Korea
A case of contested legitimacy
B.K. Gills

Taiwan and Chinese Nationalism
National identity and status in international society
Christopher Hughes

Managing Political Change in Singapore
The elected presidency
Kevin Y.L. Tan and Lam Peng Er

Islam in Malaysian Foreign Policy
Shanti Nair

Political Change in Thailand
Democracy and participation
Kevin Hewison

The Politics of NGOs in South-East Asia
Participation and protest in the Philippines
Gerard Clarke

Malaysian Politics Under Mahathir
R.S. Milne and Diane K. Mauzy

Indonesia and China
The politics of a troubled relationship
Rizal Sukma

Arming the Two Koreas
State, capital and military power
Taik-young Hamm

Engaging China
The management of an emerging power
Edited by Alastair Iain Johnston and Robert S. Ross

Singapore's Foreign Policy
Coping with vulnerability
Michael Leifer

Philippine Politics and Society in the Twentieth Century
Colonial legacies, post-colonial trajectories
Eva-Lotta E. Hedman and John T. Sidel

Constructing a Security Community in Southeast Asia
ASEAN and the problem of regional order
Amitav Acharya

Monarchy in South-East Asia
The faces of tradition in transition
Roger Kershaw

Korea After the Crash
The politics of economic recovery
Brian Bridges

The Future of North Korea
Edited by Tsuneo Akaha

The International Relations of Japan and South East Asia
Forging a new regionalism
Sueo Sudo

Power and Change in Central Asia
Edited by Sally N. Cummings

The Politics of Human Rights in Southeast Asia
Philip Eldridge

Political Business in East Asia
Edited by Edmund Terence Gomez

Singapore Politics under the People's Action Party
Diane K. Mauzy and R.S. Milne

Media and Politics in Pacific Asia
Duncan McCargo

Japanese Governance
Beyond Japan Inc
Edited by Jennifer Amyx and Peter Drysdale

China and the Internet
Politics of the digital leap forward
*Edited by Christopher R. Hughes and
Gudrun Wacker*

**Challenging Authoritarianism in
Southeast Asia**
Comparing Indonesia and Malaysia
*Edited by Ariel Heryanto and
Sumit K. Mandal*

**Cooperative Security and the
Balance of Power in ASEAN and
the ARF**
Ralf Emmers

**Islam in Indonesian Foreign
Policy**
Rizal Sukma

Media, War and Terrorism
Responses from the Middle East and
Asia
*Edited by Peter Van der Veer and Shoma
Munshi*

**China, Arms Control and
Nonproliferation**
Wendy Frieman

Communitarian Politics in Asia
Edited by Chua Beng Huat

**East Timor, Australia and
Regional Order**
Intervention and its aftermath in
Southeast Asia
James Cotton

**Domestic Politics, International
Bargaining and China's
Territorial Disputes**
Chien-peng Chung

**Democratic Development in
East Asia**
Becky Shelley

**International Politics of the
Asia-Pacific since 1945**
Michael Yahuda

Asian States
Beyond the developmental perspective
Edited by Richard Boyd and Tak-Wing Ngo

**Civil Life, Globalization, and
Political Change in Asia**
Organizing between family and state
Edited by Robert P. Weller

Civil Life, Globalization, and Political Change in Asia

Organizing between family and state

**Edited by
Robert P. Weller**

Routledge
Taylor & Francis Group

LONDON AND NEW YORK

First published 2005
by Routledge
2 Park Square, Milton Park, Abingdon, Oxon, OX14 4RN

Simultaneously published in the USA and Canada
by Routledge
270 Madison Ave, New York NY 10016

Routledge is an imprint of the Taylor & Francis Group

Transferred to Digital Printing 2007

© 2005 editorial matter and selection, Robert P. Weller;
individual chapters, the contributors

Typeset in Baskerville by
Keystroke, Jacaranda Lodge, Wolverhampton

All rights reserved. No part of this book may be reprinted or reproduced or
utilised in any form or by any electronic, mechanical, or other means, now
known or hereafter invented, including photocopying and recording, or in
any information storage or retrieval system, without permission in writing
from the publishers.

British Library Cataloguing in Publication Data
A catalogue record for this book is available from the British Library

Library of Congress Cataloging in Publication Data
A catalog record for this book has been requested

ISBN10: 0–415–34301–1 (hbk)
ISBN10: 0–415–45706–8 (pbk)

ISBN13: 978–0–415–34301–5 (hbk)
ISBN13: 978–0–415–45706–4 (pbk)

Contents

List of tables   ix

Notes on contributors   xi

Acknowledgments   xv

1   **Introduction: civil institutions and the state**   1
    ROBERT P. WELLER

2   **The Development of NGOs under a post-totalitarian**
    regime: the case of China   20
    KIN-MAN CHAN

3   **NGOs, the state, and democracy under globalization:**
    the case of Taiwan   42
    HSIN-HUANG MICHAEL HSIAO

4   **Friends and critics of the state: the case of Hong Kong**   58
    TAI-LOK LUI, HSIN-CHI KUAN, KIN-MAN CHAN, AND
    SUNNY CHEUK-WAH CHAN

5   **Civil associations and autonomy under three regimes:**
    the boundaries of state and society in Hong Kong,
    Taiwan, and China   76
    ROBERT P. WELLER

6   **From state-centric to negotiated governance: NGOs**
    as policy entrepreneurs in South Korea   95
    HYUK-RAE KIM AND DAVID K. McNEAL

7   **The development of NGO activities in Japan: a new**
    civil culture and institutionalization of civic action   110
    KOICHI HASEGAWA

 8 **The state, local associations, and alternate civilities
    in rural northern Vietnam**   **123**
    HY V. LUONG

 9 **Nongovernmental organizations and democratic
    transition in Indonesia**   **148**
    PHILIP ELDRIDGE

10 **Constrained NGOs and Arrested Democratization in
    Singapore**   **171**
    BENG HUAT CHUA

    Index   190

Tables

2.1   Types of registered social organizations in China, 2000   26
2.2   Most urgent needs of registered social organizations in Guangzhou,
      China   31
2.3   Revenue sources of registered social organizations in Guangzhou,
      China   33
3.1   Founding years and types of NGOs in Taiwan   47
3.2   Size of NGOs in Taiwan   48
3.3   Self-characterization of NGO functions in Taiwan   49
4.1   Social and political participation by types of civic organizations in
      Hong Kong   70
5.1   Major sources of income for civil associations by city   82
5.2   Types of civil association by city   86
6.1   Year founded, number, and percentage distribution of Korean
      NGOs   100
6.2   Types and number of political actions taken by Korea's People's
      Solidarity for Participatory Democracy (PSPD)   104
6.3   Types and number of political actions taken by Korea's Citizens'
      Coalition for Economic Justice (CCEJ)   107

Notes on contributors

Kin-man Chan received his Ph.D. from Yale University and is now Associate Professor of Sociology at the Chinese University of Hong Kong. His recent work includes "Towards an Integrated Model of Corruption: Opportunities and Control in China," *International Journal of Public Administration*, 23, 4 (2000): 507–51, and "When the Lifeboat is Overloaded: Social Support and Enterprise Reform in China," *Communist and Post-Communist Studies*, 32 (1999): 305–18 (with Haixiong Qiu). His current research interests focus on the development of civil society and private enterprises, and their impacts on democratization in China.

Sunny Cheuk-wah Chan is Associate Professor in the Public Administration School, Macao Polytechnic Institute. His research interests are the political economy of East Asian development, public sector management, and economic sociology. He has recently finished his doctoral thesis on "The Politics of Banking in Hong Kong" (Chinese University of Hong Kong, 2002). He has published the articles "Comparing the Social Welfare Institutions of Hong Kong and Singapore" in *Contemporary Social Issues of Macao and Hong Kong* (Macao Polytechnic Institute, 2002), and "Hong Kong and its Strategic Values for China and Britain, 1949–1968" in the *Journal of Contemporary Asia*, 28, 3 (1998).

Beng Huat Chua is Professor of Sociology and Coordinator of the Southeast Asian Studies Programme at the National University of Singapore. His research interests are urban planning and public housing, comparative politics in Southeast Asia and the emerging consumerism across Asia. His political analysis of Singapore is published as *Communitarian Ideology and Democracy in Singapore* (Routledge, 1995) and *Political Legitimacy and Housing: Stakeholding in Singapore* (Routledge, 1997). He is editor of *Consumption in Asia: Lifestyles and Identities* (Routledge, 2000). He is currently founding co-executive editor of the journal *Inter-Asia Cultural Studies*.

Philip Eldridge is Honorary Research Associate, School of Government, University of Tasmania, Hobart, Australia, following his retirement as Associate Professor of Political Science in 1997. He recently completed *The Politics of Human Rights in Southeast Asia* (Routledge, 2002). An Indonesian translation is planned of his earlier book *Non-Government Organizations and Democratic Participation in Indonesia* (Oxford University Press, 1995).

Koichi Hasegawa is Professor of Sociology at the Graduate School of Arts and Letters, Tohoku University, Sendai, Japan. He specializes in social movements, NGO activities, environmental sociology and social change. His publications include *A Choice for Post-Nuclear Society: The Age of New Energy Revolution* (Shinyosha, 1996) and *Environmental Movements and the New Public Sphere: The Perspective of Environmental Sociology* (Yuhikaku, 2003), both in Japanese.

Hsin-Huang Michael Hsiao is Research Fellow, Institute of Sociology, and Executive Director, Center for Asia-Pacific Area Studies (CAPAS), both at Academia Sinica, Taipei, Taiwan. He is also Professor of Sociology, National Taiwan University. His current research interests are local sustainable development in Taiwan and civil society and democratic governance in Asia-Pacific new democracies. His most recent books include *Sustainable Taiwan 2011* (co-author, 2003), *Exploration of Middle Classes in Southeast Asia* (editor, 2002), *Sustainable Development for Island Societies* (co-editor, 2002), *The Paradigm Shift in Taiwan* (author, 2002), and *Chinese Business in Southeast Asia* (co-editor, 2001).

Hyuk-Rae Kim is Associate Professor and Chair of Korean Studies Program at the Graduate School of International Studies at Yonsei University. His most recent work includes the edited volumes of the *Korean Studies Forum* (Yonsei University Press, 2002), *Politics and Markets in the Wake of the Asian Crisis* (Routledge, 2000), and articles in *The Pacific Review, Journal of Contemporary Asia, Asia Pacific Business Review*, and *Asian Business and Management*. His recent research interests lie in economic and social governance, civil society in East Asia, and methodology.

Hsin-chi Kuan is Professor of Government and Public Administration at the Chinese University of Hong Kong and Director of its Universities Service Centre for China Studies. He is an editorial board member of several journals in the China field including the *Journal of Contemporary China*. His main research interest lies in political culture and development. He has published in *Asian Survey, The China Quarterly, Democratization, Electoral Studies*, and elsewhere.

Tai-lok Lui is Professor in the Sociology Department, Chinese University of Hong Kong. His recent publications include *City-States in the Global Economy* (Westview, 1997), *The Dynamics of Social Movement in Hong Kong* (co-edited with Stephen Chiu, Hong Kong University Press, 2000), *Consuming Hong Kong* (co-edited with Gordon Mathews, Hong Kong University Press, 2001), and *Light the Darkness: Story of the Hong Kong Red Cross, 1950–2000* (Hong Kong University Press, 2001).

Hy V. Luong is Professor and Chair of the Department of Anthropology at the University of Toronto. His major publications include *Discursive Practices and Linguistic Meanings* (1990), *Revolution in the Village: Tradition and Transformation in North Vietnam* (1992), *Culture and Economy: The Shaping of Capitalism in Eastern Asia* (1997, co-edited with Timothy Brook), and *Postwar Vietnam: Dynamics of a Transforming Society* (2003, edited volume). His current and major projects focus on discourse, gender, social stratification, rural-to-urban migration, and political economy in Vietnam.

David K. McNeal received his B.A. in History at the University of Michigan and his M.A. in Korean Studies at the Graduate School of International Studies at Yonsei University. He is currently Adjunct Professor in the Department of English Language at the Singu College.

Robert P. Weller is Professor of Anthropology and Research Associate at the Institute on Culture, Religion, and World Affairs at Boston University. His recent books include *Alternate Civilities: Chinese Culture and the Prospects for Democracy* (Westview, 1999), *Unruly Gods: Divinity and Society in China* (co-editor with Meir Shahar, University of Hawaii Press, 1996), and *Resistance, Chaos and Control in China: Taiping Rebels, Taiwanese Ghosts and Tiananmen* (Macmillan, 1994). His work currently concentrates on environmental attitudes and behavior in China and Taiwan, and how they affect policy.

Acknowledgments

This book began as a combination of two projects. The first was a pair of workshops on Nongovernmental Organizations and the Nation in a Globalizing World, which brought together a range of scholars from various fields to discuss the role of NGOs around the world. Although this volume ultimately evolved into something focused on Asia alone, the broader discussions and circulation of papers were crucial in shaping everyone's thinking about the issues. I am especially grateful, then, for the participation of colleagues whose excellent contributions did not fit within the confines of this particular book: Arun Agrawal, Helmut Anheier, Peter L. Berger, Ann Bernstein, Mark Edelman, Peter Dobkin Hall, Saliha Hassan, Janos Matyas Kovacs, Violetta Zentai, and Annette Zimmer. I also acknowledge with great thanks the financial support of the Pew Charitable Trusts, the Bradley Foundation, and the Himalaya Foundation, and the generous hosting of the Institut für die Wissenschaften vom Menschen in Vienna and the Asia-Pacific Research Program at the Academia Sinica in Taiwan.

The second project was a collaborative research project comparing social organizations in four Chinese cities under three quite different political regimes: Guangzhou, Hong Kong, Taipei, and Xiamen. Generously funded by the Himalaya Foundation, this project led to the four papers in this volume on Chinese societies. In addition to the authors of those papers, I want to thank the other major collaborators on the project: Yang Guoshu, Huang Shunli, and Qiu Haixiong.

I also want to thank Donald Halstead, Allyne Awad, and Molly Delano Brennan, who did a skillful job copy-editing this volume. Finally, the Institute for the Study of Economic Culture (now the Institute on Culture, Religion, and World Affairs) at Boston University fostered both projects from the beginning: this book would not have been possible otherwise.

1 Introduction

Civil institutions and the state

Robert P. Weller

The confluence of several sources has made civil organizations, especially in the form of legally incorporated nongovernmental organizations (NGOs), increasingly visible and influential over the past two decades. A trend toward smaller government has swept much of the world, from China to the United States, and that has promoted greater reliance on NGOs to provide social services. International development aid has also begun to rely heavily on local civil organizations to provide social analysis and carry out programs on the ground.[1] Through a rather different dynamic, since the 1980s NGOs themselves have been insistently pushing for a stronger role in forming national and international policy, and local advocacy NGOs regularly draw on international allies for funds and to pressure their own governments. These groups are thus beginning to reframe the nation-state both from below, by taking over social functions that the state previously performed, and from above, by their ability to mobilize political and financial pressure from beyond the bounds of national politics. From bans on land mines to the needs of the environment, they try to represent interests they perceive as ill served by the current structure of markets and nation-states.

NGOs' influence was already clear by the time of the 1992 United Nations Earth Summit in Rio and was reinforced further at the 1995 United Nations Women's Conference in Beijing. Nowadays, international NGO leaders routinely get seats at major policy meetings, from the United Nations to Davos. The World Bank has been systematically including NGOs in its decision making for a decade, while the United States Agency for International Development, to cite just one national-level example, now routinely builds NGOs into all its country plans, with the explicit expectation that they encourage democracy. Academics and policy-makers have generally promoted this trend with some enthusiasm, in hopes that newly vibrant civil organizations in the form of NGOs will lead to stable democratic politics, or at least to more effective governance.

On the academic side, the most important source of thinking about issues of NGOs and democracy has been the burgeoning body of work on civil society. The events of 1989 in Eastern Europe inspired a renaissance in thinking about the role of civil society in fostering democracy. While not primarily about Eastern Europe, Robert Putnam's work on Italy and then the United States has been pivotal in bringing attention to the problem of what he calls "social capital" – horizontal ties of trust, seen especially in formal organizations – and its influence on democracy (Putnam 1993, 1995). NGOs are a particular form of this phenomenon and have created an enthusiastic literature of their own. This includes work that views NGOs as the forefront of a new global civil society as well as local and national promoters of democracy (see, e.g. Boli and Thomas 1999a; Edwards 1999; Fisher 1997).

The essays on East and Southeast Asia in this book allow us to look closely at a region that has undergone tremendous political change during the period of rapid NGO growth. Japan has been a procedural democracy for the longest period, but significant changes ensued even there as the Liberal Democratic Party's monopoly on power finally faltered; Taiwan and South Korea have undergone rapid and apparently very successful transformations from authoritarian rule to democracy; countries like Indonesia are still in the throes of a difficult change; others, including both nominal democracies (e.g. Singapore) and communist countries (e.g. Vietnam, China), have had fewer obvious structural changes in their politics, but even there we can trace attempts to shrink the direct control of government in favor of newly empowered societies.

These essays begin an empirical examination of some of the most basic questions that come out of the policy and academic literature on NGOs and civil society. NGOs have increased dramatically in all these cases, but have they been important engines of democratic transitions, or are they the result of those transitions? Do they contribute directly to procedural democracy (i.e. regular election of political elites), or do they democratize in some other, more general sense? How do they relate to other forms of social organization, especially less formally organized sectors like social movements? Phrased more broadly still, have NGOs fostered a civil society that, as it is usually formulated, will limit tyranny?

NGOs and civil society

As the authors of these essays met in various groups to discuss these issues at several workshops over the course of three years it became increasingly clear that the questions themselves might need to be rephrased. Much of the framework for discussions of civil society comes out of European cases and does not translate easily to Asia. Two problems in particular loomed large. First, the potential contribution of less modern-looking groups, especially those based on older communal ties of kinship and village or those less formally institutionalized, has generally been ignored in most writing on civil society. Second, the idea of social capital tends to underplay relations of hierarchy that characterize all organizations, which has in particular led many studies to downplay the continuing power of the nation-state. Therefore, as a group, these essays make a strong case for rethinking assumptions about the opposition between state and society.

Before turning to these issues in more detail, it is worth spending a little time on the issue of definitions, particularly of the core terms of "civil society" and "non-governmental organization." As the term has evolved in English, "civil society" has several important features (see Seligman 1992). First, civil society groups are voluntary: membership is not based on ascriptive ties of kith or kin, but on the free choice of autonomous individuals. Civil society therefore exists as an intermediate world between the family and the state. Second, civil society groups must show a basic tolerance to other groups. Recognizing the right to disagree differentiates civil society groups from uncivil societies like the Ku Klux Klan. In most uses of the term, civil society thus indicates voluntary, institutionalized groups that stand in some kind of opposition to the state.

NGOs are a subset of civil society organizations. However, when one looks at them closely, they soon become quite difficult to define. Some analysts include religious groups, while others avoid them; some insist on nonprofit status, but others do not – and so on. One result has been a confusion of overlapping acronyms that ultimately shed little light on the phenomenon: people write of NGOs, INGOs (international NGOs), QUANGOs (quasi-NGOs), BONGOs (business-organized NGOs), RINGOs (religious international NGOs), GONGOs (government-organized NGOs), CSOs (civil society organizations), NPOs (non-profit organizations), and many more. Crosscultural surveys require consistent definitions, and one influential formulation has come from Lester Salamon's group, for whom the key features are that groups be organized, private and self-governing (i.e. independent of the state), nonprofit, and voluntary (Salamon *et al.* 1999: 3–4). In many ways, this definition operationalizes the assumptions behind the idea of civil society itself.

In the end, it may be best to understand NGOs simply as the subset of social organizations created by the relevant laws of a particular state. As the essays that follow show, those laws vary widely in detail but generally include some kind of tax advantages for nonprofit status, and some definition of the minimal institutional structure and financial base to constitute an organization. Specific formulations, however, mean that very different kinds of groups may count as NGOs in different countries – lineages count in Taiwan but not in China, for instance. One particularly important line of variation is whether all social organizations outside the state must conform to these laws, or whether room is left for other kinds of less formal grouping.

The contributors to this volume share a concern about how well these definitions will work in Asia, particularly how well fundamental ideas about civil society will work. When we met to discuss these issues, it was clear that, while we were all writing about NGOs in some form, we did not share a common definition. In part, this reflected the very different legal constructions of social organizations in the various countries, but it also revealed our different theoretical perspectives. After some discussion, we ultimately agreed that a single shared definition would only cover up important differences among the cases. Each of us has been clear about how we use these terms in our essays, and readers should take the differences to represent both intraregional variations and theoretical differences among us.

Thus, when Kim and McNeal explicitly limit their scope to voluntary groups in South Korea, while Luong explicitly includes communally based groups in Vietnam, we have in part a disagreement about the nature of social organization under modernity. However, when Lui and his co-authors concentrate more on social welfare groups than the other essays, it represents primarily the particular nature of Hong Kong's legal field for NGOs.

In spite of these definitional differences, this collection seeks to push the boundaries of the literature on NGOs and civil society by questioning several key sets of assumptions. The first might be called the "modernity problem." The authors of these essays undermine the idea that only social groupings that fit standard assumptions about modernity – institutionalized and voluntary groupings of autonomous individuals, in contrast to earlier ties of religion, community, and kinship – are important to developing civil societies.[2] In fact, all the essays envision the possibility of alternate modernities or civilities that do not simply reiterate the history of North America and Western Europe.

While some of the essays retain the language of voluntary and institutionalized groups, all of them are concerned about the relationship of such groups to other forms of social organization that may be more informally organized or based on older communal ties. This view helps the authors open up issues that are crucial for understanding political transitions, like the relationship between social movements and more institutionalized groups like NGOs. This relationship tells us in part exactly how dissent is institutionalized in a society and is thus central to our consideration of political change.

Luong's essay on Vietnam, with its retired veterans' associations and Buddhist groups of elderly women, makes the most explicit case for looking at the range of local associations that do not fit easily as NGOs. But we also see such ties lurking below the surface in Chinese lineages (Chan's essay) and Singaporean Islamic groups (Chua's essay), while they are more implicit in most of the other cases. This concern with how earlier tradition interacts with the bureaucratized modernity of legally defined NGOs grows in part out of the specifics of these Asian cases. The experience of modernity is still new in each of these cases (except for Japan), and all of them show how social arrangements that are not pre-modern at all (no matter how old their histories) are vital ways through which these societies have often very successfully adapted to modernity, though an earlier generation of "modernization theory" often dismissed them as traditional and therefore irrelevant.

Another set of assumptions addressed here might be called the "social capital problem." While Putnam's work on social capital and civil society was inspirational for this volume, it has also tended to encourage a naive and sometimes romantic understanding of social groups as inherently good.[3] Some groups with lots of social capital – organized crime, terrorists, and revolutionaries, to name but a few possibilities – are of course not civil at all. More importantly, all groups incorporate inequalities of rank, and often also of gender, age, class, and all other possible markers of social difference. These can act both within groups and in decisions about who can join groups.

Of course, broadening our scope to less formally organized or less voluntary groups exacerbates the problem. While village life is often a web of multistranded social ties creating potential groups whose mobilization could affect broader political life, it is also a set of entrenched divisions that these webs of ties both reflect and re-create. As Chan notes in his essay, social protest in China often has roots in local social ties, but that need not make it civil. Political opposition itself need not be civil – that implies a mutual acceptance of the rules of the game. Both Hasegawa's essay on Japan and Kim and McNeal's on Korea show the move from social protest movements that were not always civil to NGOs that are.

Even formal groups organized along "modern" lines – that is, the lines envisioned by the legal codes in all of our cases – contain similar internal tensions. NGOs vary widely in their internal structures, although relevant laws often limit the formal possibilities. In general, however, they do not have clear mechanisms to hold them accountable to the people or causes they claim to represent.[4] For instance, some rely on the charismatic qualities of a powerful leader whose departure can mean the end of the organization – some are in fact little more than a powerful leader and some staff. This is sometimes possible when sufficient wealth allows someone to organize alone, but also through the possibilities of new electronic media (as in Chua's case of Sintercom in Singapore). Other NGOs speak for people they do not represent (e.g. peasants, minorities, the unemployed, land mine victims); that is, they are often not elected or funded by their "constituents," nor do the leaders come from those groups. Many cases are more complex than this, but overall accountability through procedural democracy – the process NGOs are said to encourage at a national level – is rare. NGOs may thus create a great deal of social capital, but the extent to which this constitutes civility may have to be qualified.

Finally, this brings us to the issue of how NGOs and other social organizations relate to the state itself. More than anything else, this book re-examines the assumptions about how an increase in social institutions may lead to political change toward democracy. The limited comparisons within Asia allow us to ask how different types of states incorporate NGOs, as even the least democratic of our cases do. Related to this is the issue of how the line between state and society is drawn. Some of our cases involve a more antagonistic relationship than others, but none allow an easy split between state and society.

The relationship between states and societies

Many models imply that state and society are the players in a zero-sum game: society can grow only if the state shrinks, and states grow only by diminishing society. This is the philosophy that has driven many state attempts to return responsibilities for many social services from the state to the NGO or other social sectors. Such thinking helped drive Ronald Reagan's policies in the United States and Margaret Thatcher's in the United Kingdom. Explanations for the rise of NGOs due to state failure use a similar logic, arguing that social organizations come to the fore when states fail to fulfill their social responsibilities. At the broadest level, these views reflect the assumption that state and society are independent and usually antagonistic entities. A civil society is thus one that successfully resists tyranny.

The idea that NGOs should represent society to the state, from a position of independence, characterizes much of the literature. NGOs themselves have worried a great deal about evidence suggesting that as much as 80–95 percent of their funding in developing countries comes from governmental or intergovern-mental (like the United Nations or the World Bank) sources (Hulme and Edwards 1997: 7). Globally, Salamon and Anheier (1994: 95) estimate that 43 percent of NGO funding comes from official sources. In exchange, NGOs give up some autonomy, at the very least by allowing heightened state oversight and regulation of their activities. For example, the leaders of Sarvodaya, an important Sri Lankan NGO that is often taken as a global model, lamented that increased financial support from external donors undermined local control and ultimately threatened to destroy their entire vision (Perera 1997). Even widely emulated civil associations like this one are not just independent representatives of society.

Even in the United States, where such views are especially prevalent, the empirical evidence suggests that NGOs are not so independent of the state. As Peter Dobkin Hall argues, the enormous growth in the American welfare state in the middle of the twentieth century accompanied and supported a rapid growth in philanthropic organizations and similar NGOs. State and society grew together, not at each other's expense. The conservative revolution of the 1980s, he writes, did little to change this in a fundamental way, but simply recognized trends that were already long established (Hall 2002). State and society were and remain closely entwined.

This kind of relationship is probably quite widespread. Shigetomi (2002), for example, argues that, in relatively poor countries with political systems open to social input (from NGOs or other social groups), NGOs will in fact push for bigger government because it promises more resources for them.

The need to question an assumed opposition between state and society is even clearer in Asia, where the underlying political principles often share little with the American founders' concern about social resistance to state tyranny. While they varied over time and space, the Confucian traditions of statecraft tended to see family, society, and state as smaller and larger versions of the same kinds of relationships: they related as microcosm and macrocosm, not antagonists. Nor was this opposition central to the Hindu or Islamic visions of the state that were historically important in much of Southeast Asia. The twentieth century saw the importation of a range of Western models of the state – colonial, democratic, communist – but all of them merged with earlier institutions and ideas. Furthermore, with a few interesting exceptions, regimes of both the Right and the Left tended to minimize state–society distinctions. These range from Lee Kuan Yu's argument that Western civil liberties are inappropriate to Asian value systems, to the totalizing attempts of Cultural Revolution China to dissolve society into the state.

Our case studies vary in how well the zero-sum or state-failure models help to explain the rise of NGOs. With its long-standing division of labor between state and society, Hong Kong may fit the zero-sum model best. The colonial history of British rule permitted a lively social sector, but only within circumscribed political limits. Anything that attempted to move beyond those limits was either carefully co-opted or forced to remain marginalized. Here, colonialism encouraged a state–society split and, according to Lui and his co-authors, little has changed since the return to Chinese control. Most of the countries described in this book experienced long periods of colonialism. However, unlike the end of colonial rule in many other cases, Chinese control in Hong Kong remains an exercise of outsiders; as a result, the split between the state and society remains more relevant than in places like Singapore or Malaysia, where colonialism was thrown off. The closest comparison to Hong Kong might be Taiwan after World War II, in which 50 years of Japanese colonial rule ended with a Chinese regime that came in from the outside. In the absence of genuine democracy above the most local levels, the nationalist state in Taiwan had trouble claiming to be the organic representative of society there.

The cases collected here suggest that a broad relaxation of state power also encourages a state–society split. The most obvious cases are the transitions from authoritarian rule in the Taiwanese and South Korean cases, where a long history of popular struggle culminated in democratic transformation. In both cases this has left a legacy of social organizations that value their autonomy from the state and are quick to question state controls.[5] Even the much milder political opening of Japan in the 1990s has helped make a state-failure model seem more compelling there. Hasegawa suggests that Japanese NGOs became more important because the long-term political status quo fell to a weakening of state control in the 1990s. However, he also finds the state-failure explanation inadequate and gives equal weight to what he calls "family failure."

Taken together, these cases suggest that colonialism and democratic openings encourage people to understand society as relatively independent from the state, and thus encourage NGO growth. While it is difficult to measure this objectively across the cases, this hypothesis appears to offer a rough guide to what the authors found. China, which had the least history of direct colonialism and is also the least democratic, appears to have the most dependent NGO sector, and autonomy is not an important goal for them (see the Chan and Weller essays). South Korea and especially Taiwan, with their histories of colonialism and popular organization against the state, are at the other end of the continuum.

All this is relative, however. As a group, these cases show only a weak sense of a state–society split, and the NGOs themselves give autonomy a fairly low priority. This is no surprise in more authoritarian states that promote an explicitly corporatist model of state–society relations in which each social sector gets one representative organization that is granted a monopoly in exchange for basic loyalty. Cultivating strategic links with political powerholders in authoritarian states is therefore a crucial strategy for NGOs. It is the only way to promote their agendas within the legal framework; indeed, it is often the only way to survive.

Even in the more democratic cases, however, the relationship between NGOs and states looks more symbiotic than antagonistic. In Taiwan, for example, a startlingly large percentage of NGO leaders try to gain better access to the state by becoming the state: they run for office (see Weller's essay). In their essay on South Korea, Kim and McNeal coin the term "negotiated governance" to describe this symbiotic relationship, and it would also work in the other cases. While the essays as a whole suggest a range in how important a state–society split is, they also show that such a split cannot be taken for granted. In none of our cases do the actors consider the autonomy of NGOs from the state to be the overriding issue that the general literature on civil society and the specific literature on NGOs seem to imply.

Social organizations under authoritarian rule

While the NGOs and other social organizations in these essays grow out of society, they represent a wide range in how autonomous they are from the state. Just as it is for many situations around the world, an antagonistic model of society versus the state does not really describe any of the Asian cases described here. One important finding related to this is that authoritarian states can work closely with an organized social sector in ways that remain stable over long periods of time. NGOs need not correlate with democracy.

While several of our cases are now democracies, none of them have long democratic histories. The longest is Japan's, which only goes back about half a century, and which a single party managed to dominate throughout most of that period. Japan was also one of the last to see really strong growth of its NGO sector: as Hasegawa discusses, it only developed systematic laws to enable NGOs in 1998. In contrast, undemocratic China vaunts its NGO sector, and all of our cases outside Japan had cooperative arrangements between authoritarian states and NGOs, either now or in the recent past.

Chua's essay shows the way Singapore carefully manages and manipulates the social sector through both legal tools and a broader ideological agenda based on the overriding need for the tiny nation's survival. The registration requirements are sufficiently vague and the ruling party's control of the courts sufficiently powerful that NGOs and similar organizations end up engaging in strenuous self-censorship.[6] Both Taiwan and South Korea also had explicitly corporatist models for the social sector before they democratized.

The People's Republic of China emulated these arrangements when it first drafted its own NGO laws, and the legally registered social sector there is also extremely cautious and conservative. Such groups are not wholly nominal – they really do lobby for the interests of the sectors they represent, but do so very gently, knowing that overstepping the boundaries will cause their demise. Chan's essay on China, for example, shows business groups pushing for their interests, but never to the point of direct antagonism. China has thousands of such thriving NGOs that cooperate closely with the state. This is typical of all our authoritarian cases, where NGOs and the state have reached a long-term accord. Such co-opted social organizations may well help improve governance by bringing the voices of their constituents to the government, but they can hardly be expected to promote competitive procedural democracy that would undermine the system they have adapted to.

Officially sanctioned NGOs, of course, are only a subset of the social organizations that exist between family and state. Even fully totalitarian regimes have not completely succeeded in snuffing out all independent social life, and the authoritarian regimes in these cases are not really trying. They typically require groups to register legally and make registration difficult; nevertheless, many unregistered organizations exist. They tend to be more informal and more localized, and their legal position leaves them open to repression. China, for example, closely monitors any groups large enough to cross provincial lines, but tends to be more relaxed about groups that remain local and apolitical.

One strategy for reform-minded groups under such a political system is to form what might be called "proxy" NGOs. These are groups that occupy the few available niches for genuine social activism under authoritarian rule, in the hope that they can eventually promote a broader agenda by applying pressure where it is possible. The same sectors seem to offer this opportunity in nearly all of our cases: environmental protection, consumers' rights, and sometimes women's rights. These issues are safe to pursue because the authoritarian regimes themselves embrace them, at least nominally. No regime can take a stand in favor of poisoning air and drinking water, of selling false merchandise to its people, or wife beating. It is no coincidence that these are the most active and boldest NGOs in China, Malaysia, Singapore, and in Taiwan before its democratization.

Groups that fail in their attempts to establish corporatist relations with the state – those that reject such relations, or that just fall below the state's ability to monitor – tend not to develop the formal trappings of NGOs. As extra-legal (or sometimes illegal) organizations, they need not meet the formal requirements of registration; in fact, formal institutionalization (legal incorporation, for instance) would only attract unwanted attention. Such groups can sometimes grow large and powerful, but their distance from the formal political machinery often reduces those with political goals to less than civil behavior. South Korea's labor and *minjung* "people's movements," whose demonstrations often became violent, were one example of this. The quick turn to parastatal group violence against Indonesian groups, as Eldridge describes, is also a legacy of their weak incorporation into politics. Lui and his co-authors describe something similar in Hong Kong, where street protest became the only outlet for groups that the colonial state did not co-opt.

Many other groups, however, appear to have few political interests and neither join corporatist arrangements nor take to the streets. They seem to thrive in the cracks left by systems of authoritarian control, and are often tolerated so long as they remain small, informal, and apolitical. While such groups are not the major focus of this book, they do crop up in many of the cases, and they have enormous potential significance, especially for consolidating an eventual democratic transformation. In the absence of strong institutional organization, such groups both rely on and help create ties of social capital that can be very important to democratic politics (see Weller 1999). Under some circumstances they can also translate directly into political action.

We can see this clearly in Luong's essay on Vietnam, where loosely organized and very local groups have become powerful agents pursuing political corruption. The most important have been war veterans' associations, which normally functioned primarily as mutual aid societies, followed by local Buddhist associations. By providing concrete mechanisms to mobilize local social ties, these initially apolitical groups have become important political players. Chua shows how Islam provides a similar undercurrent in Singapore, where it largely escapes formal state control, while Chan discusses a range of informal associations in China, like temple groups and lineages, that are important locally, in spite of their marginal legal status.

As a group, these essays show that NGOs can exist quite comfortably with authoritarian regimes, and that such accommodations can continue for many decades. Yet they also show that cracks in the system of control allow more independent kinds of social organization to survive. The danger here is that marginalized groups may have no alternative but to turn to uncivil means to promote their agendas. On the whole, social organizations under authoritarian rule are not well placed to push regimes strongly to democracy. Some have been successfully co-opted, while others are forced into nondemocratic modes of behavior. Even so, we should not underestimate their achievements. Even highly accommodating NGOs can, within limits, promote their own agendas. Furthermore, in the absence of formal democratic methods for communicating dissatisfaction to the political elite, they can in principle lead to better governance by creating a flow of information from citizens to the state.

Democratic transitions

As this implies, our evidence offers little support for the idea that formalized NGOs push authoritarian regimes toward procedural democracy. On the other hand, NGOs are part of a broader world of social ties that often does play an important role, especially through social movements. These are less institutionalized than NGOs, especially under authoritarian regimes that do not allow them a more formal structure. Some are little more than *ad hoc* reactions to immediate issues, but even they can sometimes evolve into longer-term commitments. Many environmental activists, for instance, begin with opposition to a single problem close to home, but later develop a more general commitment. While social movements are not the main focus of this book, they appear frequently as precursors to political change. The essays on Japan, Taiwan, South Korea, and Indonesia root NGOs in a background of social movements that led to political loosening (Japan) or fundamental political transformation (the other three cases).[7]

These cases suggest that large numbers of formalized NGOs are the result of political loosening, rather than its cause. In every one of our cases where there has been significant political relaxation, the number of NGOs has greatly increased soon afterwards. The most dramatic and obvious changes are in the democratic transitions of Taiwan and South Korea (and arguably Indonesia). It also occurred to a lesser extent in Japan, where an existing democratic system became more competitive, and in Vietnam and China, where political changes have created much more open space for social organization, but without any intention to democratize. At the same time, the number of NGOs in the regimes with the least political opening in recent years (Hong Kong and Singapore) has increased far less dramatically.

Significantly, we see a marked fading of the social movement sector in favor of NGOs after democratic openings. The essays on Japan and South Korea are especially clear on this. As the state becomes more willing to work openly with a broad range of social groups, some social movement activists become attracted to the potential advantages of institutionalized organizational structures and of closer ties to the state. Protest is no longer the only lever they have to effect political change under such systems.

In all cases of transition, older corporatist NGOs (or mass organizations, in China and Vietnam) may continue, with some slipping into irrelevance while others reshape themselves for the new conditions. Based on the limited evidence presented here, the "proxy" NGOs appear to have the best chance of continuing to thrive after the transition, since they are always less tied to the older regime. The particulars of the regimes involved also make a significant difference in the shape of the NGO sector that evolves. The most obvious differences are between the communist cases and the others, but we can also see more particular and local differences. As Eldridge writes in his essay, for example, the tendency toward violence in Indonesia has roots in the old authoritarian regime. He also shows how earlier conservative and liberal discourses continue to shape the NGO sector in the post-Suharto era: some invoke the ideals of harmony and consensus enshrined in the old Pancasila ideology, while others look more toward a model of antagonistic group interests leading to a redefinition of the power structure.

While the numbers of NGOs correlate with political opening up, most NGOs themselves are not democratic in their internal structures. This in itself may not be a serious problem: businesses are even less likely than NGOs to function democratically in their internal structure, but they are perfectly compatible with political democracy. More important is the issue mentioned earlier, that NGOs generally claim to represent people (or occasionally aspects of the environment) whose voices would not otherwise be heard, and whose interests are not well served by either the market or politics.[8] This problem of representation without accountability implies a fundamentally undemocratic mechanism at work, where university intellectuals become the voice of the poor, and urban professionals define the environmental interests of rural people.

Even unaccountable NGOs, however, may promote democracy in another sense. Although most do not contribute to a procedural democracy that leads to direct representation, they do democratize in a looser sense by broadening the range of voices that can potentially influence political decisions. Even with all the problems of doing this without procedural democracy, all the essays that follow show how NGOs have contributed to better governance by bringing information to the state through mechanisms that go beyond polls, ballot boxes, or democratic centralism. They thus contribute importantly to political transitions, even when they do not directly cause those transitions.

Globalizations

The enormous increase in NGOs in the last few decades, and even the spread of the idea of NGOs since the nineteenth century, reflect the waves of globalization that have swept the world over that time. This global nature has also sparked some thinking on the political consequences of their spread, encouraging some analysts to begin talking about a global civil society with NGOs as the leading edge. Boli and Thomas, for example, suggest that international NGOs are "the primary organizational field in which world culture takes structural form" (1999b: 6), while Helmut Anheier and his colleagues also argue strongly that NGOs constitute the avant-garde of a new "global civil society" (2001).

More goods, information, and people have flowed over national borders in the last few decades than at any other time in the centuries since nation-states came to dominate world politics. While world trade and migration have had earlier peaks, especially in the years before the First World War, the current trend surpasses everything that came before in both speed and quantity. Among the many structural changes that have resulted are various challenges to national sovereignty. These include, to cite just a few examples, pressure on economic policy from global rule-makers like the IMF and the WTO, the ability of international traders to influence national economies (as with currency speculation and Thailand), and the power of multinational capital flight (or just its threat) to influence national decisions.

Furthermore, global migrations, both legal and illegal, have forced a rethinking of the concept of citizenship, while the international human rights movement has similarly encouraged thinking about how the rights of individuals may supercede the rights of citizens (see Sassen 1996, 34–5). The Internet and other breakthroughs in information and communication have also helped to dissolve boundaries. To bolder analysts, these effects and others like them have been powerful enough to suggest the end of the era of nation-states. The mid-1990s thus saw two different books published under the title *The End of the Nation-State*; other influential works speak of an "emergent post-national order" (Ohmae 1995; Guehenno 1996; Appadurai 1996).

Globalization is not the simple expansion of a single world culture and economy. Instead, people everywhere have met it with reassertions of local identity, culture, and economy, though the specifics vary widely, from union demands for protectionism to religious revivals. A study of McDonald's in East Asia, for instance, shows how even this archetype of globalization can become localized (Watson 1997: 37). Several authors suggest an inherent tension between local revivals and globalization: Anthony Giddens (2000) calls it fundamentalism versus cosmopolitan tolerance; Benjamin Barber (1995) refers more cynically in his title to *Jihad vs. McWorld*.[9] This formulation does not necessarily predict the end of the nation-state, but leaves it a relatively minor player, caught between the broader antagonisms of the local and the global.

But the nation-state is clearly not dead yet. The most powerful global bodies – the United Nations, World Trade Organization, International Monetary Fund, and the rest – are structurally tied to the system of nation-states. Multinational corporations, just like international NGOs, are also ultimately grounded in the legal framework of a particular state, and many crucial aspects of the nation-state remain unchallenged, including core functions like taxation and control of armed force. Even the boldest predictions of the nation-state's demise recognize that we are still in the early stages of this transformation, and that their arguments are as much hypothetical as empirical.

In the particular case of NGOs, the essays that follow show how national structures continue to shape the sector. The national particulars of the legal code, for example, exert a strong force on how social organizations evolve – the varying models drawn from Britain, Germany, or the United States, and the variation between more corporatist and more open legal concepts of society continue to have a powerful influence on the political possibilities of the sector. The short and harsh history of the Falun Gong movement in China provides a good example of the limits of global influence. A sort of religious exercise movement, Falun Gong effectively established itself at a global level, brought in international support, and used various new media with enormous skill. The result, however, has been a backlash by the state that caused the near total destruction of the movement within China, the repression of many related groups, and the tightening of regulations relating to social organizations.

The particular focus of this volume in fact evolved out of an argument about the importance of globalization in the development of NGOs and in their broader significance. Globalization began as one of our primary foci in a series of two workshops that intended to cover all parts of the world, not just Asia. As the discussion matured, however, an interesting geographical split became apparent. Globalization and its consequences for both local and global civil society drove the discussion in the session attended primarily by the Europeanists, Americanists, and Africanists. They did not entirely agree with each other, of course, and argument centered on the extent to which loss of national sovereignty (e.g. control over South Africa's elephant population and its financial potential) was problematic. The Asianists, however, tended to find this issue far less compelling and urgent than the question of how NGOs might contribute to political transformation.

The reasons for this difference are not hard to see. Both groups could agree that the whole range of issues was significant: the difference was over what they felt most urgently needed to be addressed. One reason, of course, is that for most of the Asian countries, political transformation has been one of the most pressing and exciting issues of the last two decades. Nearly every country included here is undertaking, consolidating, or at least thinking hard about such changes. For the Western Europeans and North Americans, however, such issues seem less pressing. A second reason is simply that global pressures are not the same everywhere. The poorest parts of the world find themselves relying heavily on funds and expertise from international NGOs, and thus worry about a significant loss of their sovereignty. They are also more limited in their ability to foster their own thriving NGO sectors. The relatively wealthier Asian cases, on the other hand, tend to have livelier internal NGO developments and can afford to resist international policy pressures.

We can see a range of quite different relationships to globalization, even among the Asian countries represented in this book. Indonesia, for example, relies much more heavily on both international NGOs and intergovernmental organizations like the IMF. At the other extreme, Japan and the other wealthier cases rely little on such groups, and may even be global exporters in their own right. As Hsiao's essay shows, Taiwan is especially interesting when seen in this light: its isolated diplomatic position and relative wealth have both discouraged many international groups from operating there, and encouraged a uniquely high amount of indigenization and export of their own international groups.[10]

The possibility of working with international groups raises tantalizing visions of financial support and expert help for local groups, but it also brings significant dangers. As Chua shows in Singapore's case, for example, working with international groups, or even just relying heavily on their financial support, can leave organizations open to accusations of being un-nationalist. China (in Chan's essay) shows a very similar pattern: groups must often turn to international donors for support, but this can also undermine their moral authority at home. In Indonesia, which is currently far more open to political argument than China or Singapore, Eldridge shows that we still see a similar split, especially focused around arguments over whether the country's problems stem primarily from failings within the Indonesian political and social system or from external agents of globalization.

Various NGOs take different positions on this split. The Indonesian government does not drive the issue as strongly as China or Singapore, but it nonetheless represents a largely similar dynamic. In still other cases, the potential influence of international NGOs is simply not very high (Japan, Taiwan, South Korea) or salient (Vietnam).

In general, the groups in our case studies are aware of globalization's potentials and problems, but these issues are secondary to their individual agendas and broader political positions within their specific countries. In no case does globalization appear to have threatened the nation-state itself: more than anything else, the variations among our cases reflect the character of the particular national regime. The NGO movement quite clearly responds to globalization, but it takes quite different forms in each country, with the most obvious variation showing up between corporatist versus more fully democratic institutionalization of state–society relations and between communist and market-based histories. Let me turn to this issue of intraregional variation in more detail.

Regional diversities

While it is true that the Asianists in our workshops have strong interests in political transformations that not all the others share, it does not follow that Asia is regionally unique or united. Other parts of the world, like Central and Eastern Europe, have an equally compelling interest in the relationship between social organizations and political change. Just as important, the variation among our Asian cases is enormous.

We can see this most clearly by concentrating at first just on the three Chinese cases – Taiwan, Hong Kong, and the People's Republic of China. These cases formed the core of a collaborative research project that later inspired the broader comparisons in this volume. The essays by Chan, Hsiao, and Lui and his co-authors began with that project, although each has also grown to include the authors' other work. Weller's chapter summarizes the findings of the project as a whole. These cases come about as close as we can to a controlled experiment in the social sciences: they have long, shared, political and cultural histories and similar ties to world trade, but widely different political systems in the twentieth century and beyond.

The social role of NGOs and similar organizations among these three Chinese societies varies enormously. For example, China's history of socialist mass organizations created a legacy in the union movement and women's movement that is quite different from anything in Hong Kong or Taiwan; Hong Kong's roots in British law and its colonial history have created an NGO sector that is both more oriented to service and more isolated from some core political processes than the other cases; and while an earlier Taiwan showed us a classically corporatist pattern of social organizations, its recent democratization has encouraged more advocacy groups than the other Chinese societies and a clearer state–society split. The essays themselves show these differences in great detail. Here it is enough to point out that differences in political history appear to trump cultural similarities.

As we expand our gaze to the full range of East and Southeast Asian cases, political regime type and economic history still seem to be the most powerful shapers of the NGO sector. Among the countries represented in the cases that follow, Japan, Taiwan, and South Korea are both the wealthiest and the ones with the most developed multiparty democratic systems. In all three cases we see an NGO sector that has developed in response to new democratic openings, in which NGOs have partially replaced social movements that had arisen in response to early governments that were less open to input from nongovernmental groups. These new associations have a more stable legal position than their precursors and often strive for positive relations with government in order to achieve their goals. None of our cases show a really antagonistic split between state and society, but these three come the closest to having an independent social sector.

In spite of these similarities, the three cases also differ significantly from each other. Japan, in spite of being an older democracy and an economic powerhouse, has a relatively undeveloped NGO sector. This is partly because Japan's democracy took its basic form before the broad globalization of NGOs in the 1980s and did not develop out of the decades of social struggle that Taiwan and South Korea experienced. Korea, as Kim and McNeal explain, is unusual for having an NGO sector dominated by a few enormous umbrella groups that cover an enormous range of issues – a kind of social version of its *chaebol* business groups. The reasons behind this pattern still require further research.

China and Vietnam are the two communist cases, and both have followed similar trajectories away from the old mass mobilization model of state–society relations to a more corporatist model. For social organizations, this has meant the end of the monopoly of the old mass organizations (e.g. unions, peasant associations, youth leagues, women's federations) and the creation of a new NGO sector, but one heavily dependent on government ties. Registration procedures are stringent and aim more at political control than financial accountability – just the reverse of the situation in Japan, Taiwan, and South Korea. Political autonomy is not a realistic possibility or even strong goal for most NGOs in China or Vietnam.

However, both of these countries have very active sets of ties at the local, informal level, probably as a result of the obstacles to creating formal social institutions in each (see the essays by Chan, Luong, and Weller). Under these regimes we tend to see a split social sector, characterized by a gulf between a well-institutionalized and politically cautious formal sector and a set of small, local, weakly organized, informal groupings. The informal groups are not NGOs but can have important civil consequences – they are the main mechanism for the frequent expression of rural unrest in China, and Luong's essay shows how they are affecting politics in northern Vietnam.

Compared to the other cases, Singapore (and Malaysia, which is similar) falls somewhere in between. In spite of its nominal democracy, Singapore, like China and Vietnam, has a very tightly controlled social sector. Like Japan, South Korea, and Taiwan, however, it lacks the history of mass organizations and attempts at totalitarian dissolution of society into the state. Singapore has a legal system that allows for a social sector but has copious mechanisms allowing for groups to be disbanded. The result, as Chua shows in his essay, is that most groups self-censor quite effectively, so that more draconian legal penalties only rarely come into play. The government also combines repression of dissent with an attempt to deliver goods and services to voters, which has led to high degrees of political apathy.

Nevertheless, other possibilities remain. While Chua shows how other kinds of social ties, like Islam, remain active below the surface in Singapore, Indonesia before the 1998 fall of Suharto might have been described in similar terms. That country remains very much in a state of flux, but Eldridge's essay shows the ways comparable underlying social resources could become mobilized under a new political situation.[11]

Hong Kong is unique among the cases collected here. Although it has now returned to the political umbrella of China, it has a longer and much more recent colonial history than any of the others. The legacy of this is another social split that partially resembles what we see under all the more authoritarian regimes, and especially in Vietnam and China – one set of organizations was co-opted into close work with the government, while all others were either marginalized or forced away from the political arena into service delivery. On the other hand, as long as they avoid politics, the nonpolitical groups have considerably more freedom of organization and activity than we see in the other cases. Chinese rule has so far not fundamentally altered this situation, although attempts to revise the sedition law and recent large demonstrations may indicate the beginnings of a change.

Is there anything particularly Asian in any of this? Culturally, probably not. The similarities among these cases stem instead from their shared economic and political features. By world standards, these are all relative economic success stories, even in the aftermath of the financial crisis of the late 1990s. This means they have relatively little dependence on intergovernmental organizations or foreign-based international NGOs compared to much of Africa and Latin America. They vary, of course, from wealthy Japan to struggling Indonesia, and in these essays we can see that concern over ties to foreign funding becomes more pressing as countries depend on them more. As a region, however, these countries show relative independence from international funding. This volume thus reflects less worry about national policy autonomy or about northern NGOs taking over southern ones than comparable work on other parts of the world.

Compared to the general literature on NGOs, these studies found a relatively close working relationship between NGOs and the state. This is especially obvious in the more authoritarian and corporatist cases, where NGOs tend to come to terms with the nature of the state, rather than pushing for democracy. Yet even in newly democratic Taiwan and South Korea, which have developed the strongest state–society split, most NGOs appear to work within some concept of "negotiated governance," as Kim and McNeal put it. In fact, these cases suggest that assumptions of such a split may grow more out of theoretical presuppositions than empirical evidence. Rather than showing the fundamental difference of the Asian cases, they suggest the need to re-examine these assumptions elsewhere.

Notes

1 For details on this process in the World Bank, see Fox and Brown (1998).
2 Work on NGOs has gravitated toward such assumptions in part because of assumptions about how modernity works, but also because legally institutionalized groups are far easier to track using the formal survey methods that have most shaped the literature.
3 Much earlier work on social movements and "moral economy" had a similar effect. See, for example, Scott (1976) and Thompson (1971).
4 For a general discussion of this problem, see Fox and Brown (1998).
5 Indonesia may develop in similar ways, but the changes there are still so recent and the situation so unstable that it is too early to draw conclusions.
6 Malaysia also permits a lot of social organizations, but the corporatist legal framework and the threat of coercion also keep them docile.
7 Note that in his essay Hsin-Huang Michael Hsiao uses the term "NGO" in a broad sense that includes both formalized NGOs and the social movement sector. He does this to call attention to the relatively institutionalized nature of the social movement sector in Taiwan.
8 The Kim and McNeal essay on South Korea and Eldridge's essay on Indonesia bring this problem up most clearly.
9 Thomas Friedman makes the same point in his title reference to *The Lexus and the Olive Tree*, where the Lexus is the world economy and ownership of olive trees is what people fight over locally (2000).
10 These wealthier cases successfully resist direct political influence by international groups, but they remain very much part of broader globalization processes based on market exchange and information flow.
11 The fiscal crisis of the late 1990s and Anwar Ibrahim's *Reformasi* policies similarly resulted in more political room for NGOs in Malaysia.

References

Anheier, Helmut, Marlies Glasius, and Mary Kaldor. "Introducing Global Civil Society." In *Global Civil Society 2001*, edited by Helmut Anheier, Marlies Glasius, and Mary Kaldor. Oxford: Oxford University Press, 2001.

Appadurai, Arjun. *Modernity at Large: Cultural Dimensions of Globalization*. Minneapolis: University of Minnesota Press, 1996.

Barber, Benjamin R. *Jihad vs. McWorld*. New York: Times Books, 1995.

Boli, John, and George M. Thomas. "INGOs and the Organization of World Culture." In *Constructing World Culture: International Nongovernmental Organizations since 1875*, edited by John Boli and George M. Thomas. Stanford, CA: Stanford University Press, 1999a, pp. 13–49.

——. "Introduction." In *Constructing World Culture: International Nongovernmental Organizations since 1875*, edited by John Boli and George M. Thomas. Stanford, CA: Stanford University Press, 1999b, pp. 1–10.

Edwards, Michael. *Future Positive: International Co-operation in the 21st Century*. London: Earthscan, 1999.

Fisher, Julie. *Nongovernments: NGOs and the Political Development of the Third World*. Bloomfield, CT: Kumarian, 1997.

Fox, Jonathan A., and L. David Brown, editors. *The Struggle for Accountability: The World Bank, NGOs, and Grassroots Movements*. Cambridge, MA: MIT Press, 1998.

Friedman, Thomas L. *The Lexus and the Olive Tree: Understanding Globalization*. New York: Anchor Books, 2000.

Giddens, Anthony. *Runaway World: How Globalization is Reshaping Our Lives*. New York: Routledge, 2000.

Guehenno, Jean-Marie. *The End of the Nation-State*. Minneapolis: University of Minnesota Press, 1996.

Hall, Peter Dobkin. "Philanthropy, the Welfare State, and the Transformation of the American Public and Private Institutions, 1945–2000." Presented at the Workshop on NGOs and the Nation in a Globalizing World. Vienna, 24–6 May 2002.

Hulme, David, and Michael Edwards, editors. *NGOs, States and Donors: Too Close for Comfort?* New York: St. Martin's Press, 1997.

Ohmae, Kenichi. *The End of the Nation-State: The Rise of Regional Economies*. New York: Free Press, 1995.

Perera, Jehan. "In Unequal Dialogue with Donors: The Experience of the Sarvodaya Shramadana Movement." In *NGOs, States and Donors: Too Close for Comfort?* edited by David Hulme and Michael Edwards. New York: St. Martin's Press, 1997, pp. 156–67.

Putnam, Robert D. *Making Democracy Work: Civic Traditions in Modern Italy*. Princeton, NJ: Princeton University Press, 1993.

——. "Bowling Alone: America's Declining Social Capital." *Journal of Democracy*, 6, 1 (1995): 65–78.

Salamon, Lester M., and Helmut K. Anheier. *The Emerging Sector: An Overview*. Baltimore, MD: Johns Hopkins University Institute for Policy Studies, 1994.

Salamon, Lester, Helmut K. Anheier, Regina List, Stefan Toepler, and S. Wojciech Sokolowski. *Global Civil Society: Dimensions of the Nonprofit Sector*. Baltimore, MD: Johns Hopkins Center for Civil Society Studies, 1999.

Sassen, Saskia. *Losing Control? Sovereignty in an Age of Globalization*. New York: Columbia University Press, 1996.

Scott, James C. *The Moral Economy of the Peasant: Rebellion and Subsistence in Southeast Asia*. New Haven, CT: Yale University Press, 1976.

Seligman, Adam B. *The Idea of Civil Society*. New York: Free Press, 1992.

Shigetomi, Shinichi. "The State and NGOs: Issues and Analytical Framework." In *The State and NGOs: Perspective from Asia*, edited by Shinichi Shigetomi. Singapore: Institute of Southeast Asian Studies, 2002, pp. 1–33.

Thompson, E.P. "The Moral Economy of the English Crowd in the Eighteenth Century." *Past and Present*, 50 (1971): 76–136.

Watson, James L. "Introduction: Transnationalism, Localization, and Fast Foods in East Asia." In *Golden Arches East: McDonald's in East Asia*, edited by James L. Watson. Stanford, CA: Stanford University Press, 1997, pp. 1–38.

Weller, Robert P. *Alternate Civilities: Democracy and Culture in China and Taiwan*. Boulder, CO: Westview, 1999.

2 The development of NGOs under a post-totalitarian regime

The case of China

Kin-man Chan

Introduction

China's economic reforms since the late 1970s have not only dramatically changed its economic structure by expanding the scope of markets and private owner-ship, but have also had major impacts on the social and political arenas, changing it from a totalitarian to a post-totalitarian regime (Linz and Stepan 1996: 44–5). One indicator of this political change is the expansion of social space for people to associate with each other in the pursuit of common interests and values, as can be seen from the exponential increase in the number of NGOs during this period. However, since the regime is far from being liberal–democratic, these NGOs have to constantly negotiate with the state on where their boundaries will be drawn.

Contrary to the expectation of most Western observers, these NGOs do not always struggle for independence from the state. Rather, they may strategically turn to the state to secure the political and economic resources required for their development. On the other hand, if they need to seek funds from foreign sources, such as US-based foundations, even organizations established by the party–state will strive to cut their official connections to make themselves eligible to receive foreign support. This happens more frequently in certain types of social groups in Beijing and other major coastal cities. In this respect, globalization, in terms of funding from developed countries, enhances the independence of NGOs in countries like China, where the regime is still suspicious of any autonomous social force and the people have yet to fully appreciate the significance of supporting civil society.

Economic reforms, liberalization, and the transition from totalitarianism

The reforms in China over the past 20 years follow Deng Xiaoping's ideas on restructuring the economy while maintaining political stability. Their focus is to give market and private ownership a more important role in economic devel-opment. Before these reforms were implemented in the late 1970s, all farms and factories in China were owned by different levels of state authorities under its command economy. Markets were minimally involved in allocating goods and determining prices, and private enterprises and farms were prohibited in the name of socialism. One result of this was the extensive wastage and low-quality production that are so typical of the "soft budget constraints" in most socialist countries (Kornai 1989: 45).

The eradication of markets for goods and labor also made people completely dependent on the state for meeting their basic needs. Before the reforms, the Chinese people were organized into different types of *danwei*, or work units (Walder 1986), especially in state enterprises in cities and production teams in rural areas. Their jobs were assigned by the state, usually for life, and workers could only enjoy social welfare provisions such as housing, medical care, and pensions through these units. Furthermore, since these goods and services were not available in the market and people could seldom change jobs, they were completely controlled or "encapsulated" by the state.

During the Cultural Revolution, China in many ways resembled a totalitarian regime as defined by Linz (Linz and Stepan 1996: 44–5). First, there was no significant economic, social, or political pluralism: the Chinese Communist Party (CCP) had a monopoly on power and allowed no space for a "second economy" or "parallel society" to develop. Second, communism as the official ideology provided a basis for policy formation and a sense of mission for leaders and their followers. Third, the party–state initiated extensive mobilization of people on a massive scale for political movements and development projects, while private life was decried. Fourth, as a charismatic leader, Mao ruled with undefined limits and great unpredictability. Recruitment to the top leadership was highly dependent on an individual's ideological commitment and Party performance. The only problem with this totalitarian imagery is that it emphasizes overt conformity to the state while it neglects subtle resistance to the regime, including people using personal connections with officials to circumscribe state power in everyday life (Walder 1986; Scott 1990).

The reforms that began in the late 1970s were the regime's response to the stagnant economy and legitimacy crisis that had emerged earlier in the decade. The expanded role of markets in the economy led to the reinvention of private markets in rural areas as well as the "separation of the state from enterprises" in the cities, which had significant implications for the restructuring of state–society relations. State enterprises were given more autonomy in what they produced to meet market demands. As a result, factory managers put aside their political role in controlling workers and focused on making their enterprises profitable: they took steps to improve their products and services, cut back welfare packages, and even laid off unproductive workers. At the same time, skilled workers were rewarded with higher salaries, and a labor market gradually emerged. In the past few years, many state-owned enterprises have been privatized or even gone bankrupt, signifying the state's determination to retreat from directly interfering in the economy. This fundamental change will eventually lead to the loss of political control over the people through the work unit system, as workers find jobs as well as goods and services through markets (Walder 1991).

The development of private enterprises has also dramatically changed the landscape of wealth distribution. In 1978, the proportion of industrial output accounted for by state enterprises amounted to 80.8 percent – by 1986 it had declined to 68.7 percent and in 1997 to a low of 26 percent. During those two decades, the state lost its monopoly on the economy, while the blooming of the second economy created a middle class comprised of private entrepreneurs, managers, and professionals. The state then donated some resources to the budding civil society and began to liberalize the social lives of the people to reduce political tensions and promote consumption and production.

These social and economic changes have gradually brought China close to what Linz defines as post-totalitarianism. First, limited social and economic pluralism (though without political pluralism) has emerged, especially with the phenomenal growth of the second economy. Second, though the guiding ideology still at least officially exists, the commitment to utopia has weakened: "socialism with Chinese characteristics," "primitive stage of socialism," and the paradoxical "market socialism" are examples of how doctrinal Marxism has been diluted. Third, only sporadic mobilizations have been launched to achieve a minimum degree of conformity and compliance with the official agenda: boredom, withdrawal, and ultimately privatization of the population's values have become accepted facts. Fourth, top leaders are seldom charismatic. Recruitment to top leadership is restricted to Party officials, but leaders increasingly come from technocratic backgrounds. This transition to a post-totalitarian regime has now opened up spaces for the development of NGOs.

Small government, big society: the role of NGOs in the reform era

When Zhu Rongji was made premier of China, his vigorous program for furthering marketization and streamlining bureaucracy made the first meeting of the Ninth National People's Congress (NPC) in 1998 a milestone in China's reforms. But because the spotlight was on the Chinese political leader's determination to tame state intervention in the economic arena, little attention was paid to its implications for the role of society. In fact, the government's report to the ninth NPC stated that, along with the plan to cut the size of the government, "intermediate social organizations," a social structure to mediate between individuals and the state resembling NGOs, should be promoted to enhance the development of market socialism.

This idea of restructuring state–society relations has been much discussed in recent years. At the First National Conference on the Management of Social Organizations, held in September 1992, a state councilor suggested that "small government, big society" would be a trend in China's political reform.[1] In 1993, participants at another official conference reiterated the suggestion that a new form of social administration under the Chinese socialist market economy should be created.[2] They argued that "social organizations" (*shehui tuanti*) such as business, professional and social service organizations should play a more active role in linking the Chinese state with business, as well as social and cultural sectors. They also urged that social organizations should be given more autonomy to achieve the "three selves" (*sanzi*) – self-governance, self-management, and self-support (*zizhu, zili, zili*) – in order to become truly nongovernmental.

The state therefore encouraged the development of NGOs, as they could assist it in implementing a new form of social administration in several ways (Chan 1999). First, the economic reforms required state enterprises to be market oriented, so that these enterprises would eventually have to face "hard" budget constraints. As these enterprises could no longer rely on government departments or planning commissions to enhance their production and sales, business organizations and especially industry associations and research societies with close ties to industries were swiftly established to promote market exploration, technological advancement, and other common concerns.[3]

Second, China's economic reforms created a large group of enterprises, professionals, and workers in the private sector who were not subject to political control or welfare provision in state work units. New forms of organization, like associations of private enterprises and lawyers' associations, were therefore needed to serve as bridges to the state, so these organizations could when necessary seek government support (e.g. applying for visas for business trips).

Third, the economic reforms created many social problems like unemployment, inequality, and increased pollution, but at the same time greatly reduced the state's welfare commitment to workers through traditional work units. Many NGOs were established to tackle these issues with impressive developments in the areas of environmental protection, women's services, and providing basic education in the country's impoverished interior regions.

Fourth, the emergence of more leisure time due to the state's promotion of consumption (by, for instance, reducing the work week from six to five days) and people's withdrawal from politics encouraged the development of hobbies and other cultural and religious pursuits. Since the work units could not cater to these needs, NGOs like hobby and friendship groups grew phenomenally. The development of NGOs in China can therefore be seen as an emerging public space catering to the social needs that the state, families, and markets could not accommodate.

The transition from a totalitarian regime has, however, left many public issues unresolved. Some of these are partially absorbed by families, such as laid-off workers who are financially supported by their families (Chan and Qiu 1999a); others are absorbed by the market, such as the handling of some communities' sanitation and public order problems by property management companies. But many other problems are either beyond the capabilities of families to solve or do not provide profitable market opportunities, and it is here that the "third sector" or NGOs emerge as public responses to these problems.

Citizens' participation not only provides an alternative way to solve problems and fulfill needs more effectively, but also creates "social capital" in terms of trust, norms, and social networks that the state and markets are unable to produce. The Chinese government readily understands that these NGOs could become an independent force that could threaten the regime at time of crisis like the 1989 Democracy Movement in Tiananmen Square. The government has therefore imposed strict legal and administrative controls over these groups, to ensure cooperation from these groups and to minimize their potential danger. As a result, many of them are not really nongovernmental, and researchers find it extremely difficult to identify the NGOs in China.

Distinguishing NGOs from other registered groups

If an NGO is defined as an unofficial, not-for-profit, autonomous and voluntary organization that aims at enhancing social and economic development (Zhang 1995a: 94; Shaoguang Wang 2001: 382–3), then some NGOs might exist in China, in the form of "registered intermediate organizations." These are legally established groups which aim at mediating among members within certain sectors of society, as well as between sectors and the state. There are three types of registered groups.

First are the "social organizations" (*shehui tuanti*) registered under the Regulation on the Registration and Management of Social Organizations, which was promulgated in 1989 and amended in 1998. Section 2 of the 1998 regulation defines social organizations as nonprofit organizations voluntarily established by Chinese citizens to pursue common goals. This definition closely resembles the Western concept of NGOs.

The second type of registered group is the nonprofit organizations (NPOs, *minban feiqiye danwei*) registered under the Provisional Regulation on the Registration and Management of Mass Nonenterprise Units, which was promulgated in 1998. Section 2 of this regulation defines NPOs as organizations providing not-for-profit social services. They can be established by enterprises, social services agencies, social organizations, or other social forces, including individuals using nongovernmental assets. Unlike the social organizations, these NPOs usually do not have a membership. They include organizations like social services agencies, schools, museums, and so on.

The third type of group includes foundations (*jijin hui*) registered under the Management Method of Foundations of 1988. This type is defined as "mass, not-for-profit organizations that exercise management over funds donated by Chinese and foreign organizations and individuals. Their objectives are to assist the development of scientific research, education, social welfare and other public services" (Zhang 1995b: 523).

Before the CCP took power in 1949, many social organizations, such as guilds, academic associations, student bodies, and religious and philanthropic organizations, had been quite active (Zhang 1995a: 95). An estimated 26,126 of these groups with a total of more than 5 million members were active in the areas controlled by the Nationalist regime, along with 9,982 commercial and industrial organizations (White *et al.* 1996: 19). They were later abolished or replaced by state-controlled social organizations, especially after the promulgation of the Provisional Method for Registration of Social Organizations (*shehui tuanti dengji zanxing fa*) in

1950. By 1965 only 100 social organizations at the national level and 6,000 plus at the local level remained (Kang 2001: 4).

The number of these groups is believed to have grown dramatically during the reform period that started in the late 1970s, but accurate figures are lacking. One internal source estimates that there were 1,600 social organizations at the national level in 1989. However, after the implementation of the Regulation on the Registration and Management of Social Organizations in 1989, the number of social organizations at the national level declined to 1,200 and to 80,000 at the local level.[4] Since 1991 the number of social organizations can be determined by using the *China Civil Affairs Statistical Yearbook*. It shows 107,304 social organizations in 1991, with their number peaking at 184,821 in 1996. A new round of stringent inspections was then carried out before and after the new amended regulation was enacted in 1998, and by 2000 their number had dropped to 130,768. These figures indicate how the growth of social groups, including NGOs, is curtailed by the state's vigorous registration procedures. Each year, thousands of social organizations are removed from the registration list: 35,236 registrations were cancelled in 1999 alone.

An analysis of the 1998 regulation shows that the Chinese government is promoting a form of social administration similar to "corporatism" (Schmitter 1974; Unger and Chan 1995; Chan 1999), a system of interest representation in which a limited number of constituent units are created and recognized by the state as monopolizing representatives of their respective sectors. The aim of this system is to create consensus and cooperation within and across different sectors and to facilitate rules based on interest representation.

The 1998 regulation stipulates that only one social organization of its kind is allowed to register within the same administrative region, which has largely curbed the growth of social organizations in China, including NGOs. The regulation also stipulates a practice of "dual supervision" in which each organization must find a relevant state unit (government department or official social organization) that will be its "business supervisory unit" (*yewu zhuguan danwei*) and then register with the civil affairs departments at different levels. The supervisory unit is then responsible for inspecting the organization's activities and finances, a burden that discourages government units from sponsoring any registration applications unless there are material interests or personal connections involved. Many organizations are therefore unable to register because they fail to find sponsors. This regulation helps the state steer the direction in which these groups develop (Kang 2001: 4). Academic, business, and professional groups are the main types of social organizations to have registered successfully (Table 2.1).

Ever since the Falun Gong incident, when a religious group was declared an "evil cult" after launching a sit-in outside the central government's headquarters in 1999, the government has rigorously inspected many "associational groups," like friendship and hobby groups. In fact, early in 1992 the government issued an internal circular that discouraged the establishment of alumni clubs.[5] This indicates how the state encourages the development of social groups in the economy-related sector for pragmatic reasons rather than out of respect for freedom of association.

Table 2.1 Types of registered social organizations in China, 2000

Type	No.	%
Academic	40,152	30.7
Business	36,605	28.0
Professional	34,849	26.6
Associational	16,361	12.5
Foundations	1,273	1.0
National*	1,528	1.2
Total	130,768	100.0

Source: *China Civil Affairs Statistical Yearbook, 2001*

*Note: Indicates total registered social organizations at the national level.

The practice of dual supervision also enables the supervisory units to intervene in the selection of these organizations' leaders. In fact, most leading positions in these organizations are occupied by the leading figures from their supervisory units, while their assistants are usually officials who have transferred from these departments. White's study showed that 77 percent of social organizations were led by party–state officials (1996: 135). Only cultural, sport, and religious organizations are able to elect their leaders by using relatively democratic methods (Wang *et al.* 1995: 157).

In our 1997 survey in Guangzhou, we found that the boards of directors in about 50 percent of the social organizations were completely filled by government officials (official), some 30 percent were partly filled by government officials (semiofficial), while only in 20 percent of the cases were the boards filled by ordinary members (popular) (Chan and Qiu 1999b). The first and second types are usually called "GONGOs," for government-organized nongovernmental organizations (White *et al.* 1996: 112), while the third type is closest to the Western idea of an NGO. Using this 20 percent figure as a yardstick, we estimate that in 2000 approximately 26,000 registered social organizations in China could be considered authentic NGOs in the Western sense.

Friends of Nature (FON), established in 1994 by the historian Liang Congjie, is one such group. This NGO focuses on environmental education and habitat–wildlife conservation and has developed and published a primer of environmental readings for schoolchildren and organizes field trips and summer camps. Its conservation efforts focus primarily on the golden monkey in Yunnan (a western province), where the local people's logging practices threaten the monkey's habitat. FON takes this advocacy seriously by mobilizing its members to write letters and send petitions to central government officials, with additional support from the media (Knup 1997).

Another example is the Guangzhou Handicapped Youth Association, established in 1986 by a group of handicapped persons. The association receives no funding from the government, and its board of directors is elected from among its members. The association organizes student volunteers from a teacher's college to provide home help and tutoring services to its members. It also organizes monthly mate-matching activities and runs a hotline that provides counseling services for its members.

As for the second type of registered intermediate organizations called "mass nonenterprise units," or NPOs, government statistics show that there were 3,489 in 1998, 4,508 in 1999 and 22,654 in 2000 (*China Civil Affairs Statistical Yearbook 2000–01*). However, many more have yet to register with the government; one scholar estimates that in 1999 the number of NPOs could have been as high as 700,000 (Sun 2000). NPOs are also subject to dual supervision, and though few studies have been conducted on these organizations the impact of supervisory departments on their autonomy should be similar to the NGOs.

One well-known example of an NPO is the Luoshan Civic Center in Shanghai, a social service center run by the Shanghai YMCA as designated by the Social Development Bureau of the local government (Zhu 2001). Another example is the Global Village Environmental Culture Institute of Beijing (GECIB), established in 1996 by Liao Xiaoyi. Supported by Liao's personal savings and small grants from overseas, the institute is staffed by a few workers and focuses on two main areas: producing a series of television programs, including a weekly television program, *Time for Environment*; and efforts to popularize reuse and recycling among Beijing households (Knup 1997; Sun 2000).

In the mid-1990s, the total number of foundations in China reportedly exceeded 300, of which 48 were national foundations (Zhang 1995b: 524); by 2000 their total had reached 1,273 (Table 2.1). Chinese foundations vary in scale, functions, and official affiliations. They can be organizations that look for funding, or they can dispense existing funds; they can rely on state funding to implement programs preset by the state, or they can provide a public service on behalf of an enterprise. The 1988 Management Method specifies that foundations should have an endowment of no less that 100,000 renminbi (RMB), or around US$12,000; they should not be led by government functionaries; national foundations shall apply to and be approved by the Bank of China and must then register at the Ministry of Civil Affairs, while provincial foundations shall be approved by the provincial governments and register at the provincial Civil Affairs departments (Zhang 1995b: 523).

Examples of the wholly government-funded foundations include the National Science Foundation and the National Social Science Fund. Among nongovernmental foundations, some, like the Beijing Philharmonic Orchestra Foundation, rely on membership fees, which are usually low; some, like the China Foundation for the Handicapped, rely on donations but also receive substantial state funding; while others, like the China Zhenhua Foundation (for the sciences), rely entirely on social donations, including international contributions. The first and probably the country's most successful foundation is the China Youth Development Foundation, which was founded in 1981 by the Central Committee of the Chinese Youth League of the CCP. By the mid-1990s, it had already succeeded in providing tuition for 540,000 children and had built more than 200 schools for children in underdeveloped areas through Project Hope (Zhang 1995b: 524–7).

Searching for NGOs among the unregistered groups

Beside the registered groups discussed above, there are two types of NGOs that are not registered with the Civil Affairs Department. The first type is "patronized intermediate organizations," which are groups that are sheltered by government units, state or private enterprises, official social organizations or registered intermediate organizations. The second type is "unregistered intermediate organizations," or illegal groups.

Various factors lead to the formation of these patronized (*guakao*[6]) groups. Some NGOs limit their scope of activities within certain government units or social organizations, so it is natural and legal for them to become subsidiaries of these umbrella organizations. Others may find themselves unable to meet the requirements for registering with the Civil Affairs Department, perhaps because similar registered organizations already exist in the same administrative region. Still others may deliberately seek to avoid the strict registration requirements and regular government inspections.

In some cases, these patronized groups organize activities that are way beyond the scope of their patron organizations, so that they could be deemed to be in violation of the regulations. Gao argues that over the past 20 years many "breathing exercise" (*qigong*) groups took this form to develop their networks. But as long as these groups serve the purposes of their patron organizations or at least do not bring trouble to them, their activities are protected under this quasi-legal status. Gao also observes that, beside enterprises, universities are one of the most common patrons for these NGOs (2001).

One example is the Women's Legal Studies and Service Center at the Law School of Peking University. The center was established in 1995 by a group of law school students, lawyers, and professors. By 2000, it had pro bono provided more than 6,000 legal counseling sessions to the public and represented more than 260 underprivileged women in legal actions. However, Guo Jianmei, the center's director, reports that the center faced many difficulties when it began, especially from government pressure due to its poor understanding of NGOs, insufficient legal and policy support, and lack of local funding (2001).

Although patronized groups are immune from direct inspection by the Civil Affairs Department, they can be under even stricter scrutiny from their patron organizations. For example, a famous university has promulgated an internal regulation on the administration of student bodies that requires them to apply for university permission before any activities are held, while they must seek permission from higher-level authorities for activities involving more than one organization inside or outside the university. In this case, patronized groups enjoy even less autonomy than some registered groups (Gao 2001).

Unfortunately, no systematic study of these patronized organizations has been conducted to assess their number and types, much less their degree of autonomy. What is certain, however, is that thousands of NGOs avail themselves of this semilegal protection to successfully circumvent the state's policy of limiting the growth of NGOs, regardless of how closely they may be monitored by their patron organizations.

Compared with the types of organizations discussed so far, the unregistered intermediate organizations, or illegal organizations, are the most "nongovernmental." They comprise:

1   traditional groups that receive sufficient support from their communities and local governments, so they do not bother to seek legal status;
2   advocacy groups that may not fulfill the requirements for registration but enjoy enormous support from their communities;
3   loose friendship or regional organizations that refuse to become formalized;
4   underground organizations whose existence may not be tolerated by the authorities.

Unfortunately, no systematic survey has been conducted of these groups either, so it is difficult to estimate their number.

The first type of illegal group includes traditional organizations like the "flower club" (*huahui*) in Beijing, as well as the "incense club" (*xianghui*) and the "temple club" (*miaohui*) in rural areas. These indigenous religious groups were quite active even after the CCP took power in 1949 but were forced to halt their activities during the Cultural Revolution from the late 1960s to the late 1970s. Following the economic reforms, however, these groups have revived remarkably. They collect donations from residents in their communities to organize religious activities, help the needy, and improve the local school environment. Although these groups do not seek legal status, they find ways to attain legitimacy in their communities, sometimes through traditional rituals, or by displaying souvenirs sent from, and photos taken with, government officials during public ceremonies. Moreover, since local governments always invite these organizations to help make important festivals a success, their activities extend beyond their localities (Gao 2001).

The second type of illegal organization includes environmental groups like the Green Earth Volunteers (GEV), founded in 1997. GEV organizes activities that are carried out by volunteers who generally pay their own way in order to participate in various projects, such as planting trees in the Engebie Desert. They also organize weekly discussion sessions on environmental issues. Since there are similar environmental groups in China, GEV may not qualify to register with the Civil Affairs Department. But as the founders preferred their informal style of organization and were confident that their existence was supported by the community, they decided not to seek registration (Knup 1997; Sun 2000). However, in 2003, GEV became a patronized group under the Society for Chinese Culture Study.

One of the reasons the authorities tolerate these unregistered environment groups is that China has adopted a very progressive environment-protection law. The authorities therefore find it difficult to crack down on groups that, often through educational programs and media advocacy, promote a cause that the state itself embraces. But not all advocacy groups have the same luck. In 1998 the Chinese government cracked down on an NGO "corruption monitor" based in

Henan province after it failed to register with the Civil Affairs Department as a national NGO promoting clean government. The group was denounced by the government for having illegally organized cross-regional activities, though it was obviously suppressed because of its political sensitivity and ambition to expand beyond a confined region. The authorities also deemed the existence of the group unnecessary, as "the state had already established a sound system to monitor the problem of corruption."[7]

The third type of illegal group includes many friendship (e.g. alumni) and regional groups (*tongxiang hui*), especially those established by rural migrant workers staying in coastal towns and cities. Members of these groups usually come from the same province or home town. These informal organizations provide assistance (e.g. job search and accommodation) to members, to help them settle in these unfamiliar places. They sometimes even represent members in negotiations with employers during labor disputes (Man 2001). They are tolerated by the authorities, so long as they remain a loose network and do not publicly organize collective actions.

The fourth type of unregistered organization is the underground organizations the state finds intolerable. Autonomous workers' unions are one example. In some coastal regions, like Guangdong, the authorities have cracked down on NGOs like the Male Migrant Workers' Association and the Female Migrant Workers' Association. An internal document shows that, by August 1994, 27 workers' associations and/or committees had been established by workers and retired employees in state-owned enterprises in 14 provinces. With their mission of fighting for "work, survival and food," these NGOs demanded that the authorities pay their overdue salaries and pensions.[8] Other underground organizations include religious groups, such as underground Christian churches and Falun Gong. They are under constant surveillance and their members may from time to time be forced to receive "thought education."

State funding, donations, and NGO autonomy

The above discussion shows that, while the state needs NGOs to help meet the social and economic needs that have emerged in the new era, it is worried that they might turn into an independent political force that challenges the regime. The state's solution to this has been to institute corporatist practices, such as requiring dual supervision in registration, selecting only a limited number of representatives in each sector, and regular inspections. But while the number of registered NGOs has been curtailed, many NGOs have responded by seeking protection from patron organizations or by attaining legitimacy without any legal status. However, this legal aspect only partially structures the state–NGOs relationship. Another important dimension concerns the source of NGOs' resources. This section discusses whether the state's subsidies to NGOs may erode the latter's autonomy and how NGOs have strategically responded to this issue.

One of the most difficult problems faced by the Chinese NGOs is lack of funding. In 1997, there were 1.6 million NPOs in the United States with an average annual income of $625,000. This is equivalent to 81 times the income of the largest environmental group in China, Friends of Nature (Sun 2000), and many other Chinese NGOs have far fewer resources. For instance, the Association for Handicapped Youth in Guangzhou collected only 3 RMB (less than 40 cents) in annual membership fees from each member in 1998. It relies much more on donations from enterprises to operate. This includes its premises, located on the second floor of a shabby old building, which means that its members, who are handicapped, must climb a long flight of stairs to reach the office where many of the activities are held.

Our survey of a coastal city shows that half the registered social organizations claim that their most urgent need is for more government funding (Table 2.2), and that some are willing to exchange their autonomy in order to secure these resources (only 6.8 percent indicated that having more autonomy is their most urgent need). Some NGOs deliberately invite government officials to join their boards of directors and turn themselves into semiofficial organizations just to get access to official resources in terms of direct subsidies or political connections that may facilitate their development.

For example, two private enterprise associations, one founded in Beijing, the other in Guangzhou, are both NGOs established by small businessmen. Without any political connections in the government, these associations encountered many difficulties in making visa applications, joining overseas exhibitions, and other activities. Both organizations eventually gave up their nongovernmental status and began working closely with the Bureau of Industry and Commerce (Yu and Li 2001; Chan and Qiu 1999b). Here, this "invited state intervention" can be viewed as a strategic decision by the NGOs to create space for their own development, when many public problems can only be solved with the cooperation of party–state officials.

But NGOs seeking direct state subsidies will be disappointed, because the government has been withdrawing its financial commitment, due mainly to the state's insufficient financial capability (Wang and Hu 1994). These social organizations are instead being encouraged to become financially independent through membership fees and service charges, and by establishing economic entities. As a result, the state's control over NGOs through financial means is weakening.

Table 2.2 Most urgent needs of registered social organizations in Guangzhou, China

Needs	*% (No.=145)*
More autonomy	6.8
More legal and policy support	10.1
Reduce legal and policy constraints	1.2
More government concern and cooperation	16.4
More government funds	49.2
Other	16.3
Total	100.0

Our survey in a coastal city documented the sources of revenue of these registered social organizations (Table 2.3).

Some 48.1 percent of these organizations were financially independent from the state, as they had not received any funds from the government. But since some of them had received "other subsidies" from their supervisory units, such as state enterprises or official social organizations, only 38.2 percent were completely financially independent from the state. On average, state subsidies and "other subsidies" constituted 29.6 percent and 7.4 percent of their revenues respectively, a level below the global average (see Weller's introduction). In some smaller cities in southern China, most social organizations have been able to maintain financial independence from the state.[9]

Nevertheless, without sufficient subsidies from the government, the financial situation of these organizations is bleak. Only a few are able to provide commercial services or establish their own economic entities. Thus, in our survey, the percentage of social organizations that collected more than half of their revenues through service charges or profits from their enterprises was only 3.5 percent and 5.9 percent respectively, while, on average, service charges and economic entities accounted for only 5.9 percent and 6.4 percent of revenues.

Social organizations find it difficult to raise funds from donations. Some argue on the one hand that the expanding middle class and growing number of private enterprises have become a significant source of donations. Youth participation in voluntary service is also impressive (Deng 2001). However, others argue that the lack of civic consciousness and the breakdown of institutional trust due to corruption during the reform era have deterred people from making donations (Sun *et al.* 2001). In our study, only 4.7 percent of registered social organizations could rely solely on donations – these were mainly foundations, charity groups, and religious bodies. On average, donations accounted for 13 percent of the revenues of social organizations, while members' fees accounted for 31.8 percent of revenues and was the single most important source of revenue.

The financial situation is so constrained that many of the organizations we surveyed believed their financial situation to be either "difficult" (42.7 percent) or "very difficult" (26.4 percent). As government funding has become increasingly inadequate, these organizations will have to seek funds from their communities as well as overseas, and some official and semiofficial organizations are gradually turning themselves into nongovernmental organizations to achieve this purpose. Zhang (1995a: 97; 1995b: 526) found that many government-designated social organizations and foundations, including the National Social Science Fund, were exploring ways to loosen their ties with the government in order to be able to get resources from more diverse channels. In our study, one of the leaders of a youth organization explained how its Party background had made it difficult for them to solicit donations from Hong Kong and overseas; they were therefore becoming a genuine NGO so they could be more financially independent. Thus, the lack of state funding has implicitly pushed many social organizations to rely more on community support.

Table 2.3 Revenue sources of registered social organizations in Guangzhou, China

Proportion of revenue	Source (%) (No.=149) State subsidies	Source (%) (No.=147) Other subsidies	Source (%) (No.=150) Service charge	Source (%) (No.=149) Economic entities	Source (%) (No.=148) Member fee	Source (%) (No.=151) Donation	Source (%) (No.=147) Others
0 %	48.1	86.1	85.8	89.7	34.0	69.8	87.7
Less than half*	27.9	8.0	10.7	4.4	38.6	20.2	8.8
More than half **	15.4	1.7	1.4	4.2	14.5	5.3	2.6
100 %	8.6	4.2	2.1	1.7	12.9	4.7	0.9
Total	100.0	100.0	100.0	100.0	100.0	100.0	100.0
(Mean)	(29.6)	(7.4)	(5.9)	(6.4)	(31.8)	(13.1)	(4.4)

* By combining original data ranging from 1% to 49%.
** By combining original data ranging from 50% to 99%.

To conclude, most Chinese NGOs are in the primary stage of development and are striving to survive. They have become "resources driven" and are willing to exchange autonomy for resources. Our study also showed a contradictory tendency: NGOs that seek political or economic resources from the government may turn themselves into semiofficial groups, while official and semiofficial groups that seek financial support from their communities or overseas may turn themselves into NGOs.

Thus, in some cases, the status of a social group could be a result of a strategic decision on how to attain resources. In light of this, some semiofficial groups should not be overlooked, simply because they do not fit the Western conception of NGOs. In fact, one study argues that many of these semiofficial groups are in fact embedded in civic culture, while many autonomous or illegal groups, especially those in rural areas, lack civic consciousness (Qin 2001).

This brings us to the question of what constitutes civil society. Gellner argues that not every set of autonomous groups creates a civil society. He illustrates his claim with reference to some traditional societies in which the individual is caged in by kinship groups. In his view, civil society depends upon the ability to escape any particular cage; membership in autonomous groups therefore needs to be both "voluntary" and "overlapping" if society is to become civil (Hall 1995; Gellner 1995). It is therefore important to also look at the cultural side, when we examine the development of NGOs with civil society in China.[10]

The more immediate implication of the resources-driven phenomena concerns the relationships of these social groups with the government and overseas NGOs. For instance, whether these social groups choose to enter a closer relationship with the state depends on the importance of political versus financial resources in serving their members' needs, and the importance of the state versus the local community as well as overseas NGOs in obtaining more resources. These strategic decisions are also constrained by the nature of the social groups concerned and their locale: many foreign foundations may prefer to support certain types of NGOs located in Beijing or major coastal cities. Accordingly, the following section turns to these overseas donations and their implications for the development of NGOs in China.

Globalization and the development of NGOs

If financial resources affect the relationship between the NGOs and the state, then it is worthwhile exploring globalization in terms of the funding from developed countries' NGOs to NGOs in China. This section discusses the sources, the amount, the usages and impacts of this overseas funding for China's NGOs.

Sources

The Ford Foundation of the United States, Germany's Ebert Foundation, and the Japan Foundation all have offices in Beijing. Other active foundations, such as Oxfam, the Asia Foundation, Luce, the MacArthur Foundation, the Rockefeller Foundation and Rockefeller Brothers Fund, and the Lingnan Foundation of the

United States, may not have their offices in China, but do have very focused areas of interest there (Zhang 1995b).

There is no clearly defined way for foreign NGOs to register in China; thus there is a multitude of forms. By 1998, more than 30 foreign NGOs had entered China through the International Economic and Technology Exchange Center and the China Association for the Cooperation of International NGOs. These NGOs have now sponsored more than 200 projects in more than 20 provinces (Ding 1999: 56). Other NGOs, like the Ford Foundation, are registered with the Industrial and Commercial Bureau.

Amounts

While we have no reliable estimates so far on the total amount of funding received from foreign NGOs, we can use some examples to illustrate the contribution of these donations. By 1999 the Friends of Nature (FON) had received 2.52 million RMB in contributions; some 79,000 RMB were from membership fees and the rest were from donations. Of these, foreign foundations had contributed 1.32 million RMB (around $160,000), or 52 percent of the total sum. As of the same year, Global Village (GECIB) had received a total of $390,474 from the Ford Foundation, World Wildlife Fund, and other NGOs and enterprises (Sun 2000).

In fact, no Chinese foundation has its own self-generated endowment: most of their funding comes from overseas, and Hong Kong businesspeople are one of the major sources. For instance, one-third of the donations received by the China Youth Development Foundation for Project Hope are from overseas with 90 percent from Hong Kong firms, businesspeople, and individuals. Zhang (1995b: 527) estimates that overseas donations account for 60 percent of many national foundations' total financial resources.

Uses

Foreign donations have covered a wide range of social and economic development projects, particularly in the areas of women, environmental protection, public health, poverty, and education. For example, the establishment of the legal aid center at the Law School of Peking University was supported by the Ford Foundation, while the women's hotline run by the Beijing Red Maple Women's Counseling Service Center, which has counseled more than 40,000 callers since 1992 (Xingjuan Wang 2001), was supported by the Global Fund for Women and the Ford Foundation, while the training of the online counselors was supported by the UNDP and the Turner Foundation.

Foreign NGOs like Save the Children Fund, Oxfam, and World Vision International concentrate their donations in the western region of China for fighting poverty, environmental protection, community development, education, and health. They set up successful models of development, train local talent, and enhance the transmission of technology (Deng 2001). The Ford Foundation, the Asia Foundation, and the Rockefeller Foundation also support many academic activities, such as conferences held by the Chinese Association of American Studies (CAAS). By the mid-1990s, the Ford Foundation had already contributed a total of $50,000 to CAAS in support of its academic publications (Zhang 1995a: 103–4).

Impacts on Chinese NGOs

The above discussion shows that foreign donations have contributed significantly to the establishment and maintenance of China's NGOs. Foreign funds have also helped train local talent; for instance, the Institute of Environment and Development and the Beijing Environment and Development Institute were founded by graduates of the Rockefeller Foundation's Leadership for Environment and Development training program (Knup 1997). Cooperation with foreign governments and NGOs has also helped restructure Chinese NGOs to become more transparent; the China Youth Development Foundation has, for example, changed its internal audit system due to the criticisms received from Hong Kong newspapers and collaborators. Continuous interactions with foreign NGOs have provided Chinese foundations many opportunities to learn from their experiences, systems, and mobilization strategies (Gu and Gan 2001).

In sum, foreign NGOs, and especially foundations like the Ford Foundation, have made substantial contributions in financing the establishment and main-tenance of many NGOs in China that might not have been able to receive government funding and whose contributions cover a wide range of areas including women's issues, environment, poverty, education, and public health. This funding has not only prevented some NGOs from having to turn themselves into semi-official organizations, but it has inspired some official or semiofficial organizations to restructure themselves as NGOs. Foreign funding can also improve the standard of NGO management, by sponsoring training programs for local talent and by pushing China's NGOs to meet international standards in their accountability systems.

However, this foreign influence on the development of Chinese NGOs can create tensions with the state, which continues to control this sector through strict legal and administrative measures. Foreign subsidies to these NGOs are welcome, so long as they do not fundamentally disrupt these corporatist arrangements. This also depends very much on whether the Chinese government trusts these foreign foundations and on China's changing foreign relations, especially Sino-US relations. The Chinese government has witnessed the global mobilization of both Falun Gong and Tibet's independence movement and keeps a close watch on NGOs receiving foreign assistance.

But this is not exceptional when compared to other Asian countries. In this book, Chua's essay (Chapter 10) shows how foreign donations to NGOs in Singapore are so closely scrutinized by the government that many do not accept foreign funding, while Eldridge's chapter on Indonesia shows that, when NGOs become too dependent on foreign funding, they may become targets of national resentment at a time when there is a growing suspicion towards the international community.

Chinese NGOs also need to be very prudent in striving for survival and autonomy. Either they trade their autonomy to gain political or economic resources from the state or they risk becoming politically suspect by accepting foreign funding. The long-term solution to this problem is to develop a donation culture so that the NGOs can rely on local giving, in addition to state and foreign subsidies, so that they will be able to negotiate more space for developing a truly autonomous third sector.

Conclusion

The economic reforms and political liberalization that have taken place in China over the past two decades have not only expanded the scope of markets and private ownership, but the withdrawal of the state from direct management of enterprises, the reduction of political control and welfare packages in state enterprises, the general improvement in living standards, and the time and space allowed for private and associational lives have all created needs and opportunities for NGOs to develop. But the potential of these NGOs to evolve into a liberal civil society – an autonomous social structure against the state – also poses a threat to the post-totalitarian regime. The Chinese state has responded by imposing various legal and administrative measures, particularly some corporatist arrangements and close supervision, to scrutinize these emerging social groups.

Following the 1989 Democracy Movement and the 1999 crackdown on Falun Gong, the Chinese state has become even more cautious in granting social groups legal status. The number of social organizations as a major form of registered social groups has been dropping in recent years, and most of the applications that are approved are groups of an academic, business, and professional nature. Religious, advocacy, and even friendship groups are discouraged from developing. Our study also found that around 80 percent of these social organizations were official or semiofficial in their governance structure, while 20 percent of them were truly run by their members.

But many more NGOs are able to get around state controls, either as patronized groups or without any legal status. The former seek protection from universities, state enterprises, or other established social groups; the latter include traditional kinship and religious groups, loose friendship and regional groups, advocacy groups that enjoy great community support, and underground political and religious organizations. While some of these groups may not fit the Western definition of an NGO, they have the potential to promote societal interests and to check the power of the market and the state, while the truly civil organizations are still constrained by the authoritarian regime.

The decline of the financial capacity of the Chinese state has also eroded its control over NGOs. Many registered groups complain that they are short of government funding and have gradually become resource driven. Some strategically invite government officials to join their governing boards, so as to solicit resources and support from the authorities, but many find this tactic futile. They also encounter serious difficulties in raising donations from communities that lack trust and public-spiritedness, while the state does not provide tax deductions or other institutional support that would encourage donations.

In this connection, funding from international NGOs, particularly certain Hong Kong and Western foundations, plays a crucial role in establishing and maintaining some NGOs to promote their causes more independently from political control. Besides financial support, this global exposure also helps train local talent for NGOs, just as it helps NGOs restructure their systems and practices to become more in line with international standards.

The downside of this support from global civil society is that NGOs receiving foreign support risk suspicion from the state when China's foreign relations turn sour. In the long run, the future of NGOs in China rests on how the Chinese people understand the importance of civil society in preserving and promoting their values, rights, and interests; to solve public issues that are beyond the reach of the state and families; and to help begin the transition to democracy.

Notes

The author would like to acknowledge the generous support from the South China Research program of the Chinese University of Hong Kong in conducting research for this paper.
1   The speech was given by State Councilor Chen Junsheng and is included in the "Collection of Documents on the Registration and Administration of Social Organizations" (in Chinese, unpublished).
2   The Conference on the Development of Social Organizations and Related Economic Issues under a Socialist Market Economy was held by the Institute of Chinese Social Organizations and the Chinese Science and Technology Development Foundation on 22–4 October 1993. A summary of the conference proceedings was collected in "Collection of Documents on the Registration and Administration of Social Organizations" (in Chinese, unpublished).
3   Guosheng Deng's (2001) study found that the first batch of NGOs of this type was developed in rural areas in the early 1980s. Examples include the Beekeeping Association of Bi County, and the Sichuang and Research Society of High-Quality Hybrid Paddy Rice of Niujiang Town, Enping County, Guangdong.
4   The figures cited are taken from the speech "Understand the Situation, Liberate Our Thought: New Development in the Management of Social Organizations," given by Deputy Minister of Civil Affairs Fan Baujun at the First National Conference on the Management of Social Organization, 16 September 1992.
5   "Memo on How the Problem of Alumni Clubs Should Be Handled during the Inspections of Social Organizations," Ministry of Civil Affairs, No. 120, 1992.
6   In Chinese, *gua* means "attached to" and *kao* means "dependent." "*Guakao* organizations" thus refer to groups that are attached to or dependent on other umbrella organizations for protection. Since this is a type of patronage relationship, "*guakao* organizations" can be translated as "patronized groups."
7   "Corrupt Behavior Monitor Was Banned," *Ming Pao*, 1 November 1998.
8   "Report on Properly Handling the Voluntary Organizations Established by Some Employees in Enterprises," released by the Ministry of Public Security and originating from the Office of the Central Committee of the CCP and the Office of the State Council, No. 34, 1994.
9   Yingfei Zheng, "Strengthening Management of Social Organizations, Vigorously Serving Economic Construction and Social Stability," a speech delivered at the Conference on Management of Social Organizations in Guangdong, 27 June 1995.

10 Weller (1999: 14–15) agrees that not every voluntary organization between family and state is civil. Nevertheless, he stresses that various communal ties can be compatible with civil society and did in fact play an important role in the democratization of Taiwan.

References

Chan, Kin-man. "Intermediate Organizations and Civil Society: The Case of Guangzhou." In *China Review 1999*, edited by Chor-chor Lau and Xiao Geng. Hong Kong: Chinese University Press 1999, pp. 259–84.

——, and Haixiong Qiu. "When the Lifeboat is Overloaded: Social Support and State Enterprises Reform in China." *Communist and Post-Communist Studies*, 22, 3 (1999a): 305–18.

——. "Social Organizations, Social Capital, and Political and Economic Development." *Sociological Research*, 4, 20 July (1999b): 64–74. (in Chinese)

China Civil Affairs Statistical Yearbook. Beijing: China Statistic Press, 1991–2001. (in Chinese)

Deng, Guosheng. "New Environment for Development of NGOs in China." In www.usc.cuhk.edu.hk, 2001.

Ding, Yuanzhu. *Volunteerism in China*. United Nations Volunteers–United Nations Development Programme, 1999.

Gao, Bingzhong. "The Development of Social Organizations and the Problem of Legitimacy." In *China's Social Organizations at the Crossroads*, edited by China Youth Development Foundation and Research Committee on the Development of Foundations. Tianjin: Tianjin People's Press, 2001, pp. 75–91. (in Chinese)

Gellner, Ernest. "The Importance of Being Modular." In *Civil Society: Theory, History, Comparison*, edited by John A. Hall. Cambridge: Polity Press, 1995, pp. 32–55.

Gu, Xiaojin, and Dongyu Gan. "Internationalization: An Important Direction of the China Youth Development Foundation." In *China's Social Organizations at the Crossroads*, edited by China Youth Development Foundation and Research Committee on the Development of Foundations. Tianjin: Tianjin People's Press, 2001, pp. 205–18.

Guo, Jianmei. "Survival and Development of China's NGOs: Case Study of the Women's Legal Studies and Service Center of the Law School at Peking University." In *China's Social Organizations at the Crossroads*, edited by China Youth Development Foundation and Research Committee on the Development of Foundations. Tianjin: Tianjin People's Press, 2001, pp. 335–44. (in Chinese)

Hall, John A. "In Search of Civil Society." In *Civil Society: Theory, History, Comparison*, edited by John A. Hall. Cambridge: Polity Press, 1995, pp. 1–31.

Kang, Xiaoguang. "Social Organizations in China's Transitional Period." In *China's Social Organizations at the Crossroads*, edited by China Youth Development Foundation and Research Committee on the Development of Foundations. Tianjin: Tianjin People's Press, 2001, pp. 3–29. (in Chinese)

Knup, Elizabeth. "Environmental NGOs in China: An Overview". In *Environmental Change and Security* (website: ecsp.si.edu), China Environmental Series I, 1997.

Kornai, Janos. "The Hungarian Reform Process: Visions, Hopes, and Reality." In *Remaking the Economic Institutions of Socialism: China and Eastern Europe*, edited by Victor Nee and David Stark. Stanford, CA: Stanford University Press, 1989, pp. 32–94.

Linz, Juan, and Alfred Stepan. *Problems of Democratic Transition and Consolidation*. Baltimore, MD: Johns Hopkins University Press, 1996.

Man, Chi-shin. "Exploitation, Exit and Familism: Economic Retreatism of the Migrant Workers in the Pearl River Delta." M. Phil. Thesis, Department of Sociology, Chinese University of Hong Kong, 2001.

Qin, Hui. "From Traditional Mass Charity Organization to the Modern 'Third Sector'." In *China's Social Organizations at the Crossroads*, edited by China Youth Development Foundation and Research Committee on the Development of Foundations. Tianjin: Tianjin People's Press, 2001, pp. 30–60. (in Chinese)

Schmitter, Philipe. C. "Still the Century of Corporatism?" *Review of Politics*, 36, 1 (1974): 85–131.

Scott, James C. *Domination and the Arts of Resistance: Hidden Transcripts*. New Haven, CT: Yale University Press, 1990.

Sun, Liping, Jun Jin, and Jiangsui He. "Reorganizing Societal Resources by Socialized Means: A Study of the Resources Mobilization Process of the Project Hope." In *China's Social Organizations at the Crossroads*, edited by China Youth Development Foundation and Research Committee on the Development of Foundations. Tianjin: Tianjin People's Press, 2001, pp. 130–43. (in Chinese)

Sun, Zhixiang. "Case Study of NGOs in Beijing." In *China Social Development Network*, www.csdn.net.cn/page/china/wenhua/wenhua/1114abbx02.htm, 2000.

Unger, Jonathan, and Anita Chan. "China, Corporatism, and the East Asian Model." *Australian Journal of Chinese Affairs*, 33 (1995): 29–53.

Walder, G. Andrew. *Communist Neo-Traditionalism*. Berkeley, CA: University of California Press, 1986.

Walder, G. Andrew. "Workers, Managers and the State: The Reform Era and the Political Crisis of 1989." *China Quarterly*, 127 (1991): 467–92.

Wang, Shaoguang. "Practice and Theory: Overview of the Third Sector in Other Countries." In *China's Social Organizations at the Crossroads*, edited by China Youth Development Foundation and Research Committee on the Development of Foundations. Tianjin: Tianjin People's Press, 2001, pp. 381–429. (in Chinese)

———, and Angang Hu. *Report on China's State Capabilities*. Hong Kong: Oxford University Press, 1994.

Wang, Xingjuan. "The Management Principles of the Women's Hotline." In *China's Social Organizations at the Crossroads*, edited by China Youth Development Foundation and Research Committee on the Development of Foundations. Tianjin: Tianjin People's Press, 2001, pp. 345–54. (in Chinese)

Wang, Ying, Sun Bingyao, and Yiaoye Xhe. *Intermediate Sphere in Society: Reforms and Chinese Social Organizations*. Beijing: China Development Press, 1995. (in Chinese)

Weller, Robert P. *Alternate Civilities*. Boulder, CO: Westview Press, 1999.

White, Gordon, Jude Howell, and Xiaoyuan Shang. *In Search of Civil Society: Market Reform and Social Change in Contemporary China*. Oxford: Clarendon Press, 1996.

Yu, Xiaohung, and Zizi Li. "An Institutional Analysis of the Dual Nature of the Social Organizations in Contemporary China: A Case Study of Individual Labor and Private Enterprises Association in Haiding." *Website in Institutional Analysis and Public Policy* (www.wiapp.org/wpapers/wpaper200107.html), 2001.

Zhang, Ye. "Chinese NGOs: A Survey Report." In *Emerging Civil Society in the Asia Pacific Community*, edited by Tadashi Yamamoto. Tokyo: Japan Center for International Exchange, 1995a, pp. 93–108.

———. "Foundations in China: A Survey Report." In *Emerging Civil Society in the Asia Pacific Community*, edited by Tadashi Yamamoto. Tokyo: Japan Center for International Exchange, 1995b, pp. 523–32.

Zhu, Youhong. "Social Innovation in the Third Sector." In *China's Social Organizations at the Crossroads*, edited by China Youth Development Foundation and Research Committee on the Development of Foundations. Tianjin: Tianjin People's Press, 2001, pp. 265–82. (in Chinese)

3 NGOs, the state, and democracy under globalization

The case of Taiwan

Hsin-Huang Michael Hsiao

The historical development of NGOs in Taiwan

Since the early 1980s, Taiwan has experienced far-reaching changes both in the way it is governed and in its NGO sector. From an authoritarian government that allowed little if any input from the grass roots, it has been transformed to a liberal democracy with a vibrant civil society, while its NGO sector has grown tremendously in terms of its size, functions, and realms of concern.

In this chapter, I argue that these changes were interactive: the numerous social movement-oriented NGOs of the 1980s were vital to the gradual loosening of the governance system, which helped bring about the democratization of 1987 and the subsequent transformation and consolidation of that democracy; and democratization has in turn legitimated the NGO sector and helped it to continue to grow. I will also analyze the NGO sector as it has developed since democratization in 1987 to the present.

Suppression of civil society under authoritarian rule: 1950s–1970s

Under political authoritarianism and the martial law regime of the 1950s, 1960s and 1970s, Taiwan did not have a genuine NGO sector that could engage in any legitimate or genuine state–civil society dialogue or exchange. The ruling Kuomintang (KMT) practiced state corporatism and had a Department of Social Affairs in its party apparatus to control and monitor all civic and social organizations and groups. No autonomy in a political sense was granted to existing NGOs, no new civil membership associations could be established without prior investigation, and almost all associations were under government surveillance.

NGOs in that period were de facto bureaucratic arms of the KMT party-state, part of the vertical chain of command structures in the KMT's authoritarian rule. No free and autonomous horizontal linkage or networking was permitted among NGOs, especially among politically sensitive civil organizations such as labor unions, farmers' associations, student groups, and cultural and intellectual societies. The KMT even established many NGOs, to preempt any real grassroots NGOs and to extend the party's penetration into every sector of Taiwanese society.

As for the foundation sector, only rich and powerful or politically well-connected individuals and corporations were in a position to establish charitable foundations to assist the poor and needy. No other socially or politically significant reform agenda was considered at all.

However, alongside the inactive and monitored local NGOs was a transplanted Western sector of philanthropic organizations and middle-class social clubs. To some extent, these foreign NGOs were the only real nongovernmental civil institutions at the time, but they were concerned with nonpolitical or depoliticized charitable causes and social welfare activities. The most notable philanthropic NGOs among this group were church-related organizations such as World Vision and the Christian Children's Fund. Transplanted urban middle-class social clubs such as the Junior Chambers of Commerce (JC International), Rotary Club, Lions Club, and Kiwanis represented another spectrum of Taiwan's early NGOs. Therefore, the best way to characterize the overall nature of the Taiwanese NGO arena before the late 1970s is as a form of coexistence between suppressed local NGOs and transplanted foreign charity and social friendship-oriented NGOs.

Liberalization and the rise of social movements in the 1980s

Taiwan's transition to democracy, which began in 1980, can be divided into several phases. From late 1980 to June 1987, Taiwan began a process of gradual liberalization coinciding with increasingly emboldened opposition political forces and citizens' social reform movements. Following that period there was an uncertain opening toward democracy in July 1987, with the lifting of 33 years of martial law, and in early 1988, with Vice President Lee Teng-hui's confirmation as president following the death of President Chiang Ching-kuo. The period from July 1988 until Taiwan's first change of government in March 2000 saw the complete transition to democratic rule. Since then, Taiwan has been consolidating its democracy (Hsiao and Koo 1997; Hsiao 2001).

Beginning in 1980, Taiwan began to witness the mobilization of a civil society as represented by the rise of social movements and civil protests, many of which were very contentious and demanded various concessions from government. Throughout the transitioned phases to democracy, these social movements and the NGOs have played a very significant role in creating, facilitating, fostering and ensuring Taiwan's democratization. The numbers of NGOs advocating change and reform have greatly increased since 1980, and their causes cover a wide variety of areas including consumer protection, labor and farmer rights, environmentalism and nature conservation, gender equality, minority identity, human rights, urban housing prices, and the preservation of Hakka culture.

What is striking about the emergence of Taiwan's social movements is that, from initiating issues and setting agendas to establishing and mobilizing NGOs, everything has been of local origin with no direct foreign intervention. Taiwan's diplomatic isolation since 1982, when it lost the China seat in the United Nations, has meant that UN-related international governmental and nongovernmental organizations have not contributed to the activation and mobilization of its local

NGOs. The credit for this must go to Taiwan's grassroots organizations and to their localization and indigenization of NGO initiatives.

In addition, the emergence of mobilized social movements has profoundly changed state–NGO power relations in Taiwan. The democratizing of the KMT party-state since the 1980s, which culminated in the succession of the opposition Democratic Progressive Party to the presidency in 2000 and to its control of the Legislative Yuan in 2001, has taken place with the formal legitimizing of NGOs and the tremendous growth in their number and autonomy.

Civil society, NGOs, and democratization since the 1990s

The NGO sector in Taiwan has both benefited from and aided in the consolidation of democratization. The rapid growth of advocacy NGOs and social movements in the 1980s has been matched since 1990 by the growth of many service-providing NGOs and a variety of new kinds of civil society organizations. The result is that Taiwan today has a very robust NGO sector, which has also seen a great deal of qualitative change. Taiwan's NGOs have become pluralistic and diversified, with NGOs of all types founded to meet the new demands generated by ongoing social and political changes. For example, many social movement organizations, think tanks, and corporate foundations have now redirected their orientations in response to this social and political transformation. Several contextual factors can be used to explain this remarkable growth and change in Taiwan's NGO sector over the past two decades.

The first factor is Taiwan's political liberalization, which has been conducive to the growth, expansion, and pluralistic development of the nonprofit sector. Beginning in the early 1980s, many so-called underground civil organizations and protests were initiated and organized by various social movements to exert demands on the authoritarian state. Once martial law was lifted in 1987, many more foundations and membership associations were established by various individuals active in the mobilized civil society.

The early wave of social protests and social movements was the facilitating force behind Taiwan's political liberalization, while the later waves of social movements and their formalized organizations have been the result of the institutionalization of its democracy since the late 1980s. With the demise of authoritarianism, political obstacles restricting the development of free association and expression in the civil society have been dramatically removed. Furthermore, in its struggle against authoritarianism, the political opposition has further legitimized the role of NGOs as reformers, so that NGOs are now also viewed as a necessary safeguard for a healthy and mature civil society.

Social and economic factors have also contributed to the impressive development of Taiwan's NGO sector. The spread of public education, in particular higher education, has enhanced and awakened the general public's social consciousness to demand a better society and political system, while overall economic affluence has freed the general public from worry about basic material needs, allowing them to pursue other ends, including social and political reforms. The public's freedom of access to the mass media and other sources of information and increasing opportunities to travel abroad have also equipped many citizens with the knowledge and skills to become organized in voicing their demands.

Finally, as witnessed in Taiwan's many social reform movement organizations, intellectuals and the new middle class have also played a crucial role. Many were trained and educated in the West, and this "new knowledge class" has served as a catalyst for many global values and facilitated the emergence of Taiwan's local NGOs (Hsiao 2000a).

The current state of Taiwan's NGOs

NGO typology

Taiwan's NGO sector can be categorized in several ways. First, in terms of the broad objects and strategies they employ, individual NGOs can be classified with the social movement sector–advocacy NGOs or with the nonsocial movement sector–service-providing NGOs. While the majority of the NGOs in Taiwan belong to the service-providing category, the advocacy NGOs played a crucial role in making democracy possible, even though they were relatively new constituents to Taiwan's NGO world. In general, while the service-oriented NGOs were not established with the clear objective of promoting specific social reform, many have moved beyond their traditional charitable activities and social functions and redirected their objectives to focus on emerging social concerns. Since the 1990s, both advocacy and service NGOs have further developed, so that they have on the one hand converged on a common "new reformism," while at the same time they have diverged to serve a wide variety of functions. This has made Taiwan a better society for all.

In terms of its general organizational typology, Taiwan's NGO sector can be divided into membership-centered civil associations and endowment-centered foundations. As of 2001, the number of membership associations had increased to almost 15,000, including all types of political organizations, a more than 50 percent increase since 1991. More than 60 percent of these membership associations were established in the 1980s and 1990s, which clearly reflects the dynamism of Taiwan's mobilized civil society. The three most popular types of Taiwan's social organizations are social services, public interest and charitable organizations, followed by those for academic and cultural promotion and international exchange.

By 2001 there were nearly 3,000 foundations of all types in Taiwan, about 75 percent of which had been established since the 1980s. Over 70 percent were privately funded, corporations funded about 25 percent, and the rest were mixed and governmental foundations. This sector is therefore clearly dominated by newly established nongovernment foundations that are supported by either private donations or corporate bodies. It is noteworthy that an increasing number of corporate foundations have been established since the 1980s. Their increasing importance in Taiwan's NGO arena reflects the growing involvement of the private business community in the resurrected civil society and its growing concern with public affairs.

As with the membership-association sector, the foundations with philanthropic, welfare, and charitable aims are the top categories, followed by those that promote public interest research, education, culture and the arts, international cultural exchanges, and social activism. Moreover, with few exceptions, most are operating rather than grant-making foundations. Because of this unique character, Taiwan's foundations are not readily distinguishable from what are normally defined as membership civic associations. The difference lies only in their legal definition, not in their nature or practice (Hsiao 2000b).

The legal framework

Each membership-oriented NGO is required to register as a legal entity with the relevant supervising government body and go through an administrative review and approval procedure. The civic code is the legal base for specific regulations governing the establishment and operation of NGOs, though there is a separate civil organization law which stipulates the required permit-application procedures. A minimum of 30 founding members is required to establish a membership NGO, which must then go through an internal review process by the state bureaucracy. A national association needs to apply at the Ministry of the Interior and a local association at a local government Bureau of Social Affairs. Local associations must then obtain approval from the city or county government.

Applying to establish an endowment-oriented foundation tends to be more complex, in that the particular ministry or bureau that administers the functions of that foundation must approve each one. All 13 ministries and agencies of the Executive Yuan, Taiwan's central administrative body, issue their own set of "regulations for the establishment and supervision of foundations" as legal and administrative guidelines. Provincial, county, and municipal governments can also approve and supervise foundations.

To set up a foundation, most central government bodies require an endowment of at least 30 million NT dollars (approximately US$870,000). In order to avoid conflicts of interest, public officials with supervisory duties are prohibited from taking up positions as trustees or board members. How and when endowment funds are used is also subject to legal restrictions. For example, according to the most recent regulations, no more than half of a foundation's endowment can be transferred into real estate, bonds, or stocks without authorization from the supervising government body.

Taiwan's income tax law provides that, if educational, cultural, public interest, and charitable associations and foundations are established in accordance with Executive Yuan regulations, they are exempt from paying income tax on either their own income or that of their subordinate operating units. It also grants special tax deductions or credits to individuals who make a deductible donation to nonprofit civil society organizations of up to 20 percent of their annual gross consolidated income (Feng 1999).

But what makes Taiwan's NGOs unique is not how they are governed legally but how they work. Many associations and foundations were conceived by groups of individuals pursuing similar ideals, who viewed establishing membership associations as the best way to do so. However, if someone has the financial means and wants to use an organization as a personal vehicle, they can establish a foundation whose membership can be limited, and in this way not jeopardize their control. This option is only open to the wealthy, however; those who lack the necessary funding have to set up membership associations.

Furthermore, as indicated above, the actual management and operation of many foundations are similar to those of membership associations, as the great majority of Taiwan's foundations are in fact operating foundations rather than grant-making ones. But while many religious groups, schools, hospitals, and performing arts groups have now also registered themselves as foundations in order to enjoy the tax benefits, their legal qualifications are somewhat controversial.

Characterizing Taiwan's NGOs: autonomy, advocacy, and influence

Any civil society association in the democratic world should enjoy legal recognition and protection, just as it should also be autonomous vis-à-vis the state. In today's Taiwan, all NGOs and civil society associations can easily gain legal recognition, and NGOs no longer need to go underground to prove their autonomy or independence.

However, in order to better understand the current situation of Taiwan's civil society organizations under democratic consolidation, I conducted in early 2000 an organizational survey of 266 NGOs in the Taipei metropolitan area. A total of 194 membership associations and 56 foundations were successfully surveyed, which included six types of NGOs: economic (9), religious (13), friendship (48), academic–professional (57), advocacy–social movement (30), and welfare (92); one group did not fit the categories. More than 75 percent of these NGOs had been established since the 1980s, while half (50.8 percent) were set up in the 1990s (Table 3.1). This rapid growth of civil society associations and NGOs underscores

Table 3.1 Founding years and types of NGOs in Taiwan

Established	Associations	Foundations	Total No.	%
Pre-1949	13	0	13	5.2
1950–9	7	1	8	3.2
1960–9	14	2	16	6.4
1970–9	18	6	24	9.6
1980–9	39	23	62	24.8
1990–9	103	24	127	50.8
Total	194	56	250	100.0

Note: 16 NGOs did not respond.

Table 3.2 Size of NGOs in Taiwan

| | Associations | | Foundations | | Total | |
	No.	%	No.	%	No.	%
1–19	8	3.8	21	36.8	29	11.0
20–49	29	14.1	19	33.3	48	18.3
50–99	27	13.1	9	15.8	36	13.7
100–199	29	14.1	0	0.0	29	11.0
200–499	49	23.9	2	3.5	51	19.4
500–999	20	9.7	1	1.8	21	8.0
1000–	44	21.4	5	8.8	49	18.6
Total	206	100.0	57	100.0	263	100.0

Note: 3 NGOs did not respond.

the unprecedented social and political transformation Taiwan has experienced since the 1980s.

Of the different types of NGO, membership associations tend to be large: more than 50 percent of them had more than 200 members, 24 percent had between 200 and 499, and 21 percent had more than 1,000 (Table 3.2). Foundations, on the other hand, tend to be small: 70 percent had fewer than 50 personnel, while 37 percent had fewer than 20.

The survey also found that the majority of NGOs had key members with professional and middle-class backgrounds, while their services were mainly rendered to the general public and the lower class. These class differences illustrate how the urban middle and professional classes have been at the core of Taiwan's "new reformism," which was initiated by NGOs in the 1980s. One can therefore also characterize Taiwan's NGOs as the continued manifestation of forces for social reform.

When NGOs were asked to characterize themselves using one or more than one descriptor, the largest number identified themselves as "cultural and educational organizations" (44 percent), followed by "social and community service groups" (39.1 percent), "professional organizations" (27.4 percent), "organizations to protect the socially disadvantaged groups" (26.3 percent), "charitable and welfare institutions" (24.8 percent), and "academic and research associations" (23.3 percent) (Table 3.3).

Nearly 80 percent of all NGOs surveyed organized regular activities: public seminars, lectures, and training courses were the major ones, followed by activities like publishing magazines, books, or newsletters; exchanging and cooperating with local and overseas NGOs; and providing social and community services. These findings are consistent with the fact that, under democracy, NGOs are by and large taking reformism as their primary goal.

Private donations were the most important source of NGO financing (71 percent), followed by membership dues (65 percent), and income generated from NGO activities (38 percent). Financial assistance and subsidies from the government, by comparison, were relatively small and insignificant, though 31 percent of

Table 3.3 Self-characterization of NGO functions in Taiwan (multiple choices)

	Associations	Foundations	Total No.	%
Charitable–welfare	42	24	66	24.8
Cultural–educational	84	33	117	44.0
Protecting socially disadvantaged groups	56	14	70	26.3
Self-help	41	4	45	16.9
Research–academic	51	11	62	23.3
Professional	60	13	73	27.4
Protest–pressure groups	26	4	30	11.3
Friendship	55	1	56	21.1
Social–community service	85	19	104	39.1
Total	208	58	266	

surveyed NGOs claimed to receive government support. By this, one can assert that Taiwan's NGOs are to a large extent independent of government's economic control. It is not the state, but rather the public and the citizens, especially the rising middle classes, who stand behind and with the NGO sector.

However, this does not mean that Taiwan's NGOs can financially survive without public sector support or that government can no longer dominate NGOs through financial manipulation. In fact, 29 percent of the NGOs surveyed had an annual budget of less than NT$1 million (US$30,000), 13 percent had annual budgets of NT$1–2 million, and 10 percent had budgets of NT$2–3 million. This means that about half of the NGOs in the sample had an annual budget of less than NT$3 million (less than US$100,000).

There was also a sharp difference in financial condition between membership associations and foundations: about 20 percent of the latter had annual budgets of more than NT$50 million (about US$1.6 million), but more than half of the associations' budgets were less than NT$2 million (about US$60,000). This financial gap has also created the popular public image of "poor associations" and "rich foundations." In the government's eyes, foundations are viewed as more creditable because of their financial endowments and organizational capabilities.

The issue of autonomy for NGOs should be looked upon in relative terms, as it does not necessarily mean total separation from state connections. The survey found that 31 percent of the core leaders of Taiwan's NGOs were in fact elected officials, while 23 percent of the leaders had run for public office. However, these NGO officials were elected, and the impetus is always from the bottom up rather than top down. Aspiring politicians sometimes use NGOs as a springboard to electoral politics, but NGOs are not subject to their control. Rather, they are a medium they engage in, to raise their social prestige and political influence.

Autonomy

For an NGO to be truly autonomous, its administrative and financial decisions must be free from all types of interference and dominance from outside forces. With this criterion in mind, the data from the survey found that Taiwan's NGOs were independent in numerous ways. For example, only 2 percent said that a single family had control over personnel decisions, while 4 percent responded that there were close family and kin ties within the decision-making core; 11 percent were financially established by a single business or corporation, and 21 percent were originally set up by governmental funding. These figures tend to show that, in today's Taiwan, no significant domination from family, business, and government was detected in NGOs' decision-making processes.

One way for an NGO to avoid being dominated by outside forces is to develop horizontal networks with other like-minded NGOs. In Taiwan, 63 percent of the NGOs interviewed claimed to have such interorganizational cooperation with other Taiwanese NGOs, about 30 percent had developed exchanges and networking with international NGOs and local business on various joint efforts, while 13 percent said they had cooperation with political parties. It can therefore be asserted that Taiwanese NGOs have quite successfully built up interorganizational resource linkages with other local or international NGOs and, to a lesser extent, even with the business sector.

It is easy to understand why cooperation between NGOs and government has been limited. Under authoritarian rule, any NGO's "cooperation" with government or the ruling political party meant that it was being controlled or dictated to by the political power. Now, even under the new democracy, NGOs do not yet have full confidence in government, just as government is still not comfortable working with NGOs.

The survey also indicated that NGO leaders considered the relationships between NGOs and governments at different levels to be mixed. On the one hand, 46.2 percent of NGOs interviewed criticized laws and regulations as being unsuitable to the reality of civil society, and 32 percent contended that central government officials were authoritarian and bureaucratic in dealing with NGOs. On the other hand, 38 percent considered the central government happy to cooperate with civic associations, and 25 percent asserted that the government respected civil organizations' professionalism and even listened to their policy inputs.

There was similar ambivalence in the case of NGO–local government relations: 41 percent and 29 percent viewed relations as "cooperative" and "respectful," while 30 percent and 24 percent said they were "out of touch with reality" and "bureaucratic."

All maintained that the NGO and government relations have gradually changed in favor of NGOs, though the NGOs still have to deal with what remains of the legacy of past authoritarianism.

Advocacy

The spirit of reformism is quite prevalent among Taipei's NGO sector. The survey found that 74 percent of NGO leaders agreed that "we should improve the social condition through gradual reform steps"; only 9 percent insisted on complete reconstruction, while 7 percent maintained that "we should keep the status quo and resist any radical changes"; 51 percent of NGOs surveyed were more inclined to take the view that "we should try hard to narrow the gap between the poor and the rich," and 65 percent agreed that "environmental protection is necessary to prevent Taiwan from being polluted." In addition, 38 percent took an ambivalent stand on the issue of individuals vs. the government in terms of who should be responsible for the general condition of the public's livelihood, while 44 percent felt that balance was needed between emphasizing people's participation vs. government's efficiency.

Taiwan's NGOs have very much stressed their role as advocates for social reform. The survey results indicate that the most popular approaches to performing this advocacy role are in the forms of "engaging in dialogue with government officials" (29.3 percent), "proposing recommendations to the government" (24.8 percent), "organizing seminars on policy issues" (22.2 percent), "signing petitions" (20.7 percent), "calling a press conference" (17.7 percent), and "staging a sit-in or rally" (12.8 percent). All these are more or less moderate in spirit though diverse in style.

The survey also found that more than a quarter of NGOs surveyed had participated in protests or advocacy activities, and more than 60 percent had ever sought support from other civic organizations in advocacy activities. These advocacy actions are expected to lead to "bringing about new ideas" (43.2 percent), "offering charitable activities" (33.8 percent), "concern for public problem issues" (28.2 percent), "changing government's policies" (25.6 percent), "envisioning further social reforms" (10.9 percent), and "enhancing civic consciousness" (9 percent).

Influence

Besides being autonomous and advocacy driven, Taiwan's NGOs have also been influential in shaping government policies and public life. More than 50 percent of NGOs identified their primary objectives as "monitoring government policies" and "lobbying on related laws and regulations," while about a quarter indicated they had been participating in the government decision-making process. The ways they have exerted influence on government include "consultation to relevant agencies" (33.8 percent), "monitoring policy implementation" (17.3 percent), "discovery of new social problems and policy issues" (15.4 percent), "changing government officials' attitudes" (15.4 percent), and "lobbying for public policies and legislation" (14.7 percent).

All in all, precisely half of the NGOs' leaders interviewed disagreed with the statement that "government officials do not care about NGOs' opinions," while another 42.5 percent agreed that "government officials still do not take NGOs seriously."

As for their social influence, NGOs claimed that they have "provided direct services to needy individuals and social groups" (58.3 percent), and "educated the public" (57.1 percent). They also maintain that NGOs' social impacts include "caring for disadvantaged social groups" (38 percent), "promotion of new ideas and new values for the public" (36.8 percent), and "extension of social services and promotion of public participation" (32.7 percent). It is therefore quite evident that NGOs in today's democratic Taiwan already enjoy both policy influence and social impact.

However, another new phenomenon has occurred in the relations between some of the advocacy NGOs and the current DPP state. Former protest and movement allies prior to the DPP taking power in 2000, these two groups have had some difficulty in adjusting to each other's new roles. To be fair, the DPP government has been trying hard to realize as soon as possible many of its campaign platforms on various labor, welfare, and environmental policy concerns. But due to the unfavorable political relations with the opposition KMT and People First Party (PFP) and its own inexperience in governance, the DPP government has not performed well enough to meet public satisfaction since it came to power in mid-2000.

The advocacy NGOs for labor, social welfare, and the environment have often found themselves at odds with the DPP government on various policy issues. Of particular importance is that these NGOs began to criticize the new regime for its not being able to deliver on its campaign promises or to initiate progressive policy visions. The emerging relations between the advocacy NGOs and the state can be characterized as precarious and tense between 2000 and 2002.

The DPP state is quite aware of the dilemma and has tried to resolve the problems. It hopes to renew its progressive alliance with those NGOs by accommodating their demands, while at the same time not jeopardizing its new interest coalition with other sectors in society. It is important to note here that the DPP state now has a hard time balancing its new relations with the business groups and its old relations with the labor, environment, and social welfare groups, as these two groups are in conflict with one another on various issues.

This emerging issue in the NGO–civil society and state relations is still in the making, and it is likely to have some bearing on the future course of democratic governance in Taiwan.

The regionalization and globalization of Taiwan's NGOs

Throughout the 1990s, Taiwan's NGOs increasingly broadened their perspectives and expanded their activities beyond the domestic boundary. Several cases can be drawn to illustrate these new directions.

The Kaohsiung-based Asia-Pacific Public Affairs Forum (APPAF), an operating foundation, was established by business and academic leaders in 1996. They embarked on their stated mission of developing a new path to cooperation and partnership among individuals, NGOs, and the business and public sectors to work together to confront common problems in the rapidly changing global environment. APPAF aimed from the beginning to develop itself into a global organization, which sets it apart from most other nonprofit organizations in Taiwan.

Under its two guiding principles, partnership and network building, APPAF has established extensive institutional linkages with NGOs, academic institutions, and foundations in East and Southeast Asia, Australia, New Zealand, Central America, and the United States. APPAF does not limit itself to local concerns but regards the greater Asia-Pacific as its geographic orientation and focus of identity. It also participated in the CIVICUS Second World Assembly 1997 held in Budapest, Hungary, becoming the first of Taiwan's civil society organizations to do so. It has also continued to work closely with CIVICUS, a large international NGO with an emphasis on linking and strengthening civil society organizations around the world in building a global civil society. This involvement has indeed increased Taiwan's visibility in the emerging global community.

The Chinese Children's Fund (CCF, formerly Christian Children's Fund), World Vision of Taiwan (formerly World Vision), and the YMCA Taiwan – three philanthropic foundations originally transplanted from abroad – have indigenized, while simultaneously ensconcing themselves in global networking and linkages. From being dependent on external funds from the overseas philanthropic community, they have not only become self-sufficient in their Taiwan activities but even provide humanitarian assistance to less developed nations. In the summer and fall of 1997, CCF, and the YMCA took steps toward regionalization and globalization in their outreach activities, by jointly organizing East Asian regional conferences in Taiwan. The CCF sponsored the Third East Asian Fundraising Workshop, which attracted a sizable international attendance, while the YMCA organized the East Asian Deliberation on Empowerment, inviting representatives from East Asian YMCA-affiliated organizations to attend (CCF 1999; World Vision of Taiwan 2000).

Taiwan's three major Buddhist organizations, Buddhist Compassion Relief Merit Society (Tz'u-Chi), Buddha Light Mountain (Foguangshan), and Dharma Drum Mountain (Fagushan), have all set up foundations to promote cultural and welfare causes beyond Taiwan's borders. The Tz'u-Chi Foundation has very active global social relief and development programs in more than 40 countries. It is noteworthy that these sacred and revitalized neotraditional Buddhist organizations embraced worldly concerns and adopted a secular, Western-style NGO model as they globalized.

Taiwan's NGOs have also acted to promote peace and stability by extending their activities to China. Over the past decade, Taiwan–China philanthropic links have been steadily growing, with more and more of Taiwan's philanthropic resources flowing to the mainland. Aside from their work in disaster relief, Taiwan's NGOs have engaged in various people-to-people activities involving exchanges of persons in the areas of media, religion, sports, literature and arts, and scholarship. There are cross-Taiwan Straits partnerships between universities, research institutions, and publishing houses. Usually Taiwan's NGOs are the donors while their Chinese counterparts are the recipients. Taiwan's most notable NGO engaged in Taiwan–China philanthropy and exchange programs is the Tz'u-Chi Foundation.

The continuing tense political relations between Taiwan and mainland China have not stopped Taiwan's NGOs from developing genuine people-to-people relations across the straits. Many who live in this highly unstable region hope that the civil society forces on both sides will someday be able to reshape political relations between Taiwan and China. They have a vision of the civil society organizations of Taiwan, Hong Kong, and at least some parts of the South China coastal provinces developing more equal and cordial relations that in the near future will improve the environment for rapprochement and a more imaginative framework for peaceful coexistence and prosperity among the three Chinese societies, China, Taiwan, and Hong Kong.

Furthermore, inspired by the success of democratic development, since the mid-1990s Taiwan's many social movement NGOs have become increasingly involved in what Keck and Sikkink (1998) have described as "transnational advocacy networks," a clear move toward globalization. According to Chen (2000), Taiwanese NGOs' regional and global involvement has recently concentrated in five advocacy areas: human rights, indigenous peoples, migrant workers, environmental protection, and women's issues.

Human rights

The Taiwan Association for Human Rights and the Fishermen's Service Center (a Kaohsiung-based NGO concerned with the well-being of the 30,000 Filipino fishermen hired in Taiwan) have actively participated in the drafting and launch of the Asian Human Rights Charter.

The Eden Social Welfare Foundation has become a national member of the International Campaign to Ban Landmines and has been active in developing global networks in its campaign to clear landmines in Jinmen and Mazu, along with its long-standing efforts to protect the rights of Taiwan's disabled.

Indigenous peoples

The Alliance of Taiwan Aborigines was a founding member of the recently established Asian Indigenous Peoples' Parliament (AIPP), which has been a leading advocacy network on Asian minority issues since its birth in 1998. It now has 18 member organizations and three associated member organizations from nine Asian countries.

Migrant workers

The Hope Workers' Center and Migrant Workers' Concern Desk have maintained close linkages with the Migrant Forum in Asia, a Manila-based network.

The Taiwan Grassroots Women Workers' Center has also developed extensive collaborative relations with other Asian NGOs working on migrant worker problems in Japan, Korea, the Philippines, Thailand, and Indonesia.

Environmental protection

The Taiwan Environmental Protection Union has participated in the Anti-Nuclear Alliance in Asia for many years, in order to increase its leverage in campaigning to stop a fourth nuclear power plant from being built in Taiwan. The Green Frontline and the Green Consumers' Foundation have worked with the Environmental Investigation Agency, Tusk Force, and the Shepherd's Foundation, all international NGOs, in banning the consumption of rhino horn and tiger bones in Taiwan.

The Life Conservationist Association has become a member of the British-based World Society for Protection of Animals and has aggressively worked with many other international NGOs, such as the People for Ethical Treatment of Animals, the Royal Society for Prevention of Cruelty to Animals Australia, and the Humane Society, in campaigning against the mistreatment of animals in Taiwan. In 1997 the Life Conservationist Association and its global partners led a very successful international protest campaign to improve the condition of stray dogs in Taiwan, which pressured the government to pass the Animal Protection Law the following year.

Women's issues

Taiwan's NGOs have long been involved in global linkages and regional networks on women's rights issues. Taipei Women Rescue Foundation, the Garden of Hope Foundation, the Taiwan National Committee to End Child-Prostitution in Asian Tourism, Women Awakening Foundation, and the Homemakers' Union and Foundation are the most dynamic ones. Taiwan's women's issues NGOs participated in the biennial East Asian Women's Forum in Tokyo (1994), Seoul (1996), and Ulan Bator (1998). They also sponsored and hosted the 2000 East Asian Women's Forum in September in Taipei, a landmark event for Taiwan's women's issues NGOs.

On another women-related advocacy front, the Taipei Alliance of Licensed Prostitutes (TALP) was formed when the Taipei city government decided in 1997 to abolish licensed prostitution. It immediately went international and sought global support from similar NGOs in many other countries. In May 1998, TALP, along with two other local NGOs, the Solidarity Front of Women Workers and Pink Collar Solidarity, organized a three-day International Forum on Sex Worker Rights and Sex Industrial Policy in Taipei. It was held to parallel the World Forum on Capital Cities, which was hosted by the Taipei city government. The sex workers' forum was attended by 17 delegates who represented sex-workers'-rights NGOs from 11 countries. The forum denounced Taipei city government's policy as moralistic, and came up with a declaration of sex workers' rights, to prevent discrimination and exploitation and to empower them in the fight against AIDS, and so on. Taipei's brothels were reopened in 1999, after a two-year struggle.

Concluding remarks

To summarize, the development of Taiwan NGOs can be divided into three phases. In the 1950s, 1960s and even the early 1970s, bona fide and autonomous NGOs were by and large nonexistent in Taiwan. They were either suppressed by the authoritarian state or became part of the control structure of KMT-government state corporatism. The only real NGOs that were outside of the KMT's control were the charitable social welfare-oriented NGOs and the middle-class social networking organizations that originated in and were transplants of Western philanthropic organizations.

But the environment for NGOs has changed dramatically since the 1980s, allowing for many active and autonomous NGOs to become established completely by local initiative and organizational resources. The social movement NGOs established in this period facilitated and fostered Taiwan's democratic transition and profoundly transformed the power relationship between the state and civil society. Here, Taiwan's NGO sector stands apart from most other countries, in that it drew on indigenous resources with no direct international or global NGO intervention and was based on local issues.

In the 1990s, many of Taiwan's locally initiated NGOs went regional and global in their outlook and networking activities. Both advocacy and service-providing NGOs have extended their scope of activity to the Asia-Pacific region, in some cases to the entire world. Owing to the political tensions across the Taiwan Straits and Taiwan's diplomatic isolation, the government did not assist in the regionalization and globalization of Taiwanese NGOs, whose globalization path is characterized by its genuinely nongovernmental nature.

But the globalizing Taiwanese NGOs have nevertheless internationalized the state in an interesting way. It may not be so relevant to NGOs in many other countries in Asia (Serrano 1994), but many of Taiwan's NGOs are seeking to upgrade the political status of the Taiwan state, a task that the pubic fully supports them in. This is the unique external role Taiwan's NGOs have been playing since the 1990s. At the same time, Taiwan's NGOs have internally created more trust, social networks, and social capital, all of which are necessary for sustaining a viable civil society in this newborn democracy.

References

Chen, Jie. "Love with Frontier: Trans-nationalism of Taiwan's Social Movement NGOs and the Nation State." Paper presented at the 6th Annual Conference of the North American Taiwan Studies Association, Harvard University, 16–19 June 2000.

Chinese Fund for Children and Families in Taiwan (CCF). *CCF: Happy Birthday of 50 Years*. Taichung: CCF, 1999.

Feng, Joyce Yen. "Taiwan." In *Philanthropy and Law in Asia*, edited by Thomas Silk. San Francisco: Jossey-Bass Publishers, 1999, pp. 315–31.

Hsiao, Hsin-Huang Michael. "Taiwan's Knowledge Class," in *Correspondence: An International Review of Culture and Society*, Vol. 6 (2000), p. 41. New York Council on Foreign Affairs.

Hsiao, H.H. Michael (ed.). *Nonprofit Sector: Organization and Operation.* Taipei: Chiu-Liu Press, 2000b. (in Chinese).

——. "Sociocultural Transformation in Taiwan since the 1980s." In *Taiwan's Economic Success since 1980*, edited by Chao-Cheng Mai and Chien-Sheng Shi. Cheltenham, UK: Edward Elgar, 2001, pp. 156–208.

——, and Hagen Koo. "The Middle Classes and Democratization." In *Consolidating the Third Wave Democracies: Themes and Perspectives*, edited by Larry Diamond, Marc F. Plattner, Yun-han Chu, and Hung-Mao Tian, Baltimore, MD: Johns Hopkins University Press, 1997, pp. 312–33.

Keck, Margaret and Kathryn Sikkink. *Activists beyond Borders: Advocacy Networks in International Politics.* Ithaca, NY: Cornell University Press, 1998.

Serrano, Isagani R. *Civil Society in the Asia-Pacific Region.* Washington, DC: CIVICUS, 1994.

World Vision of Taiwan. *Vision beyond the Millennium: International Relief and Development Conference.* Taipei: World Vision of Taiwan, 2000.

4 Friends and critics of the state

The case of Hong Kong

Tai-lok Lui, Hsin-chi Kuan, Kin-man Chan, and Sunny Cheuk-wah Chan

Introduction

Hong Kong has never been short of civic organizations.[1] Right from the early years of its colonization by the British in the nineteenth century, local Chinese gathered in temples and discussed how to protect and promote their interests in a sociopolitical environment of foreign rule. *Kaifong* (neighborhood, or neighbor) and *tungheung* (native place) formed the social and cultural basis of the formation of collective identity and of the mobilization for collective action. Furthermore, though Hong Kong's population has always been in flux, with migrants arriving at different critical phases of its social development, for more than 160-odd years its residents have had the will and ability to form voluntary bodies and self-help groups to deal with the social, economic, and political issues they encounter in their everyday lives.

Indeed, the Chinese community has uninterruptedly played an active role in forming various kinds of voluntary bodies serving very different purposes, though at the same time their diverse interests and political orientations have often divided them. One of the major features of contemporary Hong Kong society is its vibrant civil society which reflects this long tradition of "organizing from below," and serves to almost fill the gap, particularly in the domain of social services and social welfare, between a bureaucratic state that always avoids directly intervening in the local society and an economy driven by largely unrestrained market forces.

This chapter, based upon a review of secondary literature and drawing upon the findings of a survey of local NGOs carried out in 2000, reports on the development of civic organizations in Hong Kong. In our discussion, we will first review the historical development of civic organizations in Hong Kong; we will then examine the development of NGOs in contemporary Hong Kong. Our observations can be broadly summarized into three points.

First, a "soft," nonintrusive yet authoritarian colonial ruling strategy allowed various kinds of voluntary groups to proliferate within the Chinese community. Though some of these groups were not detached from either local or mainland politics, they were relatively free and autonomous from political interference, as long as they stayed within the parameters prescribed by the colonial state. That most civic organizations continue to enjoy a reasonably high degree of autonomy constitutes one of the distinguishing features of NGOs in Hong Kong.

Second, in various ways, civic organizations articulate the interests and opinions of their represented communities, and they assume different roles and profiles in different historical contexts. Civic organizations have played a critical role in facilitating popular mobilization and in opening social and political spaces for more political participation, since the mid-1960s, while in the 1970s and 1980s their involvement in oppositional politics was highly pertinent to the loosening of colonial–authoritarian political control. Yet, the contributions of these civic organizations in circumscribing the scope and power of the state lie more in the formation of a loosely organized pro-democracy camp than in being a critical social force.

Third, while some civic organizations have long been co-opted by the state, others continue to stay outside the political establishment. The structure of relations between the state and civic organizations is therefore dichotomous. The state has adopted a selectively inclusive strategy towards civic organizations and reserves places in the political establishment for friendly organizations – a selectively inclusive strategy made possible because of the previous colonial nature of the bureaucratic state and lately because of the partial democratization prescribed by the institutional arrangements of "decolonization without independence" (Lau 1990). However, those organizations critical of the state and active in mobilizing the public against various state initiatives fall out of the orbit of the state's "administrative absorption" strategy (King 1972).

Therefore, in the eyes of the powerholders, civic organizations are both friends and enemies. They can be effective agents between the state and the market in meeting the emerging needs of the local population; however, in articulating those interests and opinions, civic organizations, particularly those excluded from power sharing, quite often become vocal critics of the government. They are therefore agents both of cooperation and of opposition.

The historical development of civic organizations in Hong Kong

The first hundred years

As mentioned earlier, Hong Kong's NGOs have long played an important role in the mediation between the state and society.[2] Largely a result of the British colonizer's ruling strategy of avoiding direct confrontation with the Chinese community, the locals, many of whom migrated from neighboring regions and continued to see themselves as sojourners, found themselves reasonably free to form groups to deal with emerging issues brought about by the continuous influx of incoming population. Neighborhood groups were formed as early as the 1850s:

> *Kaifongs* (local residents of the same neighborhood) used temples as the venues for public gathering and discussion. Among them, the Man Mo Temple,

constructed at Hollywood Road in 1847 and refurbished in 1851, was the
largest. It became the main venue of public gathering and meeting for the
Chinese community.

(Yu and Liu 1994: 407)

The growth of the Chinese community and the resulting changes in its
social composition and structure, particularly the emergence of a Chinese elite
and local leadership (Chan 1991: ch. 3), increased both the number and the
size of local Chinese groups and associations. The establishment of the District
Watch Committee (a body to set up local patrols for maintaining social order
in the Chinese community though it also carried the implications of being a self-
governing body for local Chinese affairs) by Chinese notables in the 1860s is an
example of these changes (Lethbridge 1978). The formation of trade associations
like Nam Pak Hong Guild (1868) and Chung Wah Wui Koon (1896) further
demonstrates the expansion of the Chinese trading networks in Hong Kong and
the rise of a class of Chinese merchants.

Even more significant was the establishment in 1872 of the Tung Wah Hospital.
This hospital was never confined to providing medical services: it functioned as
a charitable organization for the Chinese community and is a powerful example
of that community "surpassing the traditional format of neighborhood organizing
with local temples as the centers of activity and going beyond the constraints
imposed on organizing by the ties of blood, place of origin, and trade" (Yu and Liu
1994: 408). It was "the first permanent Chinese association which could justifi-
ably claim to represent the whole Chinese community, and more importantly, to
be recognized by the government as an elitist group" (Sinn 1989: 4). Together with
the Po Leung Kuk (founded in 1878 and known in English as the Society for the
Protection of Women and Girls) and with other associations like Lok Sin Tong
(another local Chinese charitable organization), the District Watch Committee,
and the Tung Wah Hospital "formed a system" (Lethbridge 1978: 113) within the
Chinese community. This was a social system stratified according to "prestige,
influence, and power": the District Watch Committee being "the apex of a
pyramidal and hierarchical structure, at the base of which were local-based
associations, and guilds of employers" (Lethbridge 1978). This system worked as a
mechanism of mediation between the colonial government and the Chinese
community, allowing the Chinese to manage and to regulate their own affairs
within the parameters prescribed by the former.

Altogether 17 regional associations, as compared with 10 up to 1910, were
formally established in the decade 1911–20 (Sinn 1997: 377). Partly a result of the
enactment of the Societies Ordinance in 1911, "which forced many informal
societies to become formally established" (Sinn 1990: 166), and partly an outcome
of the changing socioeconomic and political environment in the mainland after the
1911 revolution, an upsurge of regional associations began around 1910.

The development of these regional associations mirrors the changing configuration of Hong Kong society and its population (Sinn 1990: 174–5, Sinn 2002a).
Most of the *tongs* (a term commonly adopted by various kinds of traditional Chinese

associations) established in the 1870s to the 1900s were rather locally oriented, focusing mainly on the welfare of their native countrymen staying in Hong Kong. The regional merchants' associations that emerged as the dominant form of regional association from the 1900s onwards "participated more widely in local matters than the earlier *tong*" (Sinn 1990: 175) and were also more actively engaged in social (e.g. disaster relief) and political (e.g. nationalist campaigns related to the 1911 revolution) affairs in the mainland. The *tungheungwooi* (association for people of the same native place) that proliferated in the 1930s showed strong nationalist sentiments and responded actively to the mobilization of the Chinese war effort against the Japanese invasion.

The development of trade unions and the labor movement was also closely tied with the political environment and emerging political projects on the mainland. While a strike protesting against an ordinance levying a poll tax was recorded as early as 1844 (Hong Kong Government 1932; Chan 1991: 158; Tsai 1993: 40), strike actions with wider sociopolitical repercussions were the 1884 anti-French strike and boycott, the 1920 mechanics' strike, and the 1922 seamen's general strike (Chan 1991: 160–81; also see Tsai 1993). Of course, none of these major strikes can be reduced to a single cause, be it nationalism or class conflict (see for example Sinn 1982). However, it is fair to say that, whether for popular mobilization or discrete political maneuver and political participation of the Chinese elite (Chung 1998), Chinese politics on the mainland always had an impact on shaping the political horizon and on civic and political group formation in Hong Kong. This connection to national politics continues to be a critical factor in the structuring of Hong Kong's political development.

While thus far we have discussed the growth and development of civic groups organized by the locals, the arrival of Protestant and Catholic missionaries brought social services organizations and charity groups with religious backgrounds to Hong Kong. For example, the Chinese YMCA of Hong Kong was established in 1901, the Hong Kong YWCA in 1920, and the Hong Kong Salvation Army in 1930. Local social services like the Children Playground Association (1933) and the Boys and Girls Clubs Association (1936) were set up in the 1930s to address emerging social issues, such as the growing population of children. In 1936, the Social Service Centre of the Churches was established "to provide family casework, material relief and the co-ordination of agencies' services" (Webb 1977: 134–5). It laid the foundation for the subsequent establishment of the Hong Kong Council of Social Service and the Hong Kong Christian Service in the post-war years.

Without going further into the details of the growth and development of civic organizations in Hong Kong's first century, suffice it to say that the range of these civic organizations was fairly comprehensive, and they were actively involved in different domains of social life.[3] While it would be quite wrong to assume that the colonial government was relaxed in regulating the activities of these civic groups – it was in fact very cautious in managing trade unions and other groups, which was most evident in its rather hostile and repressive measures towards radical organizers and unions after the 1925–6 general strike (Tsai 2001: 162–4), in which might politicized the social environment under its colonial administration – it is fair to say that most of these groups developed autonomously. Together with the reasonably vibrant English and Chinese press media (see for example Sinn 2002b), these local groups and organizations had come to constitute a lively social and public space in Hong Kong.

Furthermore, the colonial government selectively co-opted the leaders of quite a number of these civic organizations into its broader colonial administrative framework. Many of these groups functioned as part of the political machinery for integrating the local elites into the administrative system and for maintaining arm's length but accommodating relations with the Chinese community.

Early post-war decades: coping with the influx of refugees

Following the end of the Sino-Japanese War, the civil war in China triggered another wave of immigrants into Hong Kong, whose population swelled from around 1.6 million in 1946 to almost 2.5 million in 1955. Unlike previous waves of population influx, in which people would return home once conditions in the mainland had stabilized, this round of immigration, and the continuous arrival of legal and illegal migrants from across the border in the many years that followed, had longer-term social, economic, and political implications.

For one, despite the Communist victory in 1949 and the Nationalist govern-ment's retreat to Taiwan, the tensions and rivalry between these two political parties and regimes continued to have their impacts on Hong Kong. Trade unionism and the labor movement were structured by the cleavage between the pro-Communist and the pro-Nationalist camps. In the early post-war years, many neighborhood groups and regional associations were also divided into two major camps according to their political affiliation and stance in the Communist–Nationalist rivalry. Indeed, popular mobilizations in the early post-war years, as in the strike wave in 1946–50 (Leung and Chiu 1991) and the 1956 Kowloon and Tsuen Wan riots, are best seen as extensions of this kind of "Chinese politics on Hong Kong soil" (Lee 1998: 158–9).

The colonial government meanwhile had to deal with both reconstruction and recovery in the midst of a war-torn economy and a rapidly growing population. It had to find both the financial and organizational means to provide housing, medical services, public hygiene, and education to the local population as well as an expanding migrant community. More critically, it soon became apparent that these migrants would not return to their home towns once the political turmoil on the mainland had subsided.

The colonial government therefore continued to rely on the local Chinese organizations to assist in providing social welfare services. In addition to enlisting the assistance of established groups like the Tung Wah and the Po Leung Kuk, the colonial administration also began a campaign to mobilize community self-help and mutual aid. As a result, 21 *kaifong* associations had been established in various urban districts by 1954 (Wong 1972). These philanthropic associations were expected to contribute to the provision of relief (especially to the poor and immigrants), education, and other welfare services at the neighborhood level.

Newly formed social service agencies and voluntary charity groups were another source of assistance in providing welfare to migrants and the poor. For example, the late 1940s witnessed the establishment of the Hong Kong Anti-TB and Thoracic Association, the Hong Kong Family Welfare Society, and the St. James Settlement (a social service group based primarily in the Wan Chai district, which was active in relieving poverty). By the early 1950s:

> the above local agencies were joined by several international social service organizations, the majority of which were Christian . . . Most of these organizations were involved in direct relief work, such as the distribution of food and clothing from donor churches overseas or as the channel for government aid, mainly from the U.S.A. but also from European countries, Australia and New Zealand.
>
> (Webb 1977: 137)

The 1950s and 1960s are sometimes characterized as the golden decades of voluntary services, when both local and international agencies played an important role in providing social services. In the 1970s, as Hong Kong gradually became capable of feeding, sheltering, and educating its people, more local voluntary service groups developed new programs and moved into new areas of service provision, such as community development. Furthermore, as Hong Kong became capable of supporting its own welfare services through government subvention and the newly established Community Chest (a fundraising body adopting an organized approach to finance services of small voluntary welfare agencies), many international agencies reduced the scope and scale of their programs, became localized, or began to leave Hong Kong. Local charity and voluntary service groups became less dependent upon overseas support and subsequently developed a wide range of philanthropic bodies to support local services and charities in other parts of the world (Yip 1994; Noda 1995).

The emergence of local politics

The colonial government's ruling strategy worked quite smoothly in an environment where most migrants still saw themselves as refugees or sojourners and shied away from public and social affairs. But the fragility of its anachronistic political system and ruling strategy was exposed as Hong Kong stepped into the modern times of industrial production and it encountered a new generation of young people who had grown up locally, had found the inequalities under colonial rule problematic, and were less prepared than their parents to swallow their pains quietly. The 1966 Kowloon riots, which spontaneously broke out because of a hunger strike against an increase in the fares of the Star Ferry, and the 1967 riots, which were largely shaped by radical politics in the mainland under the influence of the Cultural Revolution, marked a turning point in Hong Kong state–society relations. In response to popular grievances, the colonial state was quick to recognize areas of its administration that were sources of conflict. In 1968 it enacted the Employment Ordinance – "the primary source of legislative protection for Hong Kong workers generally" (England and Rear 1975: 123) – to cope with workers' discontents. It also launched the City District Officer Scheme to bridge the widening gap between the government and the grass roots. In short, the colonial government took an active role in restructuring the state machinery and state–society relations in order to strengthen colonial rule in the post-riot years (Scott 1989).

The colonial state was also quick to enlist support from local voluntary groups in its efforts to expand social services. Voluntary welfare agencies were described as partners of the government, while the latter, instead of taking up the role of direct service provider, significantly broadened its scope of social services by financing projects initiated or carried out by the voluntary agencies. Meanwhile, the colonial state became more active in grassroots organizing in its attempt to strengthen social integration at the community level and to enhance a sense of belonging among the locals. Community mobilization was carried out in the early 1970s to launch the "Keep Hong Kong Clean" and "Fight Violent Crime" campaigns. Following these mobilizing efforts and in response to growing complaints in connection with management issues in multistory buildings, the idea of establishing the Mutual Aid Committee was introduced in 1973 (Leung 1982: 162).

However, despite greater governmental efforts to cultivate a sense of belonging, strengthen its community linkage and develop a responsive and benevolent image of the colonial state, more collective actions soon followed in the late 1960s and early 1970s: first college and university students, then grassroots communities defending their rights and living environment, and then independent unions who championed the welfare of local employees, including those in the civil service (on various social movements, see Chiu and Lui 2000). Indeed, the most distinctive feature of the development of Hong Kong NGOs in the 1970s and 1980s is the emergence and growth of spontaneously organized interest groups and pressure groups that actively used collective action as a means to articulate the interests of concerned parties and to confront a bureaucratic colonial regime.

The early 1970s witnessed several waves of collective action by social movements whose characteristics are as follows. First, most of these collective actions were protest actions whose main strategy was to rally the support of third parties in order to exert pressure on the government. This reveals the movement organizations' limited resources for mass mobilization and their relatively weak bargaining position vis-à-vis the colonial state. Second, these protest actions were an outcome of the institutional configuration of political action under the so-called consultative democracy and the administrative absorption political arrangement (King 1972). Prior to the reform of local administration through the establishment of district boards and related elections in the early 1980s, the channels for open political participation were confined to electing the Urban Council.

More important, within this "consultative democracy" framework, the administrative state was politically insulated from society, and the colonial administration's ruling strategy was depoliticization. In this context, while elitist interest groups could gain access to the government through the appointment of representatives or related persons to consultative bodies and exert political influence on the bureaucrats (Rear 1971; Davies 1977), political demands made by the general public were channeled to the noninstitutional arena. Simply put, the design of the colonial state and its system of representing political interests drove popular political claims and demands to assume the form of protest actions.

By the end of the 1970s, there were signs that a social movement industry was forming. The proliferation of different types of collective action had greatly broadened the scope of contentious politics. A variety of interest groups were mobilized and began to make claims and demands, while protest and pressure groups were formed to sustain mobilization. The growing importance of pressure groups – as for instance the Hong Kong Professional Teachers' Union and the Society for Community Organization, as well as the formation of an *ad hoc* alliance for joint action mobilization under the leadership of these groups – illustrates a change toward the consolidation of social protest through pressure group politics.

In essence, pressure group politics were a continuation of the protest actions of the early 1970s. Though some pressure groups were co-opted into the colonial administrative system through appointment to advisory committees (mainly on an individual, not a group, basis), most of the pressure groups were active outside formal institutional politics. Indeed, the fact that most of them were outsiders to institutional politics helped create a tacit understanding among pressure groups, social movement organizations, and grassroots protest groups. In the joint actions organized in the late 1970s and early 1980s, these various groups and organizations could easily get together and form *ad hoc* organizations for a common cause (e.g. the 1980–1 campaign against a bus fare increase). Their affinity was largely a consequence of the restricted opportunities for political participation in the period. By the early 1980s and on the eve of the Sino-British negotiations over Hong Kong's future, this loosely knit network of pressure groups, social movement organizations, and grassroots protest groups was playing the role of an oppositional force to the colonial administrative state.

Political transition: the separation of electoral politics and popular mobilization

The Sino-British negotiations over Hong Kong's future and the subsequent agreement to return the colony to China on 1 July 1997 brought drastic changes in both the agenda and parameters of Hong Kong politics. Overall, the settlement signaled the beginning of the decolonization process. Without going into the background of different phases of political reform carried out in the 1980s, it is safe to say that changes in the political design restructured Hong Kong's political arena. The new question on the political agenda was how a new political order would be instituted within the parameters of decolonization without independence (Lau 1990) and the diplomatic politics between Britain and China. Meanwhile, in the realm of *realpolitik*, the 1980s was a period of political contention through electoral politics.

Studies of social conflicts in the 1975–95 period (Cheung and Louie 2000; Lau and Wan 2000) show that conflicts related to constitutional matters and political and civil rights issues drastically increased from 1984.[4] Before then, constitutional matters rarely appeared in the agenda of local social movements, though this was not of course because of political indifference among the activists. But prior to the political reforms of the 1980s, most activists saw the question of democratization as an issue that was unlikely to have any practical meaning in the face of a closed colonial administration.

The growing importance of political issues in social conflicts reveals the opening of new political opportunities brought about by decolonization and a shift of attention towards political participation in formal institutional politics by pressure groups, social movement organizations, and grassroots protest groups. The major concern of the activists in the 1980s and 1990s became the struggle for democracy – both for deepening political reform before 1997, and then for democratizing the political structure of the future Special Administrative Region of the People's Republic of China (SAR) government.

The opening of new political opportunities driven by decolonization had a double-edged effect on the development of social movements in Hong Kong. On the one hand, there were new opportunities for political intervention in the sphere of electoral politics and in the process for designing Hong Kong's future political structure. After a short spell of initial hesitation, activists quickly came to form new political groups to prepare for elections at different levels and to articulate political programs for the blueprints of the transitional arrangements and post-1997 administration to the Chinese government (Lui 1999). The proliferation of political groups in the 1980s can be seen as a response to the emerging political order triggered by the decolonization process (Cheng 1984). Indeed, the development of the democracy movement in the 1980s best illustrates how the former pressure groups, social movement organizations, and newly formed political groups had developed a loosely defined group of democrats through previous collaboration and a tacit understanding of the need to fight for the democratic cause (on the pro-democracy movement, see Sing 2000).

The early 1980s was a time when many activists saw the 1997 question as an opportunity of societal mobilization: previously suppressed political agendas (e.g. democratization) would now become real political matters for public discussion. The moves towards the establishment of a representative government in 1985 and 1988, in which for the first time in colonial history Hong Kong elected (indirectly, through functional constituency and electoral college) members of the legislature, further politicized pressure groups and social movement organizations. Political parties were subsequently formed to consolidate the existing networks of activists and concerned groups.

On the other hand, participation in formal political institutional politics had given rise to divisions among the loosely connected active groups in local social movements. The twists and turns during the Sino-British talks about Hong Kong's political reforms, the political structure of the future SAR government, and the emphasis on convergence towards a social and political system that

China would find acceptable posed new questions for political groups and social movement organizations.

The choice between accepting the parameters prescribed by China and continuing to play the role of an oppositional force created divisions among these politically active groups, especially after the Tiananmen Square incident in 1989. The loosely formulated consensus found among active groups in the 1970s lost its relevance: solidarity among the so-called democrats was weakened, and informal political networking was replaced by formal party participation and interorganizational linkages. At the same time, electoral and party politics became the focus of contentious politics in the transitional period. Discussions about the decline of grassroots protest groups reflected the gradual separation of grassroots mobilization and community action on the one hand and party politics on the other (Lui 1993).

It should be noted, however, that the colonial government was not passive in the face of grassroots mobilization and the emergence of social movements and contentious politics. As mentioned earlier, the colonial government had started its own initiatives in community organizing in the early 1970s. These efforts were linked with the broader framework of its district administration, ensuring that the colonial government could continue to recruit potential leaders from local communities.

The colonial government continued to practice the co-optation strategy by selectively recruiting leaders into its administrative structure through appointment to committees and various other advisory bodies. When it finally had to introduce elections to the legislature in the 1980s, the colonial government set up a channel of functional representation to formalize the political representation of business associations and professional groups (Leung 1990). This was intended both to encourage more political participation from those with vested interests in the established social system and to counterbalance more radical voices that had been growing stronger in the context of the political transition.

The mass mobilization before and after the Tiananmen Square incident did not really change this picture. While more than one million people joined the street rallies and marches to protest the suppression of the student movement in Beijing, the pro-Chinese democracy movement quickly lost support following the crackdown (Wong 2000). Nor did controversies over the political reform program put forward by the governor, Chris Patten, trigger another round of pro-democracy popular mobilization. As Hong Kong approached 1997, it was increasingly difficult to mobilize the public and to stage open confrontational action against China.

In a sense, the process of politicization facilitated by political changes since the Sino-British negotiations did not really bring social movements into institutional politics. While we witnessed the participation of pressure groups, social movement organizations, and protest groups' leaders in electoral politics in the 1990s and 1980s, this did not necessarily imply the political transformation of social movements. Popular demands expressed in collective actions were brought to public discussion in the electoral bodies, but they were mediated by party and electoral politics.

The odd situation in Hong Kong was that a kind of party politics operated in a political institutional setting that, given the constraints of the political design, did not allow parties to assume decision-making power. This shaped party and electoral politics into a type of oppositional politics, maintaining a close connection with grassroots social movements, but its agenda and room for maneuver were significantly restricted by Hong Kong's peculiar decolonization process. The very fact that Hong Kong's politics had to be accommodated within the broader framework of Chinese politics and that the crafting of the SAR blueprint was restricted to diplomatic talks between the Chinese and British governments made it very difficult for oppositional electoral politics to convince residents of the viability of a form of alternative politics that could go beyond the restrictions imposed by the decolonization framework.

At the same time, the issues and questions brought about by 1997 drove almost all active political participants to concentrate on political matters, especially those concerning China–Hong Kong relations. Issues such as the impacts of industrial relocation and the consequences of a bubble economy, which were most relevant to grassroots mobilization and became more apparent after the economic recession that began in late 1997, were not successfully articulated to the 1997 political agenda. This reinforced the separation of party and electoral politics from social movements and popular mobilization.

Contemporary civic groups: organization, outlooks, and action

Organizational profile

The brief review above offers a diachronic view of the development of civic organization in the context of Hong Kong history. In this section, based upon the findings of a survey we carried out in 2000, we will give a snapshot of Hong Kong's civic organizations.[5] The observations taken by the diachronic and synchronic perspectives largely echo each other. First of all, our survey findings confirm that civic organizations in Hong Kong have a relatively long history: 19 percent of the surveyed NGOs were established in or before 1945. More interestingly, the years these NGOs were established are fairly evenly spread across the post-war decades: 13 percent were founded in 1946–59, 14 percent in 1960–9, 17.5 percent in 1970–9, 18 percent in 1980–9, and 18.5 percent from 1990 onwards.

This finding is consistent with the observation that, while the colonial government was always cautious in handling NGOs that tried to politicize and radicalize social and political participation, in general it did not explicitly suppress freedom of speech and assembly. There is no indication of a repressive period wherein people's efforts to organize were driven underground, nor of a time when civil society bounced back from containment and/or suppression. Hong Kong's NGOs generally grew and developed in a reasonably open and stable sociopolitical environment.

The surveyed NGOs varied in membership size: 28.6 percent had fewer than 100 members, 32.6 percent had 100–499 members, 36.9 percent had 500 or more members, and about 2 percent declared that they only had organizational members. The main source of NGO finances came from membership dues (38.2 percent); fundraising (22.2 percent) and government subvention (16.4 percent) were the other sources that financed their activities. Of the surveyed organizations, 83.5 percent employed part- or full-time staff. Only 2 of the 206 NGOs surveyed said that they were not formally registered.[6]

Social and political participation

In our review of the historical development of Hong Kong's civic organizations, we found that voluntary groups played a critical part in the interface between the state and society, not only fulfilling a bridging function for communication but playing a crucial role in the delivery of services. The government was therefore always accommodating and often approached these organizations to recruit potential local leaders. On the other hand, these groups quite often became agents for popular mobilization, articulating the interests of the grass roots, and were watchdogs of government policies.

In other words, there is a dualism in Hong Kong's civil society. On the one side, local civic organizations – particularly business associations, government-sponsored neighborhood groups, professional organizations, and Chinese charity groups – are targets of the government's strategy of administrative absorption and have been given access to decision-making channels or advisory bodies either through appointment or special institutional arrangements, like the functional constituency to the legislature. Others, like social service organizations, are gradually integrated into the framework of government regulation and administration by building up a partnership through government subvention.

Put differently, whether it is the colonial state or the SAR, Hong Kong's government has always practiced a selectively inclusive strategy in handling civic organizations; it is also well aware that it needs their support when launching and carrying out social policies and state-building measures at the community level (in the sense of both geographical entity and functional group). On the other side, there are civic organizations that largely stay outside the political establishment. They constitute a loosely organized network of oppositional political force, assume the role of pressure group, and articulate the interests of neglected communities.

This dualistic development is clearly shown in terms of different groups' participation in social and political affairs (see Table 4.1). The contrast between business–professional associations and advocacy groups is obvious. Business and professional associations show limited attempts in participating in elections at different levels yet are able to secure positions in the legislature and the Executive Council. Indeed, the partially democratized political arrangement allows the SAR government to ensure that established business interests and socioeconomic elites (such as the professionals) have access to the channels of decision making. These groups organize actions to support the government, but, with the possible exception of legal professionals, they largely stay out of confronting the state.

Table 4.1 Social and political participation by types of civic organizations in Hong Kong

Political participation/ types of group %	Business and professional groups %	Religious groups %	Neighborhood groups %	Academic and research organizations %	Advocacy groups %	Social service groups %	All %
Organized actions in support of the SAR government	36.6	22.2	37.5	50.0	29.2	39.5	36.5
Organized or participated in social action	20.7	55.6	20.0	0.0	84.0	51.1	36.8
Core members participated in district board elections	16.3	0.0	56.3	16.7	40.0	15.2	21.5
Core members participated in urban council or regional council elections	7.6	0.0	12.5	0.0	16.0	6.5	8.2
Core members participated in legislative council elections	29.3	11.1	25.0	33.3	28.0	15.2	24.6
Core members having positions in district board	8.8	25.0	25.0	16.7	37.5	15.9	16.3
Core members having positions in urban council or regional council	4.4	12.5	0.0	0.0	16.7	4.5	5.8
Core members having positions in the legislature	17.6	0.0	12.5	33.3	25.0	9.1	15.8
Core members having positions in the Executive Council	5.5	0.0	0.0	0.0	4.2	4.5	4.2
Core members having positions in advisory committees	38.2	22.2	42.9	33.3	56.0	55.6	43.9

Source: The Hong Kong Civic Organization Survey, 2000

Advocacy groups, on the other hand, are active in many elections. Bearing in mind that some of them are pro-government (e.g. the pro-China Federation of Trade Unions) and are able to secure access to positions in the top power echelon, they generally need to work a lot harder than the business and professional associations to obtain similar returns. Advocacy groups are more likely to be organizers of protest and oppositional campaigns, and it is mainly as a result of their own initiative of trying to enhance their influence through participation in formal politics that quite a number of them are able to find positions in the political establishment.

It is also interesting to observe that more than half (55.6 percent) of Hong Kong's religious groups organized or participated in social action. In fact, the involvement of Catholic groups in issues concerning the rights of abode (more particularly concerning the right of Hong Kong residency for local residents' mainland-born children) and the campaign against the enactment of national security legislation under article 23 of the Basic Law have drawn people's attention to changing state–church relations.

While it would be hasty to conclude that religious groups have assumed a more active role in social and public affairs in recent years, this shows that the controversies evolving around issues of justice and freedom have brought about societal mobilization across different sectors of the population. So far, however, it is social groups and organizations with religious faith and moral values, not religious groups, that have taken the offensive and come out to defend the rights of the powerless and the sense of justice.

As shown by the range and extent of social and political participation of different kinds of civic organizations (Table 4.1), the robustness of Hong Kong's civil society has not declined since 1997. Despite various criticisms of media self-censorship and of the SAR government's paternalistic style of governance, Hong Kong's civil society remains vibrant. In fact, the first six years of the Tung Chee-hwa administration were marked by waves of protest. For instance, on 25 June 2000, five demonstrations took place: doctors against the government's reform proposal, social welfare workers against the new service-funding system, local residents against the land-resumption power of the newly established Urban Renewal Authority, the pro-business Liberal Party organized a demonstration to express the grievances of property owners who were badly hit by the property slump, and a protest against the government's stand on the rights of abode.

More dramatically, half a million people, with the active participation of the middle class (*Hong Kong Economic Times* 2003), marched in the street on 1 July 2003, the sixth anniversary of Hong Kong's return to China. The main theme of the mass rally was the protest against the Basic Law's proposed article 23 legislation concerning national security. But it was also evident that many joined the demonstration not only because they were skeptical regarding the planned anti-subversion law and feared losing political freedom, but because of their growing discontent with the SAR government. Even after 1997, Hong Kong people are no less ready to voice their discontent in the public sphere and to demonstrate their solidarity in collective action.

Concluding remarks

In summarizing the development of civic organizations in Hong Kong, the main points are as follows. First, though civic organizations in Hong Kong were for a long time under an undemocratic colonial political structure and more recently a partially democratized political institution, they have to a large extent been able to flourish unrestrictedly. Voluntary groups play an active role and important part in the social and political life of the local community, a tradition that has not been undermined by political transitions either before or after 1997. The civil society is still robust, and civic organizations continue to enjoy their autonomous status. In fact, the SAR government has come to recognize the voluntary groups' significant contributions by openly expressing an interest in further cultivating the third sector and enlisting its support to deal with increasing demands for social welfare in an environment of economic downturn.

Second, while civic organizations in Hong Kong are essentially autonomous from state control, the state plays a critical part in determining their public status. The state has adopted a selectively inclusive strategy in co-opting civic organizations into its machinery of political domination, which are then often granted privileged access to political decision making. However, this selectively inclusive strategy also implies that a significant number of local civic organizations, such as grassroots pressure groups and pro-democracy political groups, have been kept away from the power center. They gain political influence either by joining local elections or by carrying out mass mobilization. Some of them have been protest groups from the very beginning that try to strengthen their bargaining power by socializing tensions and conflicts. Others are reluctant rebels that became protest groups because of state reactions to their course of action. The distinction between simply being a civic organization and a social protest (or social movement) group is therefore often quite fine.

The state has of course changed its targets of political co-optation because of the 1997 change in government. For instance, pro-China labor unions were able to change from being oppositional groups under the colonial regime to being supporting political partners after 1997, as their leaders became members of the Executive Council. In other words, the state has the power to define the status of civic organizations and indirectly shape the parameters within which these organizations try to exert their social and political influence.

Third, those civic organizations that have largely stayed outside the power center have assumed a significant role as the political opposition and have contributed to the liberalization of the political environment. This was particularly the case in the 1960s and 1970s, when the colonial government offered few openings for political participation. However, unlike civic organizations in countries undergoing democratic transition, which empower the public for democratization and a redistribution of political power, Hong Kong's civic organizations are primarily agents in maintaining a generally liberal political environment and the organizational autonomy of voluntary groups. They are more active in defending and empowering social space than seeking political power.

Nevertheless, the boundary between the social and the political is not fixed, and civic groups' defensive moves to protecting their autonomy can be politicized in the face of an authoritarian state. Indeed, the mass rally of 1 July 2003 clearly demonstrates the strengths of civic organizations in mobilizing the public in defending political freedom and in expressing political discontents in the public domain, rather than the more narrowly political organizations that focus on election campaigns and contend for power within the establishment. Civic organizations play a critical role in articulating people's discontent and in creating an effective interface for bringing frustrated individuals to the public domain of collective action.

Yet it must also be noted that the future role and development of Hong Kong's civic organizations is not simply determined by their own organizational objectives. Equally critical will be the effects of the changing political parameters defined by the state and the practice of "one country, two systems" jointly managed by China's central government and the local SAR government. We have argued that Hong Kong's civic organizations are both friends and critics of the state. They can be agents of cooperation. But they can also be agents of opposition, especially when confronted by authoritarian control from above.

Notes

1   As Yue puts it, "NGOs in Hong Kong are both comprehensive in range and high in number" (1997: 451).
2   Our account of the development of Hong Kong NGOs primarily covers those organized by the local Chinese and groups with external linkages and affiliations. We did not include groups organized by expatriates.
3   It was not our intention to cover all kinds of civic organizations in early Hong Kong in this brief review. For example, we have not touched upon sports and cultural groups run by local Chinese, nor have we reviewed the growth of professional bodies. As just one example of the latter, the Royal Institution of Chartered Surveyors (Hong Kong Branch) was established in 1928.
4   The analysis of social conflicts in 1987–95 suggests that the number of protests concerning the Basic Law has dropped significantly since 1991 (Lau and Wan 2000: 144).
5   Our survey was carried out in 2000 and covered eight types of civic organizations: business associations, professional associations, social service groups and organizations, regional and neighborhood associations, women's groups, environmental groups, academic groups, and pressure groups. While there is no official source of all registered or unregistered civic organization, we gathered a list of 1,222 organizations from different sources. Through documentary research and direct contacts, we identified 785 organizations in our list as suitable targets for interview. We mailed questionnaires and followed up by telephone to ensure responses from the sampled organizations. Altogether we collected 207 questionnaires, of which 206 were completed and suitable for analysis.
6   Of course, these descriptive statistics have to be interpreted cautiously. Given the limitations of the scale of the present study and the difficulties in accessing civic organizations that are less organized and have fewer resources, we cannot overstate our sample's statistical representation. For instance, 48 percent of our sampled civic organizations belonged to business and professional groups, which probably allowed us to gather information on groups that have a longer history and larger membership, and

are staffed with full-time employees. That said, the survey findings do allow us to make some interesting observations from this snapshot of civic organizations in contemporary Hong Kong.

References

Chan, W.K. *The Making of Hong Kong Society: Three Studies of Class Formation in Early Hong Kong.* Oxford: Clarendon Press, 1991.

Cheng, Joseph Y.S. (ed.). *Hong Kong: In Search of a Future.* Hong Kong: Oxford University Press, 1984.

Cheung, Anthony B.L., and K.S. Louie. "Social Conflicts: 1975–1986." In *Social Development and Political Change in Hong Kong*, edited by Siu-kai Lau. Hong Kong: Chinese University Press, 2000, pp. 63–114.

Chiu, Stephen W.K., and Tai-lok Lui. (eds.). *The Dynamics of Social Movement in Hong Kong.* Hong Kong: Hong Kong University Press, 2000.

Chung, Stephanie Po-yin. *Chinese Business Groups in Hong Kong and Political Change in South China, 1900–25.* Houndmills: Macmillan Press, 1998.

Davies, S.G.N. "One Brand of Politics Rekindled." *Hong Kong Law Journal*, 7, 1 (1977): 44–80.

England, Joe, and John Rear. *Chinese Labour under British Rule.* Hong Kong: Oxford University Press, 1975.

Hong Kong Economic Times. "500,000 People on the Street; the Middle Class Roared in Anger!" *Hong Kong Economic Times*, 2 July 2003, p. A1. (in Chinese)

Hong Kong Government. *Historical and Statistical Abstract of the Colony of Hong Kong 1841–1930.* Hong Kong: Government Printer, 1932.

King, Ambrose Y.C. "Administrative Absorption of Politics in Hong Kong." *Asian Survey*, 15, 5 (1972): 422–39.

Lau, Siu-kai. "Decolonization without Independence and the Poverty of Political Leaders in Hong Kong." Occasional Paper No.1, Hong Kong Institute of Asia-Pacific Studies, 1990.

Lau, Siu-kai, and Po-san Wan. "Social Conflicts: 1987–1995." In *Social Development and Political Changes in Hong Kong*, edited by Siu-kai Lau. Hong Kong: Chinese University Press, 2000, pp. 115–70.

Lee, Ming-kwan. "Hong Kong Identity – Past and Present." In *Hong Kong Economy and Society: Challenges in the New Era*, edited by Siu-lun Wong and Maruya Toyojiro. Tokyo: Institute of Developing Economies, 1998, pp. 153–74.

Lethbridge, H.J. *Hong Kong: Stability and Change.* Hong Kong: Oxford University Press, 1978.

Leung, Benjamin, and Stephen Chiu. "A Social History of Industrial Strikes and the Labour Movement in Hong Kong, 1946–1989." Occasional Paper No.3, Social Sciences Research Centre, University of Hong Kong, 1991.

Leung, C.B. "Community Participation: From Kai Fong Association, Mutual Aid Committee to District Board." In *Hong Kong in the 1980s*, edited by Joseph Y.S. Cheng. Hong Kong: Summerson Eastern Publishers, 1982, pp. 152–70.

Leung, Joan Y.H. "Functional Representation in Hong Kong: Institutionalization and Legitimization of the Business and Professional Elites." *Asian Journal of Public Administration*, 12, 2 (1990): 143–75.

Lui, Tai-lok. "Two Logics of Community Politics." In *Hong Kong Tried Democracy*, edited by Siu-kai Lau and K.S. Louie. Hong Kong: Hong Kong Institute of Asia-Pacific Studies, 1993, pp. 331–44.

——. "Pressure Group Politics in Hong Kong." In *Political Participation in Hong Kong*, edited by Joseph Y.S. Cheng. Hong Kong: City University of Hong Kong Press, 1999, pp. 149–73.

Noda, Makito. "Philanthropy and NGOs in Hong Kong and Asia Pacific Orientation." In *Emerging Civil Society in the Asia Pacific Community*, edited by Tadashi Yamamoto. Tokyo: Japan Center for International Exchange, 1995, pp. 109–20.

Rear, John. "One Brand of Politics." In *Hong Kong: The Industrial Colony*, edited by Keith Hopkins. Hong Kong: Oxford University Press, 1971, pp. 55–139.

Scott, Ian. *Political Change and the Crisis of Legitimacy in Hong Kong*. Hong Kong: Oxford University Press, 1989.

Sing, Ming. "Mobilization for Political Change – The Pro-Democracy Movement in Hong Kong (1980s–1994)." In *The Dynamics of Social Movement in Hong Kong*, edited by Stephen W.K. Chiu and Tai-lok Lui. Hong Kong: Hong Kong University Press, 2000, pp. 21–53.

Sinn, Elizabeth. "The Strike and Riot of 1884 – A Hong Kong Perspective." *Journal of the Hong Kong Branch of the Royal Asiatic Society*, 22 (1982): 65–98.

——. *Power and Charity: The Early History of the Tung Wah Hospital, Hong Kong*. Hong Kong: Oxford University Press, 1989.

——. "A History of Regional Associations in Pre-war Hong Kong." In *Between East and West*, edited by Elizabeth Sinn. Hong Kong: Centre of Asian Studies, 1990, pp. 159–86.

——. "Xin Xi Guxiang: A Study of Regional Associations as a Bonding Mechanism in the Chinese Diaspora. The Hong Kong Experience." *Modern Asian Studies*, 31, 2 (1997): 375–97.

——. "Tongxiang Associations and the Centering of Hong Kong in the Chinese Diasporic World." Paper presented at the international conference on Repositioning Hong Kong and Shanghai in Modern Chinese History, University of Hong Kong, 11–12 June, 2002a.

——. "Emerging Media: Hong Kong and the Early Evolution of the Chinese Press." Modern Asian Studies, 36, 2 (2002b): 421–66.

Tsai, Jung-fang. *Hong Kong in Chinese History: Community and Social Unrest in the British Colony, 1842–1913*. New York: Columbia University Press, 1993.

——. *Xianggangren zhi xianggangshi* [The Hong Kong People's History of Hong Kong]. Hong Kong: Oxford University Press, 2001.

Webb, Paul R. "Voluntary Social Welfare Services." In *1951–1976: A Quarter-Century of Hong Kong*, edited by Chung Chi College. Hong Kong: Chung Chi College, 1977, pp. 133–44.

Wong, A. *The Kaifong Associations and Hong Kong Society*. Taipei: Orient Cultural Service, 1972.

Wong, Pik Wan. "The Pro-Chinese Democracy Movement in Hong Kong." In *The Dynamics of Social Movement in Hong Kong*, edited by Stephen W.K. Chiu and Tai-lok Lui. Hong Kong: Hong Kong University Press, 2000, pp. 55–90.

Yip, Alice Ngan. "Private Philanthropy in Hong Kong." In *Evolving Patterns of Asia-Pacific Philanthropy*, edited by Ku-Hyun Jung. Seoul: Institute of East and West Studies, Yonsei University, 1994, pp. 111–30.

Yu, Sheng-wu and Cun-kuan Liu. *Shijiu Shiji de Xianggang* [Nineteenth-Century Hong Kong]. Beijing: Zhonghua Shuju, 1994.

Yue, Ren. "NGOs in Hong Kong: The Present and the Future." *Journal of Contemporary China*, 6, 16 (1997): 449–60.

5 Civil associations and autonomy under three regimes

The boundaries of state and society in Hong Kong, Taiwan, and China

Robert P. Weller

In the late fall of 1995 I was travelling down a bumpy road in the remote mountains of China's Gansu province, talking to my Chinese counterpart on a World Bank poverty relief project. I had raised the issue of finding mechanisms that might deliver certain benefits (like microfinance) to project participants and of identifying or creating institutions that could monitor the provincial government's success in carrying out the project. My counterpart immediately suggested that NGOs could fill these roles. I was astonished – this was a complete change from the utter reliance on state-controlled mechanisms that I had always seen in earlier work on the project.

It turned out that my counterpart had just attended the United Nations Fourth World Conference on Women, along with the associated NGO Forum on Women, which had taken place in Beijing earlier that fall, and he was swept up by the global infatuation with NGOs that took off during the 1990s. China had just created legal room for registered NGOs a few years earlier,[1] and several high-profile international NGOs were now working with the government, especially on environmental, health, and poverty issues. Other international NGOs pressured the government from the outside, particularly on human rights issues. In fact, each of the three very different Chinese polities I describe in this chapter – Hong Kong, Taiwan, and the People's Republic of China (PRC) – saw the number of legally registered indigenous NGOs increase very significantly in the course of the decade, echoing what happened all around the world.

This was a period when intergovernmental organizations like the World Bank and the United Nations Development Programme, and national development agencies like the United States Agency for International Development began to rely on NGOs to help design and monitor projects on the ground. They hoped that NGOs represented a broadening of democracy in ways that would lead to better governance. At roughly the same time, many governments began to emulate the neoliberal call for smaller government and privatization of services. China too has trumpeted the slogan of "small government, big society," even though the political results so far bear little resemblance to neoliberal visions of the appropriate role for the state.

Nevertheless, the suggestion to use NGOs for this particular World Bank project in 1995 came to nothing: we simply could not find any actual NGOs in rural Gansu. In fact, although China had thousands of registered civil associations in all kinds of fields by then, it is not clear that any of them quite fit the image that so appeals to international policy-makers. The long shadow of the state in this anecdote, and more generally in China's NGO sector, suggests the importance of taking a closer look at the relations between states and NGO structures in various Chinese societies.

This chapter details some of the results of a study of NGOs in four Chinese cities under three very different political regimes: Guangzhou and Xiamen (People's Republic of China), Taipei (Taiwan, the Republic of China), and Hong Kong.[2] Although the cases vary in important ways, none of them shows a very clear split between state and society. This is true even for Taiwan, which has historically been open to the strongest state–society antagonism.

These cases allow us to examine two versions of the hypothesis that NGOs promote democracy. First, the creation and activity of NGOs could be a precursor to procedural democracy – the regular choice of government representatives through open and fair elections. This seems to be the long-term hope behind some of the global push for NGOs. The Taiwan case is especially significant in this respect because the island has undergone a successful and peaceful transition to democracy. The second version suggests a somewhat softer kind of democratization, in which NGOs could foster better governance by offering states improved feedback from their people. New groups would gain an ability to influence decisions without any fundamental change in political structure.

The data for this essay are primarily derived from three sources: a census of registered organizations in each of the four cities, a formal questionnaire administered to at least 100 representative groups in each city, and in-depth interviews with a smaller group of association leaders. All four cities had long been parts of imperial China. They shared a unified political system and the broad outlines of Chinese culture. Like any set of places in China, however, they also varied significantly. Historically, Guangzhou was by far the most important of the cities, having long served as a provincial capital. Xiamen began its rapid development only fairly recently, primarily when its commercial opportunities greatly increased toward the end of the Qing Dynasty (1644–1911). Until very recently, it did not experience the very rapid growth seen in the other cities since about 1850, and is currently the smallest of the four. Taipei, like Taiwan, was a distant frontier city that was utterly transformed during the Japanese occupation of 1895–1945, while Hong Kong only developed into a city under British colonial rule, beginning in the middle of the nineteenth century.

Like all Chinese cities, these four have long histories of familiarity with intermediate associations – groups that were not part of the state but extend beyond the most particularistic ties of kith and kin. Contracts and the idea of share-holding associations were extremely widespread mechanisms for creating corporate institutions in imperial China. For example, in rural farm households all over China and Taiwan, it is still not difficult to find Qing Dynasty contracts that dealt with issues ranging from family property to temple finance to philanthropy (Cohen 2002; Sangren 1984). We can also find common-place-of-origin associations, common surname associations (where there is no traceable kinship tie), pilgrimage associations, famine relief associations, educational associations, and many other examples.[3] None of these were precisely NGOs in the current sense. In particular, they lacked the modern legal structures that put them in a particular relationship to the state, and many had involuntary or personalistic recruitment mechanisms that discussions of "modernity" tend to downplay.[4] Nevertheless they were clearly precursors to developments in the twentieth century, and most of these forms of association continue to this day.

Many of the international NGOs that developed in Europe and North America during the nineteenth century entered China during the waning years of the Qing Dynasty and continued at least through the Republican period (1911–49 on the mainland, and 1945 to the present in Taiwan). Prominent examples include the Red Cross and the Young Men's Christian Association. China's more urban areas quickly developed their own range of NGOs as well: unions, academic associations, fan clubs, and an extraordinary range of interest groups, including those formed to ban foot-binding, to simplify the writing system, to promote Western dress, to oppose Western dress, and on and on.

The modern legal frameworks for civil associations in Taipei, Guangzhou, Xiamen, and Hong Kong began during the late nineteenth century. The laws incorporating these groups varied, according to the different political trajectories of each site. Hong Kong (and later the New Territories) developed directly under British colonial law, which encouraged social organization, but only within a circumscribed sphere outside of politics, as Lui *et al.* describe in Chapter 4. Both Taiwan and the mainland took part in the late Qing Dynasty legal reforms, but Taiwan's crucial early development of a legal structure for social organizations came under Japanese colonialism (1895–1945), which was itself a reworking of traditions that began in Europe. The Republic of China shaped the mainland after 1911 by developing a legal framework that moved to Taiwan after the defeat of the Japanese, but which was ultimately erased on the mainland by the Revolution of 1949. In spite of the variations, all these legal developments initially grew out of the same nineteenth-century global movement that led to the first international NGOs, like the Red Cross.

The most important variant after the middle of the twentieth century is of course the People's Republic, which during the course of the 1950s generally subsumed such organizations into various mass associations. Earlier forms of association merged into new bodies like the Women's Federation, official religious groups (one for each recognized religion), and the official labor union. The alternatives were to disband or to continue in only the most informal ways. Semi-independent associations were re-created there only during the reform era after 1978.

All four sites took part in the rapid global growth of civil associations that began in the 1980s. In Guangzhou 85 percent of the registered NGOs in 1996 had been founded after the Chinese economic reforms began in 1978. In Xiamen, which experienced extremely rapid economic growth during this period, the figure was even higher: 90 percent. In Taipei, about 75 percent of the civil associations were founded after authoritarian control began to loosen up around 1980, while more than half began after 1990, when the democratic consolidation was already established. Hong Kong grew less dramatically than the others during this period, because it is the only case where these organizations had been relatively unfettered in the previous decades – about a third of its NGOs were founded after 1980.

The timing of this growth correlates closely with the global growth in NGOs, but it is important to note that the dynamics behind the increases were different in each case, as indicated by the previous chapters in this volume. In Taiwan, new civil associations skyrocketed with the political freedoms that came after the end of martial law in 1987. They were as much the result of internally driven political transformation as of global influence. The changes at roughly the same time in Guangzhou and Xiamen also stemmed in part from political transformation, but here it was a move toward state corporatism and away from state totalitarianism, which was quite different from what was occurring in Taiwan.

The changes taking place in the People's Republic did relate to the increasing role of the market, and to an attempt to reduce the role of government in some limited sectors – both global trends at the time. Yet they were hardly the result of a wave of neoliberal sentiment that helped promote NGOs in other contexts. Hong Kong may come closest to fitting the globalization model, though the speed of change there in the 1980s was less than in the other three cities. Hong Kong did not experience the large political changes that altered social life in Taiwan or the People's Republic. Even Hong Kong, however, was greatly complicated by its impending return to Chinese rule and by the colonial government's last-minute attempts at democratization.

All four cities underwent significant political changes that correlate closely in timing with an increase in NGOs, although the nature of the changes differed significantly across the three polities. The sections that follow examine each of the cases in turn to determine how these changes relate to the stronger and weaker forms of the democratization hypothesis. All four cities are at least relatively more democratic than they were two decades ago: in Taipei's case the transformation has been quite dramatic. But are NGOs the cause of these changes or the result? The answers, of course, will be more complex than the question implies; in partic- ular, they will turn on the question of how NGOs relate to state power.

Xiamen and Guangzhou

The People's Republic of China came closest to attempting a classic totalitarian project during the years of the Great Proletarian Cultural Revolution, 1966–76. At that time even the mass organizations that had been set up in the 1950s seemed potential distractions from the business of class struggle, and became relatively inactive. Institutional boundaries between state and society, and even between public and private life, became ever more difficult to maintain. Everyone was to become a revolutionary activist in all aspects of their lives – dedicated cells in the greater socialist body.

Such projects have never fully succeeded anywhere, and China began to dismantle this one formally in the late 1970s. The period of economic reforms that began in 1978 has, at the expense of central planning, ushered in far greater use of market mechanisms in all aspects of the economy. Although the Communist Party apparently has no intention of giving up one party rule, it has recognized the desirability of an independent social sector for several reasons. For one thing, it hopes to shrink the fiscal burden of the state by moving some responsibilities to the social sector. Groups that used to be formal parts of government have thus needed to raise funds in other ways. The government also recognizes that the market economy will require certain functions (e.g. accounting) to take place independently from the state, especially now that China is a member of the World Trade Organization. Finally, the government has simply abandoned the idea of controlling every aspect of people's lives, and is willing to allow self-organization where it sees no threat – primarily where the scale remains small and there are no political intentions. As a result, the new kinds of organizations that arose range from sports clubs to professional standards associations.

Chapter 2 by Chan illustrates the enormous increase in social organizations that resulted from this change from the mass organization model to the corporatist NGO model. Very few of these new organizations, however, are "nongovernmental" in any literal sense; corporatism provides a closer model for them than either NGOs in democratic societies or socialist mass organizations. Under corporatist arrangements, each social sector is allowed to organize itself, with the state granting one group in each sector a monopoly on this role in exchange for basic loyalty.

Over the previous decade, a number of scholars have characterized China as corporatist in one sense or another.[5] Indeed, this has become so widespread that something of a reaction has set in, with critics arguing that the term carries too much European baggage to be very useful in the Chinese context. In the case of NGOs, the specific anti-corporatism argument is that these groups are simply agents of state power by another name (Foster 2002). In spite of this, corporatist models of the state–society relationship have clearly shaped the Chinese legal codes that created the possibility of civil associations. These laws and regulations do not, of course, determine how organizations will actually develop, but they do indicate a way of imagining the relationship between state and society that is very influential in China.

The Chinese Constitution of 1982 guaranteed freedom of association, but typically gave no details about how that freedom could be exercised. Regulations in 1984 set a very high bar for recognition as a nationwide "social organization" (*shehui tuanti*), requiring strict control, establishment of a need for the association, and explicit permission of the State Council and the Central Committee of the Communist Party. In practice, however, the number of organizations grew significantly during the late 1980s, especially at local levels. Guangzhou, for instance, had 1,370 registered associations in 1990, and Xiamen (a much smaller city) had 320.

As Chan's chapter details, the Tiananmen demonstrations of May and June 1989 gave the Chinese government second thoughts about the proliferation of social organizations, which led it to create a new regulatory framework within the next year.[6] These new rules required approval by the appropriate government authority (either the bureau in charge of the particular activity or the Ministry of Civil Affairs) and introduced the classic corporatist limit of one organization for each social sector. In general the government is relatively tolerant of academic and professional associations. Friendship associations, according to the regulations, should be favorable to the unity of the country and the solidarity of the nation, and to political and economic stability.[7] Some, like alumni associations and traditional lineages and place-of-origin associations, have not been allowed to register. More recent regulations have largely continued along the same lines, insisting on the limitation of the one association per social sector, and making it illegal, or at least precarious, to organize without registration.[8] The intention of these laws is not so much to enable the social sector as to circumscribe it within a limited political space.

A yearlong purge of registered associations began in 1990, which aimed at removing associations that had improper social influence (i.e. those active in the events in Tiananmen) or that did not match China's "social needs."[9] These new regulations had an immediate effect. By 1991 Guangzhou's associations were reduced by 24 percent and Xiamen's by 21 percent; the total numbers were reduced by perhaps a third nationwide (Pei 1998). Yet none of this constituted a fundamental or long-term change. As in the country as a whole, both cities had recovered their earlier number of associations within two or three years and by the late 1990s far surpassed all earlier levels. Restrictive as the law may be, it has not prevented the birth of thousands of new associations in a flourishing that has not existed since the Revolution of 1949.

These laws serve in part as a statement of how the highest levels of government imagine the relations between state and society. They also create the possibility of close supervision of all social activity and a legal basis for repression of undesirable associations. They do not, however, describe social reality in any detail. At one end, many small, apolitical organizations exist without registering or by registering under false pretenses. Revived local temple cults are one typical example. Revived lineages have a similar existence, or sometimes remake themselves superficially as museums or local history associations (e.g. Yang 2001). Even large NGOs sometimes manipulate the registration system. For example, the largest environmental group in the People's Republic, Friends of Nature, registered under the Academy of Chinese Culture by claiming an artificial interest in traditional ideas about nature. Its leader refused the corporatist monopoly in favor of this less legitimized but freer position.

The quasi-religious Falun Gong also demonstrates the problems the system can create. Falun Gong was forced to withdraw from the corporatist China Qigong Scientific Research Society in 1996 and was consistently denied permission to register with any other corporatist umbrella group. This made it impossible for the group to continue to operate legally as a large organization. When it nevertheless continued to organize across provincial lines, generally to protest the increasing repression directed at it, the government finally instituted the fierce crackdown of 1999. Repression tends to occur when such organizations grow large enough to cross regional or class lines.

Our study deals almost entirely with the other end of the range, the legally registered organizations. However, even these groups do not entirely match the world that the regulatory system imagines. One of our main research goals, therefore, was to discover to what extent these groups had any significant autonomy from their supervising units in the government. The corporatist model in the regulations imagines them as representatives of social sectors, pliant and harmonious, but still able to speak for society. In practice, relations with the state are significantly more complex than this.

For example, the leadership of most organizations tends to interdigitate with government and party officials, especially from the supervising unit. A large majority of associations (75 percent in Guangzhou, 63 percent in Xiamen) reported that the government played at least some role in their creation.[10] Representatives of supervising units, including recently retired cadres, also sat on the executive committees (*lishi hui*) of a majority of associations (81 percent in Guangzhou, 54 percent in Xiamen). Many of the leaders interviewed confirmed that they preferred to have official representatives among their leadership. They saw this less as interference than as an invaluable connection to the resources and privileges of the state and party.

These organizations also intertwine financially with the state. Unlike some of our other cases, PRC law does not set a high financial bar to registration: national-level organizations need only assets of 100,000 yuan (approximately US$12,500[11]). The state also hopes to encourage financial independence among these organizations, since it has fiscal problems of its own. To help organizations meet their financial needs, in the mid-1990s it began to allow some market-based activity. However, few organizations have been able to take much advantage of this, and the state remains one of the most significant sources of funding in both Guangzhou and Xiamen, matched only by membership dues (Table 5.1). When we asked leaders what they would most like for their organizations in the future, the most common answer by far was more financial support from the government. Again, we found very little evidence of autonomy from the government or even of a desire for autonomy.

Table 5.1 Major sources of income for civil associations by city

	Hong Kong %	Taipei %	Guangzhou %	Xiamen %
Dues	38	28	26	31
Donations	22	32	15	16
Government	17	8	41	33
Activity income	15	12	6	9
Other	8	20	12	11

The Guangzhou section of the project discovered that there is a significant mismatch between organizations' actual dependence on the state and their self-conception. Kin-man Chan and Haixiong Qiu, who ran that portion of the project, classified their sample according to three categories (official, semiofficial, and popular), depending on how closely leadership, activities, and finances were tied to the government. They also asked groups to rank themselves on those categories. Chan and Qiu's independent classification of organizations' dependence on the state did not correlate at all with the groups' subjective classification of themselves. Instead, groups at both the official and popular ends of the range, as measured by behavior, tended to describe themselves as semiofficial. Chan and Qiu interpret this as a sign that these organizations tried to maximize their power to negotiate and maneuver between society and state. They think of themselves as semiofficial, regardless of their real relation to the state, because that is the position they want to occupy. In this system, genuine autonomy is not an advantage.

As an example, they cite Guangzhou's Private Entrepreneurs' Association, whose leaders come primarily from the ranks of government, but who constantly lobby their ex-colleagues against the multiplicity of taxes and management fees and for the passage of new municipal laws on private enterprise management, as a way of minimizing what members see as arbitrary interference from officials. One ex-official in a business association reported that his government counter-parts criticized him for not "knowing where his hips should sit." These results are consistent with the behaviors of similar organizations elsewhere in China (e.g. Unger 1996; Wank 1995).

If we begin with the assumption that state and society are clearly demarcated and that a primary function of civil associations like NGOs is to limit state power, then associational life in China seems very weak indeed. Nearly none of the NGOs in Xiamen or Guangzhou fills this role very well. Smaller groups that do not register officially must either disguise themselves or live in precarious legal limbo. Yet if we abandon the assumption that a strong state–society split is critical to modern life, associational life in China seems far more animated and central. The current situation is far different from anything that existed in the People's Republic before the reforms, because these new associations must answer to their con-stituents as well as to the state. This is true financially – dues are roughly equal to government subsidies in importance – as well as socially.

While I have so far considered the two PRC cities together, a brief comparison of their differences is also revealing. In general, organizations in Xiamen have considerably greater autonomy in every sphere than those in Guangzhou. One reason for this is that the survey was conducted about two years later in Xiamen, when fiscal changes had encouraged even more conversion of government departments into "nongovernmental" associations and of retired cadres into association leaders. Yet our interviews suggest that much of the difference would have appeared anyway, due to the two cities' very different political and economic histories.

Guangzhou is a major provincial capital. It has a large political apparatus that is watched fairly closely by the central government. Like most large Chinese cities, its economy before the reforms relied heavily on state-owned enterprises. Xiamen, however, was never very important in the political hierarchy. It was a small city that began to grow rapidly only with the commercial expansion of the coast in the nineteenth and early twentieth centuries. The centrally planned economy largely bypassed Xiamen after 1949, primarily because of its exposed position directly opposite Taiwan, with Taiwan's army looming visibly just offshore on Mazu and Jinmen (Quemoy) Islands. The economic reforms and the easing of tensions with Taiwan during the 1980s greatly changed the situation, and Xiamen has boomed since then.

In contrast to most comparable cities in China, Xiamen's unique position left it relatively unfettered by the old centrally planned economy and its political apparatus. We thus found greater autonomy in Xiamen because there was less government superstructure to be thrust into the private sector and because its nonstate economy is so large. This suggests that future Chinese NGOs could become more autonomous, as the government occupies less social space and the market sector of the economy continues to expand.

Let me briefly conclude this section with three points about NGOs in the People's Republic. First, the recent founding dates for the vast majority of associations reflect both global trends and specific changes in Chinese legislation since the late 1980s. They do not, however, suggest that the groups have fostered China's political changes or any of the tentative moves toward procedural democracy, like village elections. The major periods of political change in China preceded and made possible the boom in civil association, not the other way around.

Second, as I have discussed, these groups are not arrayed against the state and do not see themselves primarily as limits on state power. Instead, they act as intermediaries. They describe themselves as semiofficial, no matter their actual relationship to the state, and describe their goals as being consistent with those of the state (the state-sponsored slogan of "improving spiritual civilization" was the most popular goal for NGO leaders in both cities).

Finally, while these associations have not led to procedural democracy, they have led to improved information flow between the state and many sectors of society. That is, they have helped democratize in the weaker sense of the term, and in the process have created some pressure toward better governance.

Taipei

The Republic of China government in Taiwan did not lift the "state of emergency" from its conflict with the mainland until 1987. The immediate aftermath of that change has been a rapid embracing of electoral democracy in one of the world's most peaceful and thorough political transitions. This is a remarkable change from an authoritarian regime that exercised very tight social control by using many of the Leninist techniques that the ruling Nationalist Party (Guomindang or Kuomintang, KMT) learned during their much earlier alliances with the communists. This change included a sudden blossoming of hundreds of social organizations and interest groups covering the full range of social life, from new political parties to amateur baseball leagues.

Although some informal loosening preceded the sudden transformation of 1987, the fundamental legal structure before then was corporatist. Indeed, it was not fundamentally different from the kind of structure that the People's Republic of China has introduced since 1989. The most basic principle of one social organization to represent each social sector was the same. Regulation focused on political control, and independent interest groups found it difficult to survive before the 1980s. It should not be altogether surprising, therefore, that the social structure that resulted in Taiwan under its state of emergency resembled China today in a number of ways.

In particular, Taiwan before 1987 and China after 1989 developed a split between large, strongly institutionalized and politically tame organizations with legal recognition, and small, weakly organized and politically invisible groups that did not attempt to register. As in China now, for example, locally based environmental protest sometimes occurred, but national organizations could not become involved until the 1980s. In the area of religion, probably hundreds of small, local temple associations and sects remained unregistered, while those with grander ambitions tried to register with the Buddhist or Daoist Association. This split pattern may in fact be a common side effect of authoritarian rule based on corporatist social control. A few groups that fit state notions of modern organization and political pliancy grow large and strong, while smaller, more traditional-looking groups with no political ambitions fall beyond the grip of political control. The middle is either repressed or co-opted.

However, everything changed when Taiwan lifted martial law. The general shape of the legal system defining organizations changed from emphasizing social control to financial control. It is now legal to conduct social activities without being registered. The advantages of registration as a nonprofit organization now lie primarily in tax benefits – as in the United States, nonprofit status means exemption from income taxes, and it brings the ability to solicit charitable (and tax deductible) donations from individuals and companies.[12] Donations to public interest organizations also avoid inheritance and gift taxes, and donations of land avoid Taiwan's very high value-added tax on land.

In exchange, registered public interest nonprofit organizations subject themselves to a great deal of government oversight of their activities and finances. They also need to satisfy rigorous financial requirements. The law in Taiwan distinguishes organizations based around an endowment (foundations, which the law calls *gongyi shetuan faren*, "public interest social organizations as legal persons") from membership associations (*renmin tuanti*, "people's groups"). Civil activities are also permitted for associations that choose not to register, though they lose the tax benefits. Membership associations usually do not have to have large amounts of funds, although the Ministry of Interior Affairs (the most important registration unit) requires office space of at least 30 square meters. Foundations, however, must meet high financial thresholds: the Ministry of Interior Affairs requires they have an endowment of at least 30 million NT (approximately $1 million).[13]

Nearly all of this is aimed at ensuring that their purposes really are philanthropic, that funds are spent appropriately, and that the families who made the initial donations do not profit by funneling the money back for their own use. There are still a few political strictures – membership associations cannot promote Taiwanese independence or communism, for instance. Nevertheless, the corporatist heart of the system is completely gone, and attention has moved to providing tax incentives for society, instead of the government, to take on public interest issues. This is very different from the People's Republic, where tax incentives and financial controls play a more limited role and most of the attention falls on proper political behavior.[14] Regulation and supervision in both places are relatively strict by world standards, but the logic of the two systems is very different.

The very different conception of civil associations in Taiwan stems from their social history. Advocacy groups in areas like the environment and consumer rights had been pushing on the government for a decade, before martial law was lifted. The political undercurrent had not been allowed to organize formally until after 1987, but local elections had also been increasingly contested by an opposition that existed in all but formal name by the late 1970s, in spite of a major crackdown in 1979. While the top Nationalist Party leadership undoubtedly played an important and voluntary role in the transition, it also acted at a time when the divide between society and state was growing increasingly tense. For these reasons, Taipei has a far higher percentage of groups dedicated to social interests and advocacy than any of the other cities we studied (see Table 5.2).[15] It is also worth noting that political parties in Taiwan exist under the same sets of laws and regulations that allow other forms of nonprofit social organization.

Nevertheless, even Taipei does not easily fit a model of society versus the state. It certainly has more advocacy groups than the other three cities, but economic, professional, and friendship groups still far outnumber them. As Chapter 3 documents, the vast majority of all associations see themselves as primarily working with the government in a reformist way. They report that their most common activities are talks with government officials, exchanges of letters with the government, and running seminars. They tend to avoid more radical activities like street

Table 5.2 Types of civil association by city*

	Hong Kong %	Taipei %	Guangzhou %	Xiamen %
Economic	18	30	17	30
Religious	7	5	1	4
Friendship	26	19	38	18
Academic–professional	24	23	24	33
Social interest–advocacy	3	12	1	5
Welfare	45	37	13	10
Other	8	1	6	0

* Totals are greater than 100%, as groups could choose more than one type.

demonstrations; strikes were the single least popular method for advocating their ideas, followed closely by lawsuits.

In addition, 31 percent of the core leaders of Taiwan's foundations and people's associations turn out to be government officials, and 23 percent of the leaders had run for public office. These surprisingly high numbers are reminiscent of the rates in Xiamen and Guangzhou, but the dynamics behind them are different. A significant amount of official representation in PRC associations consists of retired party or government cadres, who are there to maintain government control and as a way of moving fiscal responsibility for their salaries to the private sector. Associations may welcome them as conduits into government power, but they are primarily placed there from the top down. In Taiwan, the officials are usually elected, and the impetus is always from the bottom up. Aspiring politicians sometimes use civil associations as a springboard into electoral politics. In addition, as in the PRC, these groups want good access to the ear of government. They hope to work with the state, not against it.

As Taipei is the only clear case of a transition to democracy in our sample, we were encouraged to look at the role NGOs may have played. The most obvious statistical fact is the sudden surge in associations of all kinds after 1987. The raw numbers show a clear correlation between democracy and associational life, but they also suggest that the great majority of NGOs in Taiwan have been the result rather than the cause of political relaxation.

The statistics don't tell the complete story, however. A handful of associations did play an important role in the loosening of the 1980s which led to the eventual lifting of the state of emergency. Under corporatist systems like Taiwan's before 1987 (and China's now), associations obtained a certain kind of independence, no matter how close their ties to government. These groups specialized in issues like environmental protection, consumer rights, social welfare, and women's rights – issues that were palatable to the authoritarian government. Unlike most professional associations or hobby groups, advocacy groups like these can provide a proxy political mechanism for political opposition when direct protest is impossible. It is no coincidence that early leaders of some of these movements became important political figures in opposition politics when the KMT first allowed competing political parties.[16] To a lesser extent, and so far on a much smaller scale, a similar pattern applies today in the People's Republic of China, where exactly the same sectors have experienced important growth in the civil realm.[17] The small numbers of such groups that can thrive under such a system may create important pressure for political change. However, large numbers of truly independent groups seem to come only after political transformation.

The fate of these pioneer civil associations may vary according to the kind of transition that occurs. In Taiwan, the most clearly cooperative corporatist groups have simply faded. To give just one example, the Buddhist Association of the Republic of China was the corporatist representative of all Buddhists and had enormous power over things like temple landholding and ordination. Now, however, it has simply fallen into irrelevance, and Taiwan's remarkable growth and export of new forms of Buddhism has left it far behind. More activist groups, however, like the Consumer Protection Foundation, went through the transition with a lot of respect and have continued to thrive.

If the People's Republic ever undergoes a gradual and peaceful transition like Taiwan's, carefully political groups like Friends of Nature (a major environmental group) and Wanghai Online (a leading consumer rights group) will get a lot of the credit. But if there is a drastic transition in the style of Eastern Europe, these groups are more likely to be dismissed as hopelessly weak apologists for government policy.

Hong Kong

Unlike Taiwan or the People's Republic, Hong Kong has a relatively uninterrupted history of civil institutions. While there were some important adjustments just before and after Hong Kong was returned to PRC sovereignty in 1997, the Basic Law, which sets the ground rules, guarantees a continuation of fundamental social and economic arrangements. Article 27 explicitly affirms freedom of association. This continuity is why only about a third of Hong Kong's NGOs have been founded in the past 25 years, in stark contrast to the vast numbers founded during the same period in the other three cities.[18]

Under British colonial rule politics remained firmly in the hands of the rulers, but social organizations were welcome when they dealt with issues beyond politics. The Hong Kong laws define social organizations' realms primarily as those concerned with charity, broadly defined as poverty relief, education, and religion. Unlike Taiwan, groups with political potential like labor unions or political parties fell under other jurisdictions. Charitable donations had financial advantages much like those in Taiwan, reducing taxes on profits, salaries, and estates.

The most important change to the Societies Ordinance, the statute which controlled the colony's NGOs, came in 1992, as Britain made its tardy attempts to institutionalize more democratic control in Hong Kong. Following the adoption of the International Covenant on Civil and Political Rights in Hong Kong's Bill of Rights Ordinance of 1991, the government further relaxed its control over NGOs. The most important change was that organizations no longer had to apply for registration, but they simply had to inform the Societies Office. All societies were supposed to do this, but many could claim exemption from registration, particularly youth groups and recreation groups. In addition, connections to foreign political organizations were permitted for the first time. This is a far more relaxed registration regime than in either the Taiwan or PRC cases. The government's legal ability to supervise NGOs is also much more limited in Hong Kong than in Taiwan, Guangzhou, or Xiamen. Most of the supervision activity appears aimed at the control of triad societies (Sanhe Hui or Tiandi Hui), which are often linked to organized crime in Hong Kong.

The People's Republic was uncomfortable with this liberalization, however, and after the handover in 1997 the National People's Congress annulled the 1992 changes. This was part of a broader dissatisfaction with the last minute changes the British had been making. In spite of this, Hong Kong's Provisional Legislative Council immediately passed another amendment to the Societies

Ordinance, essentially repeating the 1992 changes with minor alterations to satisfy the central government in Beijing. Groups that threaten the territorial integrity of the People's Republic, for example, are not allowed to register. Groups with foreign or Taiwanese political connections are also banned. Nevertheless, the very loose registration and supervision requirements have been reinstated. We see a fundamental continuity of legal policies toward NGOs, and popular demonstrations have so far succeeded in turning back attempts to strengthen the Sedition Law.

In practice, this long continuity has resulted in a very active NGO sector in Hong Kong, but one that is extraordinarily quiet politically. The British brooked no fundamental questioning of their political control and effectively co-opted any potential threats from below. Yet their ideal of indirect rule also led them to leave Hong Kong social organizations enormously free to develop within their circumscribed space. Hong Kong thus offers an unusual combination of a very free and lively NGO sector that works in close cooperation with the state.[19] As Lui and his co-authors show in Chapter 4, groups that the government did not co-opt developed into an oppositional sector, but one without much unity or power.

Such an arrangement also fits the People's Republic of China's goals for a politically tame but economically lively Hong Kong under its sovereignty. There is little evidence for significant change in the patterns of social organization since 1997. The belated British moves toward greater democracy in the 1990s and the opportunities opened by the transition in 1997 might in principle have created some space for a more confrontational social sector. In practice, however, the predominant positions of both the British and Chinese governments militated against such activity and the circumscribed status quo has more or less continued in the social sector.

We can see this in the mild-mannered techniques that groups used to advocate their causes. Much as is the case in Taiwan, the preferred methods identified by our respondents were exchanging letters with the government, meeting with officials directly, and organizing seminars. Unlike in Taiwan, however, the 206 groups in the Hong Kong survey reported that they never once resorted to more confrontational techniques like lawsuits or strikes. The government also funds about 17 percent of NGO activity in Hong Kong. This is much lower than Guangzhou or Xiamen, of course, but much higher than the 8 percent in Taipei.

Finally, only a tiny 3 percent of associations in Hong Kong identified themselves as advocacy or interest groups. This is even lower than Xiamen's 5 percent, and much lower than Taipei's 12 percent. As one might expect in a system in which this sector is defined by charitable activity, welfare-oriented groups dominate: they form 45 percent of the sample in Hong Kong, compared to 37 percent in Taiwan and just over 10 percent in the two PRC cities. It is too soon to say whether the very recent pro-democracy demonstrations in 2004 indicate the beginnings of a change in this pattern, but the pattern until then had been quiescent, especially in comparison to Taipei.

Hong Kong reminds us of the crucial role of the state in shaping the NGO world in quite a different way from the other three cities. In some ways, Hong Kong is a classically liberal regime – a small state that saw its role primarily as maintaining order and creating the groundwork for a thriving independent economy. This left a lot of room for social organizations to take on welfare functions. Politically, however, it was very much a colonial regime and the basic structure has not changed since 1997. The city thus combines a restricted political space with an open social space. The population in general has adjusted to this and we again find very little support for an image of society against the state. The organizations we interviewed tend to be ameliorist, and broader surveys show that the idea of a moral state remains current (Lau and Kuan 1988).

Conclusions

Jessica Matthews argued in an influential article that NGOs are increasingly "able to push around even the largest governments," and that they are promoting the end of the Westphalia system of nation-states (Matthews 1997: 53). This argument is a subset of the literature that sees globalization in general as undercutting the power of the state. The four cities I have examined here undoubtedly felt the effects of the global growth in NGOs over the last two decades: all of them saw marked increases in the quantity and activity of NGOs over that period, while the increase was enormous in Guangzhou, Xiamen, and Taipei. Yet there is very little evidence that NGO growth brought a decline in state power.

Events like the United Nations conference with which I began this essay, and the increasing popularity of NGOs with the World Bank and similar organizations have been crucial carriers of the global NGO movement. In certain areas, international NGOs now also carry some policy influence in China. WWF (formerly World Wildlife Fund), for example, is a primary advisor to the government on panda conservation. This does not, however, automatically imply a diminution of the state. After all, NGOs can only function if governments create legal and social space for them. The globalization of the NGO movement over the last two decades in China, Taiwan, and Hong Kong has involved a readjustment but not a weakening of all three polities. The adjustment is especially clear in the changes to the legal systems in China and Taiwan which utterly redefined how the social sector would work.[20]

The rise of NGOs has involved some reinvention of what the state is, but to a certain extent each state also invents its own NGO sector. Legal differences explain many of the specific features of NGOs in China, Taiwan, and Hong Kong, including the emphasis on welfare activities in Hong Kong and the corporatist arrangements in China. This mutual shaping is especially evident in the ways NGOs conceive of their relationships to the state in these four case studies – largely as cooperative and symbiotic rather than adversarial. These features in part grow out of the particular historical experiences of these places – China in imperial times did not make a very clear distinction between state and society (Weller 1999: 28–9). They also grow from the particular incentive structures that each polity's legal, financial, and informal political systems have developed.

Do NGOs promote democracy, or at least check the power of tyranny? These four Chinese cities do not provide much evidence in favor of the proposition. The Chinese countryside has experimented with village-level elections for a number of years now, but NGOs have had little to do with the process, and elections have not much touched the urban populations we studied. Instead, China's burgeoning NGO sector is tame, content to work largely hand in hand with the government, and pushing its issues only when they are politically safe. The combination of containing NGOs in a corporatist state structure and repressing others has been effective.

Taiwan before 1987 was roughly similar – a market-based economy and stern authoritarian rule – and shows how such a system can keep NGOs cooperative for decades on end. The real boom in Taiwanese NGOs came only after martial law was lifted. Hong Kong in the 1990s appeared to offer the greatest potential for an activist NGO sector: the British were hoping to expand democracy, and NGOs had long been well established there. Nevertheless, few NGOs actively promoted greater procedural democracy; most have been content to continue a cozy and politically circumscribed relationship with the People's Republic as they did with the British before.

In at least two other ways, however, NGOs in these cities are important to democratization. First, like elections, they provide informational feedback to the state. In principle, at least, this should help foster better governance. This feedback is not as powerful as what free and fair elections can provide, and it leaves open the serious problem of how accountable NGOs are to the people they claim to represent. But it is still a major improvement over systems in which an even more unaccountable state removes all nonstate sources of information. China first attempted to consolidate such a state in the late 1950s, and one of the key reasons the disastrous Great Leap Forward policies were continued was the lack of proper social information, even as millions were starving to death.

Second, NGOs (and social organizations more broadly) can be crucial to democratic consolidation. The corporatist arrangements in China and pre-1987 Taiwan led to a split in social organizations. At the top stand a small number of well-institutionalized groups with close ties to the state; at the bottom we can see large numbers of relatively informal groups that are not legally registered as NGOs, but are allowed to exist as long as they remain small, unambitious, and apolitical. That thriving informal sector – temple communities, recreation groups, rotating credit associations, and all the rest – provided the ties that led to the rapid expansion of NGOs in Taiwan after 1987. China tried hard to curb any space for similar informal social groups up until the end of the Cultural Revolution in 1976. Now, however, such groups are thriving all over China. Neither the apolitical and informal groups nor the large corporatist groups are likely to create a democratic China. But should the People's Republic ever undergo its own democratic transition, they will create the possibility for a successful consolidation.

Notes

1   The legal term in China is "social organizations" (*shehui tuanti*), in part because of the infelicitous political implications of "nongovernmental."

2   This was a collaborative two-year research project, Between Family and State: Intermediate Institutions and Social Change in Three Chinese Societies, led by the author, Hsin-Huang Michael Hsiao of the Academia Sinica in Taiwan, and Kuan Hsin-chi of the Chinese University of Hong Kong. I am grateful to them and to our other major collaborators in the project: Lui Tai-lok, Chan Kim-man, Yang Guoshu, Huang Shunli, and Qiu Haixiong. Major funding for the project came from the Himalaya Foundation (Taipei, Taiwan), to which I am also grateful. Some results have appeared in Weller *et al.* (2002).

3   The rapid commercial growth of the late sixteenth century also brought a large increase in elite associations, especially for philanthropic purposes (see Brook 1993).

4   I argue elsewhere that such early civil associations were not at all pre-modern, and that they continue to be important in fashioning political structures in China and Taiwan (Weller 1999).

5   For NGOs, the argument has been made most forcefully in Unger (1996).

6   The relevant regulations can be found in *Compilation of the Civil Affairs Regulations of the People's Republic of China* (Ministry of Civil Affairs). The 1984 regulation is in the "Circular on the Strict Control of the Establishment of Nation-Wide Organizations by the Central Committee of the CCP and the State Council" (p. 843). The later changes are in "Registration and Administration Provisions for Social Organizations," adopted on 25 October 1989 (also on p. 843). Further restrictions were added the next year, in the "Circular of the State Council Forwarded to the Ministry of Civil Affairs on the Clean-Up and Rectification of Social Organizations."

7   "Reply on Several Questions Relating to the Administration of the Registration of Social Organizations by the Ministry of Civil Affairs" (Ministry of Civil Affairs, p. 856).

8   The primary current regulations date from 1998.

9   Further tightening, especially of religious associations, occurred after the repression of the Falun Gong movement. "Provisional Measures to Remove Illegal Private Organizations," Ministry of Civil Affairs, 10 April 2000. Our data were collected before this, however.

10 Guangzhou data come primarily from Kin-man Chan and Haixiong Qiu, "The Autonomy of Intermediate Organizations in Guangzhou," and Xiamen data from Guozhen Yang and Shunli Huang, "Changes in Xiamen Social Organizations." Both papers were prepared for the Between Family and State project.

11 All amounts are in US dollars, unless otherwise indicated.

12 See Chapter 3 for more details.

13 Associations must register with the appropriate government unit, and the specific regulations vary significantly among them. Most of the regulatory systems were set up at different times during the 1990s. Useful summaries of the details can be found at a website maintained by the Himalaya Foundation, www.npo.org.tw.

14 In the PRC, individuals can deduct charitable contributions of up to 30 percent of their income (compared to 20 percent in Taiwan) and for-profit companies can deduct up to 3 percent (compared to 10 percent in Taiwan). More importantly, such deductions are limited to associations or state agencies that work in education, disaster relief, or poverty relief only. They must go to a small list of specified organizations that includes the Foundation for the Development of China's Youth, the Project Hope Foundation, the China Disabled Persons Association, and others. Essentially all of these have extremely tight ties to the government. Project Hope, for example, which tries to improve education in poor areas, is an offshoot of the China Youth League, one of the old mass organizations. The Disabled Persons Association is run by a son of Deng Xiaoping.

15 The data from Taipei rely on the findings of Hsin-Huang Michael Hsiao, who led the Taiwan portion of the Between Family and State project.
16 Examples include Lin Junyi, a pioneering environmentalist who was later elected to the National Assembly and served briefly as head of the Environmental Protection Administration under the first DPP government, and Annette Lu, who was an early activist in feminist issues as well as opposition politics, and was ultimately elected vice president.
17 For example, Liang Congjie, the head of Friends of Nature, was active in a relatively open journal that was repressed after the Tiananmen demonstrations of 1989.
18 In Hong Kong, 35 percent were founded after 1980 compared to 71 percent in Taiwan. We used 1978 as the cutoff date for the PRC cities, because that is when the reforms began. In Guangzhou, 85 percent were founded after 1978 and 90 percent in Xiamen.
19 Evidence for this section comes primarily from the work of Lui Tai-lok, Kuan Hsin-chi, and Chan Kin-man as part of the Between Family and State project.
20 It might be possible to argue that the state has weakened over this period in the People's Republic, although one would have to be very careful about definitions. Certainly its fiscal power appears to have decreased. No one, however, argues that NGOs had a major role in the process.

References

Brook, Timothy. *Praying for Power: Buddhism and the Formation of Gentry Society in Late-Ming China.* Cambridge, MA: Harvard-Yenching Institute, 1993.
Cohen, Myron L. "Commodity Creation in Late Imperial China: Corporations, Shares, and Contracts in One Rural Community." In *Locating Capitalism in Time and Space: Global Restructurings, Polities, and Identity,* edited by David Nugent. Stanford, CA: Stanford University Press, 2002, pp. 80–112.
Foster, Kenneth. "Embedded within State Agencies: Business Associations in Yantai." *China Journal,* 47 (2002): 41–65.
Lau, S.K., and Hsin-chi Kuan. *The Ethos of the Hong Kong Chinese.* Hong Kong: Chinese University Press, 1988.
Matthews, Jessica T. "Power Shift." *Foreign Affairs,* January/February 1997: 50–66.
Ministry of Civil Affairs, People's Republic of China. *Compilation of the Civil Affairs Regulations of the People's Republic of China.* Beijing: Ministry of Civil Affairs.
Pei, M. "Chinese Intermediate Associations: An Empirical Analysis." *Modern China,* 24, 3 (July 1998): 285–318.
Sangren, P. Steven. "Traditional Chinese Corporations: Beyond Kinship." *Journal of Asian Studies,* 43, 3 (1984): 391–415.
Unger, Jonathan. "'Bridges': Private Business, the Chinese Government and the Rise of New Associations." *China Quarterly,* 147 (1996): 795–819.
Wank, David L. "Private Business, Bureaucracy, and Political Alliance in a Chinese City." *Australian Journal of Chinese Affairs,* 33 (1995): 55–71.
Weller, Robert P. *Alternate Civilities: Democracy and Culture in China and Taiwan.* Boulder, CO: Westview, 1999.
——, Hsin-Huang Michael Hsiao, Hsin-chi Kuan, Kin-man Chan, Haixiong Qui, Tai-lok Lui, Guozhen Yang, and Shunli Huang. "Dangdai Huaren Chengshi Shehui de Minjian Zuzhi: Taibei, Xianggang, Guangzhou, Xiamen de Bijiao Fenxi" [Civil Associations in Contemporary Chinese Urban Societies: A Comparative Analysis of Taibei, Hong Kong, Guangzhou, and Xiamen]. Occasional Paper No.123. Hong Kong: Chinese University of Hong Kong, Institute of Asia-Pacific Studies, 2002.

Yang, Mayfair Mei-hui. "Spatial Struggles: State Disenchantment and Popular Re-Appropriation of Space in Rural Southeast China." Presented at the Workshop on Civilizing Discourses and the Politics of Culture in Twentieth-Century China. Fairbank Center, Harvard University, 12–13 May 2001.

6 From state-centric to negotiated governance

NGOs as policy entrepreneurs in South Korea

Hyuk-Rae Kim and David K. McNeal

Introduction

The number of civil society groups around the world has grown enormously since the end of the Cold War. Before the Berlin Wall fell in 1989, approximately 24,904 international nongovernmental organizations (INGOs) were operating worldwide (Union of International Associations 2002). Their number rapidly increased following the creation of the World Trade Organization in 1994, and by the end of 1999 one could find 43,958 INGOs working across traditional sovereign boundaries (ibid.). The situation in South Korea (hereafter Korea) illustrates this trend on the local level. Before its 1987 democratic movement, Korea had 185 NGOs working within the country, by 1996 it had 610 such organizations and by 2000 it had 843, a 450 percent increase over 13 years (Table 6.1).

These numbers help us conceptualize how the end of the Cold War and the spread of globalization via a worldwide neoliberal trading regime have greatly expanded the quantity of nongovernmental actors, but they cannot convey how this has affected governance and policy formation. Any inquiry into political power is therefore justified in studying this broadening and deepening of the third sector, even though the effects are still unfolding.

NGO development is inseparable from the neoliberal reforms and liberalization measures associated with political and economic democratization (Weiss and Gordenker 1996), as they have significantly restructured the institutional framework within which the state and NGOs interact. In an era of globalization, the state's predominant position in society is waning, and it is searching for alternative institutions and strategies through which it can articulate and pursue society's collective interest. NGOs, on the other hand, are extending their activities well beyond the not-for-profit provision of goods to include developing social governance institutions that provide leverage against traditional state-centric institutions (Hyuk-Rae Kim 2002a). We are thus living in a shift of social paradigms in which societal stewardship and development are being increasingly framed as a citizenry-centered movement that is exponentially gaining political power and influence.

Civil society as evinced by NGOs is now a verifiable entity in the decentralized institutional framework of state–civil society interaction. We have chosen the term "negotiated governance" to emphasize one of the key elements of this newly emerged decentralized institutional framework: the diffusion and dispersal of state power to organizations and institutions within civil society, such as NGOs.

The emergence of negotiated governance should be seen as both a political strategy of the state and an institutional response to civil society: the state strategically redefines its role in society under neoliberal reform programs, while NGOs actively negotiate with the state to be more involved in forming and implementing social policies and in delivering public services (Hirst 2000; Hyuk-Rae Kim 1999, 2000a, 2002a; Pierre 2000). Negotiated governance therefore challenges our conception of the state's institutional power and boundaries, and forces us to consider the role of NGOs as alternative hybrid institutions that undertake public functions through private initiatives on a range of social policies.

This essay defines NGOs as nongovernmental, nonprofit, politically neutral, voluntary, and independent organizations set up by those who agree to work together for shared goals or common goods and to empower citizens vis-à-vis a domineering state (Bratton 1989; Callahan 1998; Cohen and Arato 1992; Diamond 1994; Gellner 1994; Hall 1995; Keane 1988; Hyuk-Rae Kim 1997, 2000a, 2002). NGOs are closely linked to the state, but operate outside the parameters of the formal state apparatus. In recent years, many NGOs have become more committed and flexible in recognizing and reacting to the range of issues relating to the environment, human rights, anti-corruption, consumer protection, women's issues, and grassroots development. Owing to their involvement in these public issues, they are now being recognized as alternative quasi-public institutions.

In addition, NGOs increasingly play "the role of policy entrepreneurs, to propose and assist in the formation and implementation of policies, and to form organizations dedicated to the protection of public interests by monitoring government and business activities" (Hyuk-Rae Kim 2002a: 58). We are therefore experiencing a shift from a "centripetal" mode of state-centric governance to a "centrifugal" form of negotiated governance in which newly emerged quasi-public and entrepreneurial NGOs are pivotal in interacting and coordinating between the state and civil society (Pierre 2000: 242). Korean NGOs, for instance, have now begun participating directly in the political process, which is expanding the avenues for citizens to participate more fully in policy making.

While each country's NGO sector exhibits characteristics and strategies that are unique to its stage of economic development, geopolitical status and democratic transition, as policy entrepreneurs all NGOs share certain core activities. These include identifying policy agendas, shaping the terms of policy debates, and building networks and coalitions to propose new policy initiatives or alternatives (Conley 2001; Mintrom 1997; Schneider *et al.* 1995). Through these activities, NGOs increasingly press the state and corporate sectors to limit regulation of and intervention in citizens' daily lives, while they promote community-building and basic societal values as compensation for any inability of the state or corporate sector to do so themselves (Korten 1990; Noda 2000).

This essay focuses on the role of NGOs as policy entrepreneurs in policy formation. As an embodiment of societal change, policy formation has three distinct phases: advocacy, development, and implementation. As constituencies consolidate in civic organizations, their advocacy coalesces, and NGOs find themselves as tenable representatives of and for the populace, so long as they remain administratively and bureaucratically transparent. This authenticity allows them to assume a developmental role that legitimizes and reinforces negotiated governance in policy formation.

A model of negotiated governance can thus be established, and NGOs assume a more entrepreneurial role in the formulation of public policy with the understanding that:

> Policy entrepreneurs can be thought of as being to the policy-making process what economic entrepreneurs are to the marketplace. Policy entrepreneurs are able to spot problems . . . are prepared to take risks to promote innovative approaches to problem solving, and . . . have the ability to organize others to help turn policy ideas into government policies.
>
> (Mintrom 1997: 740)

The organizational implication of this with respect to negotiated governance is that NGOs have an intrinsic role in how policy is formulated; the theoretical dimension speaks to the growing significance of NGOs in the process of consolidating democracy.

We argue that Korean NGOs have recently attained a social authenticity that allows them to play a critical role in strategizing national public policies. While this may be the case in many other countries as well, Korea's sociohistorical trajectory is distinct not only in East Asia but across the globalized template. There are other newly developed countries that are enjoying the fruits of modernization and democracy, but Korea has arguably done so at an accelerated pace, with its recent transition from state-centric authoritarianism to democratic consolidation. The Korean third sector therefore provides social scientists with a valuable case study on how a civil society's evolution affects and is affected by political dynamics that are both unique and universal (Hyuk-Rae Kim 2000a). Furthermore, as it is still in transition, the Korean case may prove to be a benchmark by which other authoritarian-to-democratic transitions can be compared.

Using the above parameters for civil society, NGOs and policy entrepreneurship, this essay examines the emergence of Korean NGOs over the past several decades, followed by two case studies that illustrate the entrepreneurial trends of Korean civic organizations. Surveying the historical landscape of Korea's third sector reveals how rapidly it has evolved, and this recent democratic transition provides a background against which its civil society can be examined. The two case studies complete this essay by illustrating how Korean NGOs are assuming a more effective and entrepreneurial role in policy formation.

From state-centric to negotiated governance in South Korea

To understand Korea's indigenous, Confucian form of civil society, it is necessary to recognize that civil society has taken more than one historical path (Hyuk-Rae Kim 2002b). Korean civil society is not merely an East Asian version of Western civil society. As the contemporary dynamics of the Korean state and the NGO sector have not come about in a vacuum, it is necessary to establish a historical matrix upon which the state and civil society in transition as we see them today can be juxtaposed.

Social scientists have proposed various views on the origins of Korean civil society. Some see parallels between historical events in the East and West (Bratton 1989; Hall 1995) or detect a Western type of civil society particular to Korea (Chung 1995); others make out a form of East Asian civil society, or its anticipation, in Confucian doctrine (Chamberlain 1993; Cho 1997). This range of interpretations suggests the danger of generalizing from the Western model to Korea, as well as the need for a more encompassing understanding when we speak of civil society in different historical settings.

In fact the beginnings of civil society on the Korean peninsula can only be traced to the latter half of the twentieth century. While scholars debate the merits of the traditional Confucian literati's civil contributions towards restricting the monarchy, they do not meet our definition of civil society and cannot be included in this research. Furthermore, the nascent form of civil society that emerged in traditional Korea was repressed by ruling elites; later it would be severely repressed under the Japanese colonial government. Nor did the situation improve following the country's post-war division, when directive state intervention dominated Korea, leaving little room for organizational growth initiated by citizens.

Using state-centric governance, Korea's authoritarian regimes severely repressed and restricted basic democratic rights and freedoms in order to encourage rapid economic growth (Koo 1993; Moon and Kim 1996). Successive regimes excluded labor and selectively cooperated with capital to form a coalition for economic development. Although the respective roles of the state and market remain subject to debate, few dispute that state intervention was a determining force in Korea's economic development (Robison *et al.* 2000). At the same time, with a virtual monopoly on decision-making authority and jurisdiction over all social issues, state intervention impeded the growth of civil society (Hyuk-Rae Kim 2002b, 2004). Until Korea's 1987 democratic movement, successive state-centric regimes mobilized the civil society sector for economic growth and political stability by politically disenfranchising it.

However, even though rapid economic growth with pervasive state intervention impeded and distorted the development of civil society, it nevertheless enhanced its potential advancement (Hyuj-Rae Kim 2002b). For instance, government-led investment in heavy and chemical industrialization in the 1970s necessitated a larger workforce, which empowered industrial labor. Civil society was also revealed in the middle class that has emerged over the past few decades, due to the unprecedented rate of economic growth. In fact both industrial labor and the middle class played significant roles in the politics of social movements: it was collaboration and solidarity between the labor movement and the citizens' movement in the late 1980s that led to an alliance that secured and enlarged the public space to resist monopolistic capital and the dominance of state power.

Pervasive state intervention was the modus operandi of the authoritarian system of state-centric governance, which served the country well when it was pursuing rapid industrialization and economic growth but came to symbolize authoritarianism devoid of any public input or accountability. In this authoritarian era of Korea's modernization, "public" became equated with "official": government intervention was presented as a civic entity arising from and for the people (Hyuk-Rae Kim 2002a), and social movements were mainly characterized by their anti-government and -corporate positions.

In guiding capitalist development, Korean state corporatism repressed civil society. In particular, the state purposefully barred labor unions from economic and capitalist policy decisions and strategically controlled market mechanisms to thwart labor union interests. Labor movements responded to this heavy-handedness by moving to the radical Left, and the so-called people's movement groups (*minjung undong tanch'e*), composed of blue-collar laborers, peasants, the urban poor, anti-regime students and politicians, played an important role in calling for the breakdown of authoritarianism and transition to democracy (Hyuk-Rae Kim 2002b). However, this scenario has changed considerably, if not completely, since 1987, the year that is the turning point in Korea's political democratization.

Civil society and NGOs did not begin to fully form until the 1987 democratic movement, an event that also heralded Korea's passing the threshold of democratic transition and resulted in the election of Roh Tae Woo (Cho 1997; Han 1997; Hyuk-Rae Kim 2002b, 2004; Sunhyuk Kim 1997, 2000). Since 1987, Korea has been transitioning towards the political democratization of diverse social interests and interest-group politics. State repression of civil society reappeared during the Roh administration, but it has declined substantially since the 1993 election of Kim Young Sam's civilian government, which made a series of unprecedented reforms. It also further encouraged the activities of moderate civil society groups by recruiting several high-ranking public officials from within citizen movement organizations.

Until the 1987 democratic movement, successive authoritarian regimes maintained a virtual monopoly over public issues. This is exemplified by the fact that 78 per cent of Korea's 843 NGOs have been formed since then, while only 9.9 percent were established during the 1961–79 Park Chun Hee regime, a percentage that increases to a mere 18 percent with the inclusion of the 1980–6 Chun Doo-Whan regime (Table 6.1). This sharp rise in the number of NGOs founded since 1987 demonstrates how highly correlated their propagation is to the beginning of political democratization in that year.

Citizen movements have been rapidly expanding since 1987 and represent a new generation of organizations that are different from the class-based, militant (*minjung*) movements of prior years, which increasingly found themselves alienated

Table 6.1 Year founded, number, and percentage distribution of Korean NGOs

Year	No.	%
Pre-1960	34	4.0
1961–70	36	4.3
1971–9	47	5.6
1980–6	68	8.1
1987–2	179	21.2
1993–6	246	29.2
1997–2000	217	25.7
Unknown	16	1.9
Total	843	100.0

Source: *Directory of Korean NGOs* (2000)

Note: In his analysis of the Korean NGO sector, Hyuk-Rae Kim selected 843 NGOs from the *Directory of NGOs* by Citizens' Time on the basis of the following criteria: public, voluntary, and nongovernmental characteristics. The full analysis has not yet been published.

from the general public. This eventually reached a crisis in which scholars and activist leaders connected with the *minjung* groups began to seek alternative theories, ideologies, and means of organizing (Hyuk-Rae Kim 1997, 2000a). By that time, however, moderate citizens' movement organizations (*simin undong*) had begun to emerge, and both government-patronized and depoliticized organizations were becoming deeply involved in social and political issues independent of the state and began to assume the character of agents for social change in democratic transition. As a result, the organizational space for diverse interest groups expanded.

The issues and tactics that these new moderate citizen movements took up in the late 1980s starkly contrasted with the confrontational *minjung* movements of the past, and two visions of democracy competed for ascendancy (Hyuk-Rae Kim 2002b): one derived from the *minjung* movements, the other endorsed moderate and practical citizen movements focused on the procedural fundamentals of democracy. This gulf helped bring about the *minjung* crisis, as did the policy reforms implemented by the Roh Tae Woo government (1988–92) in the wake of the hyper-repressive, authoritarian Chun regime. In keeping with Roh's 29 June 1987 declaration, repression of civilians declined substantially, and he proved quite open to political opposition, as his tolerance of an independent mass media indicated. Roh also restored local political autonomy, which the military regime had suspended in 1961, and lessened government control over university policies and activities.

The Kim Young Sam government assumed power in 1993 and initiated a series of unprecedented reforms. The new government not only tolerated but encouraged moderate citizen movements, and announced initiatives that were similar to those suggested by citizens' groups. This augmented their influence. Kim filled several key public positions with leaders recruited from moderate citizen groups and even sought to normalize relationships with these groups by publicly discussing their policy proposals and accommodating some of their demands.

In this environment, moderate citizen groups prevailed. These new, citizens' movement groups abandoned class-based, confrontational strategies in favor of nonviolent lawful tactics and specific proposals for policy alternatives. This pro-democracy alliance of citizens' groups incorporated the triple solidarity of students, workers' and churches, and then encompassed the middle class. Accordingly, the relationship between these groups and the state became cooperative. Relations deteriorated, however, when Kim failed to adequately address several key issues raised in the politics of democratic transition.

Relations entered a new phase when Kim Dae Jung took office in 1998, and academics and the popular press alike noted an explosion of citizen interest in securing democracy. Owing to strong reader interest, newspapers detailed the growing power of civil groups, which had broadened their range of issues and moderated their tactics and goals, shunning radical and illegal activities. The government again sought to co-opt citizen movement leaders by appointing them to head or advise the relevant organizations.

In addition, the government and the ruling party negotiated a bill that would financially assist NGOs and provide them with other special benefits. They could now compete for financial support by submitting project plans to a screening committee. The bill also provided civil groups with free leases on buildings and offices, tax exemption for donations, postage discounts, and more, all of which strengthened and broadened their activities. Such gradual developments between the state and citizen groups also accelerated discourse on participatory democracy and the making of civil society in transition to democracy.

However, neither the growth nor the success of Korean NGOs filled the civic void that existed prior to 1987. The third sector still needs to mature (Hyuk-Rae Kim 1997, 2000a), but Korean NGOs are susceptible to the problems that afflict all civic organizations. The membrane between NGOs and the government is porous, and issues of donor–client dynamics, personnel issues, policy co-option and constituency relevance persist in Korea, just as they do nearly everywhere else.

For example, given that NGOs are self-supporting, funding is a serious issue because civic organizations must remain fiscally sound solely upon direct contributions from members, fundraising drives, or corporate or government grants. They do not run much risk of their policies being neutralized when their income comes from membership dues or fundraising, but this is not the case when they accept corporate or government sponsorship.

NGOs' nonprofit nature also affects personnel. NGOs must attract qualified staff who are willing to forgo higher salaries; raise their salaries to attract competent employees at the risk of diluting funds from a budget which should be directed more externally; or rely on short-term, project-specific staff. The first scenario is unlikely, the second threatens to compromise an NGO's mandate, and the third precludes the establishment of entrenched personal connections between employee and employer in regards to an NGO's collective long-term goals.

NGO policy runs the risk of co-option from two fronts. Donors and personnel may both pressure NGOs either to adopt new policy or to compromise existing ones for their own gain. Corporate and government donors have innate agendas that can never be fully separated from whom they give their money to. On the other hand, short-term personnel run the risk (consciously or not) of prolonging projects to sustain their employment.

But the greatest and most contentious problem facing NGOs is their relevancy towards the constituency they purport to represent. NGOs presume to speak for society, but society cannot speak for NGOs: their personnel are not elected, and their policies do not necessarily represent the *vox populi*. Therefore, as NGOs gain sociopolitical power, the danger of their becoming an embodiment of the very power elite they struggle against is all too real.

These problems pose challenges for Korea's NGOs, but it is noteworthy that, while Korean civil society has been experiencing institutionalized growing pains, it has managed them in such a way that the diffusion of democratic ideals has proceeded unabated. In this, the attention placed upon NGOs' shortcomings by the media, themselves, and each other has had the secondary effect of strengthening public interest, as well as NGOs' political presence and negotiating power. This type of critical evaluation may also internally propel Korean NGOs to take risks that they might otherwise forgo, as these risks may be avenues that lead to their improvement, development, and sustainability.

Case studies: NGOs as social entrepreneurs in negotiated governance

Having outlined the modern history of Korean civil society, our focus now turns to the two case studies that will illustrate exactly how two major Korean NGOs – the People's Solidarity for Participatory Democracy (PSPD: Ch'amyo minju sahoe simin yondae) and the Citizens' Coalition for Economic Justice (CCEJ: Kyongye chongui silcho'on simin yonhap) – have entered the realm of policy entrepreneurship. The PSPD was launched in 1994 with 200 members; by 2000 its membership had increased to around 5,000 and it had about 40 full-time employees and some 200 volunteer activists working to:

> check state power by engaging the voluntary participation of citizens from all classes and sectors, suggesting concrete policies and alternative solutions, and building a society of participatory democracy in which freedom, human rights, and welfare are fully realized by citizen action.
>
> (PSPD online archives, March 2002)

The PSPD is now composed of nine major action bodies, each specializing in an area of concern, as well as five affiliated organizations, 12 citizen circles, a policy-information committee, and a citizens' committee.

The Citizens' Coalition for Economic Justice (CCEJ), on the other hand, was founded in 1989 with the aim of eliminating economic injustice. By 2000 it had nearly 50 full-time staff and some 35,000 members. In deference to its mostly middle-class membership, it largely eschews radical political philosophies. Instead, it seeks to uncover the causes of economic justice in all levels of society and concentrates on issues of income disparity, the unbalanced distribution of wealth, real estate speculation, environmental degradation and consumer rights. At various times, it has proposed equalizing the tax structure, strengthening the antitrust and fair trade laws, breaking up *chaebol* ownership, and reforming the political system.

Both the PSPD and CCEJ have nationwide networks, endorse a wide range of policies, and resist compartmentalization. In regards to civil liberties and Koreans' quality of life, the locus of their attention is national and encompasses a broad policy spectrum. In fact, when compared with other emerging NGOs in Asia, the PSPD and CCEJ are unique, due to their umbrella-type organizational characteristics and octopus-like diversification of activities. This could be negatively construed as mirroring the octopus-like working of the *chaebols*: after all, neither the PSPD nor the CCEJ has been much involved in grassroots activities and local issues; like the *chaebols* in business, they have paid much more attention to national and global agendas. However, this may also be necessary to create a civil society umbrella that addresses the collective concerns of the population.

Policy entrepreneurship involves a transition from traditional third sector policy responsibilities (e.g. the provision of services, grassroots advocacy and education) toward a more input-oriented role. We therefore argue that the PSPD's Minority Shareholders' Rights Movement policy proposal and the CCEJ's Real Name Transaction Proposal demonstrate that Korean NGOs have made the transition from reactive to proactive civic organizations and are now policy entrepreneurs in the public policy arena.

The Minority Shareholders' Rights Movement and legislative reform

In 1997 the PSPD led a movement to "bring together minority shareholders . . . to exercise their rights under the commercial laws and securities and exchange laws" (PSPD online archives, March 2002). Since then, the PSPD has made impressive progress by a grassroots movement of the civil society. The actions taken by the PSPD include both legal and extra-legal methods such as petitions and public statements (Table 6.2).

Though seemingly confrontational, these actions actually seek negotiation, in that they proactively position policy initiatives in the public arena and place the onus of responsibility on the state and the market. Negotiation necessitates leverage, while leverage necessitates confrontation between conflicting forces. Ideally, this confrontation is benign, but agents who have power are usually reluctant to give it up. The difference between these NGOs' legal and public confrontations and those of their *minjung* predecessors is that the PSPD's actions seek to work with the system to effect change.

The PSPD has made some impressive progress in a short period. At Korea First Bank the PSPD launched the first shareholder derivative suit, which resulted in a ruling in the Seoul District Court that former bank directors and presidents had to pay 40 billion won (US$31 million) in compensation. While this case was pending in an appellate court, all the plaintiffs' shares were nullified because of the bank's

Table 6.2 Types and number of political actions taken by Korea's People's Solidarity for Participatory Democracy (PSPD)

Activity	No.
Legal action:	
Indictment	11
Litigation	13
Legislative appeal	4
Public request on legal action and others	9
Extra-legal actions:	
Public statement	38
Public comments	42
Press releases	24
Public requests	9
Press interviews	7
Public hearings and seminars	6
Social surveys	2
Signature campaigns	3
Other campaigns	3

Source: Sun-Mi Kim (2001: Table V-1)

capital reduction program. The minority shareholders therefore lost their standing as plaintiffs and their claims were dismissed, but the bank itself participated in the lawsuit with the reduced damage claim of 1 billion won (US$770,000). The appellate court agreed with the suit and ordered the directors to pay the bank 1 billion won.

In 1999 the PSPD launched another derivative lawsuit against the president of Daewoo Corporation, demanding damages of 23.6 billion won (US$18 million) to compensate for illegal insider trading with other affiliates of the Daewoo Group. This case is still awaiting the court's decision. In the case of Dacom, Korea's second largest communications service provider, the company agreed to PSPD's proposals to appoint 50 percent of the board as outside directors and to establish an audit committee with powers to supervise inter-conglomerate trading. Furthermore, at Samsung, the Korean investor group launched an injunction against preferential awards of shares to relatives of the chairman, estimated to be worth some 150 billion won (US$115 million). This share transfer has been frozen, pending further court hearings.

The most important legal decision in all this was made in the derivative suit brought against Samsung by advocates of shareholders' rights. In December 2001 the Suwon District Court ordered nine incumbent and former directors of Samsung Electronics to pay 27 billion won (US$21 million) to the company to compensate for the losses they incurred in acquiring the financially unstable Echon Electric Company, which went bankrupt two years after the acquisition. The court also ordered the directors to pay another 63 billion won (US$48 million) to the company to compensate for damages from the selling of 20 million shares of one Samsung affiliate to other affiliates at an unreasonably low price.

The government responded to PSPD's legal requests throughout this process. For example, the Ministry of Finance and Economy reflected PSPD recommendations in revisions to the Security Transaction Act and five other laws. The laws and regulations that apply to listed corporate entities are the Commercial Code (CC), the Securities and Exchange Act (SEC), and the Korea Securities Exchange Listed Company Regulations (LCR). The CC and SEC in particular have undergone a string of significant amendments in the past few years: the CC was amended three times (in 1995, 1998 and 1999), and the SEC was amended more than nine times (Jang and Kim 2001).

These amendments mandated independent directors as well as audit and nomination committees, enhanced shareholder voting and participation rights, forced boards of directors to be more transparent on major decisions, and protected stakeholders such as creditors and employees. They also include a wide range of detailed legal recommendations for enhancing and enforcing shareholder rights, monitoring related-party transactions, empowering boards of directors, and improving disclosure. However, the government has decided against introducing a cumulative voting system that would allow minority shareholders to elect board members and to punish senior management for its failures.

The government recently submitted a bill to the National Assembly to bring the Securities Related Class Action Act into being. Its purpose is to protect the interests of minority shareholders and promote transparency in corporate management through the introduction of class action suits by minority shareholders. The business sector has criticized the compulsory nature of the bill.

As is the case with many of the actions the PSPD has initiated, this movement has brought attention to and expanded the rights of minority shareholders, who were overshadowed by the arbitrary power of the *chaebols'* directors, managers, and major shareholders. The PSPD mobilized the public to articulate its demands, participated in the management of business, and eventually introduced new ideas about "the public good" into Korean society (Hyuk-Rae Kim 1999, 2002a).

The PSPD is playing the role of a policy entrepreneur that shapes the public agenda, coordinates vital public support for new initiatives, and takes legal and extra-legal actions. As a result, the Minority Shareholders' Rights Movement campaign has been described as the most influential citizen movement to affect all sectors of Korean society.

The real name transaction policy and financial sector reform

In the vacuum left by the 1979 assassination of President Park, General Chun Doo Hwan staged a military coup and seized power on 17 May 1980. Following this, Chun adopted many reforms, among which was the 3 July presidential decree to enforce the emergency order that all financial transactions be based on the real names of those involved. This reform would greatly reduce a wide range of institutionalized corruption. He also promised that a real name financial transaction system would go into effect by 1 July 1983. However, the system's implementation was postponed indefinitely, after the private sector successfully raised fears of possible decreased savings rates, a stagnant stock market, and soaring real estate prices.

General Roh Tae Woo, Chun's handpicked successor, was elected in 1988. During the campaign, Roh promised to implement a system that would bring about greater equality in the distribution of wealth. The government planned to implement such a system in 1991, but the private sector was again to scuttle it. Following the sudden changes in the political party system due to the merger of three parties, the government announced that it would defer the plan.

But the 1993 election of President Kim Young Sam ushered in a new era of civilian rule, and Kim worked hard to reform the widely criticized regulatory system through his New Economy and Globalization programs. Reform of the financial sector was at the core of the government efforts in the early 1990s, highlighted by the Real Name Financial Transaction System. This was the government's effort to do away with the old system in which financial accounts could be opened and business transactions conducted under false names, which had led to widespread illegal financial dealings and institutionalized corruption.

The Real Name Financial Transaction and Protection of Confidentiality Act went into effect on 1 August 1993. Its purpose was to contribute to the realization of economic justice and the sound development of the national economy by requiring that financial transactions be based on the real names of the persons involved and that financial institutions identify their customers when conducting transactions. Among other things this would put an end to the easy hiding of hot money. It was also expected to "bring justice in taxation, prevent inheritance of economic status, block unearned income and speculation, reduce corruption, get rid of money politics and contribute to a clean political atmosphere" (Park 2002).

However, shortly after the presidential election of December 1997, the National Assembly replaced the existing system with the Real Name Financial Transaction and Secrecy Act. The new system loosened the regulations and also indefinitely shelved the general tax formula on financial incomes exceeding 40 million won (US$31,000) a year per household until the Asian financial crisis had passed.

Civil society had been deeply involved in the legalization and implementation of the Real Name Transaction System from the start. Upon its founding in 1989, the Citizens' Coalition for Economic Justice (CCEJ) made it a top priority and immediately called for its speedy implementation. To force the issue, the CCEJ used a new social movement strategy that focused on a public campaign of statements and hearings centered on proposing alternative policies that had been formulated by experts (Table 6.3). These statements and hearings garnered great public attention and put a great deal of pressure from constituents on the National Assembly, which brought about rapid results. In all of this, the influence of the CCEJ on policy change was enormous, from the details on how interest and dividend income were to be calculated for taxes, to the stepwise implementation of the system.

Table 6.3 Types and number of political actions taken by Korea's Citizens' Coalition for Economic Justice (CCEJ)

Action	No.
Public statements	49
Public hearings and seminars	12
Public conferences	4
Social surveys	3
Policy appeals	2
Public campaigns during elections	1
Publications	4

Source: Sun-Mi Kim (2001: Table IV-4)

Conclusion

Korean civil society, as led by nongovernmental organizations, is a dynamic force in shaping negotiated governance. Korea's relatively recent democratization has been accompanied by the evolution of its civil society from a force that worked for change from the outside and was stigmatized by the state as destabilizing, to one that has been accepted by the state, the market, and the population at large.

This acceptance is not abstract but is apparent in the daily lives of individuals through NGOs' growing stature at the public policy bargaining table. Korean NGOs' newfound legitimacy has allowed them to voice their desires in terms of policy formation, to supercede the state and market at times and initiate policy, and to participate in policy implementation and the delivery of public services. This expansion of Korean NGOs has also been accompanied by a recent legitimization of their institutional efficacy, as demonstrated by the transition from policy advocacy to policy formation and governance, and as seen in the implementation of specific NGO agendas.

By establishing an input-oriented space in the policy arena, Korean NGOs are important agents in the diffusion of democratic ideas by merit of their increasing role in policy formation, and thus of negotiated governance. This is significant for the Korean people, in that their options for democratization are greater and have assumed a greater frequency and grassroots accessibility. It is also significant for civil societies and their constituents outside of Korea, in that it offers an example of the strides that can be achieved in recently democratized states.

In conclusion, the Korean case illustrates how NGOs can provide an avenue for average citizens to democratically represent themselves by supporting and thereby holding accountable civic organizations, and how policy entrepreneurship can serve to further consolidate democracy. Korean NGOs' policy entrepreneurship is far from complete, and it faces many obstacles, but its realization as the status quo has merit and deserves future research and attention.

Note

This research was supported by a grant in 2002 from the Center for International Studies at Yonsei University.

References

Bratton, Michael. "Beyond the State: Civil Society and Associational Life in Africa." *World Politics*, 41, 3 (1989): 407–30.

Callahan, William A. "Comparing the Discourse of Popular Politics in Korea and China: From Civil Society to Social Movements." *Korea Journal*, 39 (1998): 277–322.

Chamberlain, H.B. "On the Search for Civil Society in China." *Modern China*, 19 (1993): 199–215.

Cho, Hein. "The Historical Origin of Civil Society in Korea." *Korea Journal*, 37 (1997): 24–41.

Chung, Chai-sik. *A Korean Confucian Encounter with the Modern World: Yi Hang-no and the West*. Berkeley, CA: Institute for East Asian Studies, 1995.

Cohen, Jean L., and Andrew Arato. *Civil Society and Political Theory*. Cambridge, MA: MIT Press, 1992.

Conley, Richard S. "Congress, the Presidency, Information Technology, and the Internet: Policy Entrepreneurship at Both Ends of the Avenue." www.american.edu/spa/ccps/publications/pdffiles/internet.pdf, 2001, p. 4.

Diamond, Larry. "Rethinking Civil Society: Towards Democratic Consolidation." *Journal of Democracy*, 5 (1994): 3–17.

Gellner, Ernest. *Conditions of Liberty: Civil Society and Its Rivals*. London: Hamish Hamilton, 1994.

Hall, John A. *Civil Society: Theory, History and Comparison*. Cambridge: Blackwell Publishers, 1995.

Han, Sang-Jin. "The Public Sphere and Democracy in Korea: A Debate on Civil Society." *Korea Journal*, 37 (1997): 78–97.

Hirst, Paul. "Democracy and Governance." In *Debating Governance*, edited by Jon Pierre. Oxford: Oxford University Press, 2000, pp. 13–35.

Jang, Hasung, and Joongi Kim. "The Role of Boards and Stakeholders in Corporate Governance." Presented at the Third Asian Roundtable on Corporate Governance. Singapore, 4–6 April 2001.

Keane, John, ed. *Civil Society and the State*. London: Verso, 1988.

Kim, Hyuk-Rae. "Korean NGOs: Global Trend and Prospect." *Global Economic Review*, 26, 2 (1997): 93–115.

——. "Environmental NGOs and the Provision of Public Goods in Northeast Asia: Development Strategies and Prospects for Environmental Cooperation." Presented at the International Conference on Environmental Issues of Northeast Asia and the Role of Local Government in the 21st Century. Seoul, 13–14 September 1999.

——. "The State and Civil Society in Transition: The Role of Non-Governmental Organizations in South Korea." *Pacific Review*, 13, 4 (2000a): 595–613.

——. 2000b. "Contradiction and Continuity: The Independence Club and Korea's Transition to Modernity." In *Korea between Tradition and Modernity*, edited by Yun-Shik Chang, Don Baker, Ross King, and Nam-lin Hur. Vancouver: Institute for Asian Research, 2000b, pp. 184–91.

——. "NGOs in Pursuit of the 'Public Good' in South Korea." In *Collective Goods, Collective Futures in Asia*, edited by Sally Sargeson. London: Routledge, 2002a, pp. 58–74.

——. 2002b. "Unraveling Civil Society in South Korea: Old Discourses and New Visions." *Korea Observer*, 33, 4 (2002b): 541–67.

——. "Dilemmas in the Making of Civil Society in Korean Political Reform." *Journal of Contemporary Asia*, 34, 1 (2004): 55–69.

Kim, Sunhyuk. "State and Civil Society in South Korea's Democratic Consolidation." *Asian Survey*, 37 (1997): 135–1144.

——. *The Politics of Democratization in Korea: The Role of Civil Society*. Pittsburgh, PA: University of Pittsburgh Press, 2000.

Kim, Sun-Mi. "An Analysis of Korean NGOs' Negotiated Governance in Policy Making." Unpublished dissertation. Department of Social Studies, Ewha Women's University, 2001. (in Korean)

Koo, Hagen. "Strong State and Contentious Society." In *State and Society in Contemporary Korea*, edited by Hagen Koo. Ithaca, NY: Cornell University Press, 1993.

Korten, David C. *Getting to the 21st Century: Voluntary Action and the Global Agenda*. West Hartford, CT: Kumarian Press, 1990.

Mintrom, Michael. "Policy Entrepreneurs and the Diffusion of Innovation." *American Journal of Political Science*, 41 (1997): 738–70.

Moon, Chung-in, and Yong-Cheol Kim. "A Circle of Paradox: Development, Politics and Democracy in South Korea." In *Democracy and Development: Theory and Practice*, edited by Adrian Leftwich. Cambridge: Polity Press, 1996.

Noda, Pamela J., ed. *The Role of Civil Society in Domestic and International Governance*. Japan Center for International Exchange, 2000.

Park, Dong-Kyu. Policy Research Department, Citizens' Coalition for Economic Justice. Personal correspondence, March 2002.

People's Solidarity for Participatory Democracy (PSPD). http://www.pspd.org. Accessed March 2002.

Pierre, Jon. 2000. "Conclusion: Governance beyond State Strength." In *Debating Governance*, edited by Jon Pierre. Oxford: Oxford University Press, 2000, pp. 1–10.

Robison, Richard, Mark Beeson, Kanishka Jayasuriya, and Hyuk-Rae Kim. *Politics and Markets in the Wake of the Asian Crisis*. London: Routledge, 2000.

Schneider, Mark, and Paul Teske, with Michael Mintrom. *Public Entrepreneurs: Agendas for Change in American Government*. Princeton, NJ: Princeton University Press, 1995.

Union of International Associations. "International Organizations by Year and Type 1909–1999." Online. Available HTTP: http://www.uia.org/uiastats/ytb299.htm. Accessed March 2002.

Weiss, Thomas G., and Leon Gordenker. *NGOs, the UN and Global Governance*. Boulder, CO: Lynne Reinner Publishers, 1996.

7 The development of NGO activities in Japan

A new civil culture and institutionalization of civic action

Koichi Hasegawa

Introduction

Japan was the first Asian country to make itself into a modern country in which the rule of law prevails, and it has been the world's second largest economy for many years. Nevertheless, the power and the influence of its NGO sector have been very limited, despite its relatively long history in other Asian countries. In fact, until Japan's Law to Promote Specified Non-Profit Activities (the NPO law) went into effect in December 1998, volunteer organizations and citizens' groups did not qualify for corporate status. Furthermore, the law's creation and passage were mainly triggered by the government's ineffective response to the Kobe earthquake disaster and the unprecedented spirit of volunteerism that swept Japan to help the victims.

Why did it take so long for Japan to understand the importance of nonprofit organizations and extend legal recognition and protection to them? Why, for so many years, were Japan's social scientists, media, progressive parties, government offices, social movement sector activists and most of its citizens so little interested in promoting citizens' activities and in the legal non-status of NGOs? Unfortunately, the example of Greenpeace, the international environmental NGO, is all too typical. Though it was founded in 1989, Greenpeace Japan only obtained corporate status in January 2002; of Greenpeace's 27 national offices, Greenpeace Japan was the last to be founded, after Tunisia;[1] and while Greenpeace Netherlands has 600,000 members, Greenpeace Japan's membership is only 4,500, or 0.75 percent in size, even though Japan's population is eight times larger.

As described in the essays by Hsiao and Kim and McNeal in this volume (Chapters 3 and 6, respectively), NGOs in Taiwan and South Korea can dramatically influence government policy creation, especially in environmental protection and social welfare. So far, this has rarely been the case in Japan. However, following the "lost decade" of the 1990s, with its dead ends and stagnated economic and political reforms, one can now observe much progress and more institutionalized activities with Japan's NGOs and other nonprofit organizations (NPOs).

Why has this change occurred? I will attempt to shed some light on these questions by outlining the history and political background of citizens' activities and social movements in Japan.

Historical background of NGO activities and social movements in Japan

Citizens' movements and community movements

Japan's pre-war Imperial Constitution substantially limited civil liberties, and there were few NGO activities outside those by a few political parties, labor movements, and religious movements. It was not until 1960 that Japan saw the emergence of full-blown NGO activities that were primarily sustained by citizens. The social movements of the 1945–60 post-war reconstruction period were political movements of class struggle with hopes of socialist revolution, centered around labor movements led by Japan's Communist Party and Social Democratic Party (formerly the Japan Socialist Party – JSP).

Between November 1959 and June 1960, controversy over the 1960 revision of the US–Japan Security Treaty divided Japanese public opinion into pro (conservative) and con (progressive) camps. Although the opposition movement was growing, it did not prevail, because conservatives held a majority in the parliament (Diet). However, that defeat catalyzed the birth of a new citizens' movement that was supported by citizens, instead of political parties or labor unions.

In the latter half of the1960s, the public became concerned with pollution and environmental damage, which were the outward manifestations of the underside of Japan's rapid economic growth. In response, community and local citizens' movements, which were new to Japan, sprang up around the nation. The issues they addressed switched from defending the constitution and promoting peace, which had been the focus until then, to opposing pollution and large-scale industrial development, which were more concrete and closely associated with everyday life.

The first community movement to oppose large-scale development that would produce industrial pollution began in Shizuoka prefecture in 1964 and targeted the construction of petrochemical complexes in the cities of Numazu and Mishima and the town of Shimizu. In a relatively short period of time, movement members representing a broad cross-section of society – farmers, fishermen, housewives, high school teachers, researchers, blue-collar workers and others – came together and rose up to protect their communities. The movement grew rapidly and eventually caused these projects to be abandoned. Its success would significantly influence all subsequent community movements.

In the latter half of the 1960s, community and citizens' movements began to diversify. Behind this was the great number of large-scale development projects projected under the 1969 New National Comprehensive Development Plan. These were intended to expand economic development across the nation through the construction of transportation networks, including the high-speed Shinkansen trains and expressway networks, as well as huge industrial complexes. At the same time, however, the public was becoming aware of the horrific harms caused by industrial pollution, such as Minamata disease.[2]

This led to the emergence in the early 1970s of community movements around the country to stop the construction of nuclear power plants. The public closely observed the political effectiveness of exercising civil rights by registering their objections to projects through community movements, and these movements spread quickly. People formed movements that actively sought to improve their residential environments, as for instance those created by urban dwellers who had gained a new citizens' awareness and were trying to defend their neighborhoods and to build and develop communities.

This spirit also extended to the soaring populations in and around major cities such as Tokyo, Osaka, and Nagoya during the period of rapid economic growth. These newcomers were greatly dissatisfied with their residential environments and the chronic lack of infrastructure. This would lead to the nationwide flourishing of progressive local governments, as well as political actions by progressive political party support bases, in and around these cities in the latter half of the 1960s into the mid-1970s.

The end of the conservative–progressive ideological framework, 1975–94

The oil shock in the fall of 1973 brought the rapid growth of the world economy to an unavoidable end. In Japan, rapid growth gave way to stable growth, and with this transition the country's social movements began to wind down. There were several reasons for this: government began creating a system of pollution-control laws in 1970; the "progressive" socialist and communist parties grew weaker, which significantly lessened the possibility that they would take the reins of government; and the primary concerns of the media and public shifted back toward maintaining stable economic growth. Pollution had dominated the headlines from the latter half of the 1960s until about 1973, but would receive less coverage after the oil shock.

Furthermore, by this time it was no longer possible to draw a simple black and white picture of the "good guys" and the "bad guys." It was easy to identify the victims and the giant corporate industrial-polluting perpetrators with disasters like Minamata disease. But in the mid-1970s, controversy shifted to pollution from high-speed transportation facilities, such as airports and the Shinkansen, and in the 1980s it shifted again to municipal waste, litter from empty tin cans, and other problems related to daily life. These environmental problems deserved criticism, but it is also undeniable that the building of these transportation networks, for instance, stemmed from the public's demand for high-speed transportation.

Achieving rapid economic growth would eventually make Japan the world's second-ranking economic power. Prior to that, until the end of the 1960s, it was poor young people with nothing to lose who led Japan's social movements and NGO activities. Guided by socialist ideals, they dreamed of revolution and hoped to achieve political reform. But today's young are the blessed beneficiaries of this affluent society and the leading actors in the consumer society. The media and young people have become progressively apolitical since the second half of the 1970s, and the young are now referred to as the "disenchanted generation."

The most important difference to note when comparing Japan's social movements and NGO activities with those in South Korea and Taiwan is that people in the latter two countries were oppressed and deprived of their civil liberties for many years by those in power. Hence, their protest movements were led by the young and continued into the second half of the 1980s, and their students and other young people still have a strong interest in politics. Japan on the other hand gained its civil liberties just after World War II, and when affluence came in the latter half of the 1970s its young people quickly grew apolitical.

Political stability continued from the 1970s into the 1990s, when changes began slowly appearing in Japan's social movements and NGO activities. Then, Emperor Hirohito died in January 1989, which ended the Showa period. Hirohito's 62-plus year reign (1926–89) had been the longest and most turbulent in Japanese history, and the succession to the throne of the Emperor Akihito signaled the beginning of a new era (*gengo*), the Heisei. That autumn, the Berlin Wall fell, signaling the end of the Cold War. Together, these events brought a strong sense to Japan that one era had passed and another had begun.

The first change was that the end of the Cold War rendered the entire conservative–progressive ideological framework obsolete. This had been a powerful element in Japan's social movements, and they had been very critical of the Liberal Democratic Party (LDP) government, which they viewed as doing the US's bidding. The United States itself was viewed as the embodiment of capitalism: a dog-eat-dog society, replete with a cold, calculating rationalism. Furthermore, despite the civil rights, anti-Vietnam and women's liberation movements and others, they knew little about its citizens' movements and NGO activities.

This changed when the Cold War structures fell, and Japan's social movements rediscovered the United States as a country of NGOs and NPOs, a land of citizen activism, and a democratic civil society. At the same time, they lost their long-held illusions of the Soviet Union and Eastern European countries as highly developed welfare societies. In a sense, the Berlin Wall had fallen in Japan, too, and the new goal for Japan's social movements and NGOs–NPOs became the building of a liberal, vibrant civil society that would counter the country's conservative, authoritarian, and paternalistic politics.

The second change was the "liberation" afforded by the death of Emperor Hirohito, who was perhaps the most polarizing figure in post-war Japan. To conservatives, he was a pacifist who had done more than anyone else to rebuild post-war Japan; to progressives, he was an irresponsible person who had evaded responsibility for the war to remain on the throne, and the symbol of political continuity between the pre- and post-war periods. Like being pro- or anti-American, being pro- or anti-Hirohito was a defining characteristic, and his death erased a major point of divergence and hastened the end of the conservative–progressive paradigm.

The third change was the splits that occurred within the LDP, its fall from power, and the advent of an unstable political situation. The LDP and its antecedents had dominated post-war Japanese politics for nearly 50 years – through the Cold

War, the period of enormous economic growth, and much of Emperor Hirohito's reign. But the end would come in June 1993, when a series of serious political scandals split the LDP, which led to the dissolution of the lower house of the Diet, and general elections that voted the LDP out. The result was a new coalition government that combined former conservatives and progressives, primarily from the Japan New Party and the New Frontier Party, with Morihiro Hosokawa as prime minister.

But the Hosokawa cabinet, a farrago of diverse elements, collapsed seven months later, and in June 1994 the LDP formed a new coalition government along with the JSP (which had been the LDP's sworn enemy since 1955) and the New Party Sakigake (another split from the LDP). More surprising was that its prime minister, Tomiichi Murayama, was from the JSP's left wing, a previously unimaginable situation. Murayama resigned about 18 months later in January 1996, ceding the prime minister's seat to an LDP member, but the LDP–JSP coalition lasted nearly four years, until May 1998. One of this government's important achievements was the NPO law, which passed in March 1998.

The 1993 LDP split destabilized Japan's political situation, and political chaos ensued. While Yasuhiro Nakasone had served as prime minister for five years in the mid-1980s, Japan had ten prime ministers during the first decade of the Heisei period, which began in January 1989 with Emperor Akihito's ascension to the throne. Furthermore, most of them were unprepared "windfall prime ministers" who simply fell into the job unexpectedly.

Collapse of the Japanese-style system: 1995 and beyond

On 17 January 1995, Kobe, one of Japan's most beautiful cities, was severely damaged by an earthquake that killed 6,279 persons, injured over 40,000, damaged 480,000 buildings, and left over 300,000 homeless. Despite a long history of fire, flood, earthquake, and tsunami, the Japanese were stunned to witness that the government did not have a reliable crisis-management system in place. In addition, the transportation system that linked Kobe to the rest of the country had been destroyed, which further hampered the official response.

In the face of official impotence, emergent groups spontaneously formed, as community members banded together to help one another. Furthermore, thousands of people from all over Japan rushed to Kobe to help the victims, in an unprecedented outpouring of public concern. Then, two months later on 20 March 1995, leaders of Aum Shinrikyo, a "new religion" cult, committed an act of indiscriminate terror and released the poison gas sarin in Tokyo subways, killing 12 people and poisoning about 3,800.

Until then, the Japanese believed that theirs was the safest society in the world, with little crime and good public security, but the double-barreled blow of the earthquake and the sarin attacks shook the entire nation. One of the other social and political impacts of the Kobe earthquake was that it dramatically changed old attitudes towards NGOs and NPOs among Japanese citizens, business and government, opening the way for new legislation that would promote NPOs.

Under single-party LDP rule, a powerful system comprised of big business, politicians, and bureaucrats, known as the "iron triangle" or "ruling triad" (Broadbent 1998), held Japanese society in sway for about 40 years in the post-war period. During this time the public was exposed to environmental hazards, but it also enjoyed political, social, and economic stability. Furthermore, despite a never-ending series of money scandals involving politicians, the public continued to believe that Japan's chief bureaucrats and corporate leaders were upright and capable.

All of that changed with the Recruit company incident of 1989, which developed into a major political issue. Recruit was Japan's standard-bearer in the information technology sector, but it would also become the eponym for the country's greatest post-war bribery scandal. Japan was shocked by the unfolding of a series of events that led to the arrest of the company's president, the resignation of Prime Minister Noboru Takeshita (an influential leader of the biggest faction of the LDP), the arrest of two administrative assistants to top bureaucrats, as well as additional scandals that exposed collusion between big business and high-level bureaucrats in the Ministries of Finance, Foreign Affairs, International Trade and Industry, Health and Welfare, and others. Not only did the public grow even more distrustful of politicians, but this soon applied to bureaucrats, who formerly had been revered for their probity, wisdom, and leadership.

Skyrocketing land and stock market prices brought boom times in the latter half of the 1980s, but in 1990 the bubble economy burst. Japan's post-war economy had been based on the assumption that land prices would continue to rise, but sharply depressed land prices and consumption transformed stock certificates and unused land into bad debts. Bankruptcy became endemic among large construction and real estate companies and financial institutions, even though many of them had been regarded as unsinkable battleships. Even now, Japan's economy has yet to extricate itself from the shambles of the bubble economy and is struggling to dispose of its bad debts.

In recent years scandal has erupted everywhere: police, hospitals, educational institutions from elementary schools to universities, television stations, newspapers, food companies and their products, the housing industry, automakers, the nuclear power industry, electric utilities, athletes, and more. Almost no occupation or industry has been left untouched by scandal and the consequent erosion of public trust. The new keywords of the times are "distrust," "anxiety," and "risk management." People sense the declining strength of their country, and they fear unseen risks.

Can Japan become a vibrant country again? If so, where are the requisite resources? I think they can be found in NGO and NPO activities.

The development of the civil sector in the 1990s

It was not until 1998 that Japan created a system to provide NGOs with corporate status as nonprofit organizations, making it the last among the industrialized countries to do so. Why did this take so long?

The first reason is Japan's centralized, bureaucrat-led system, whose paternalistic and conservative politics, symbolized by Emperor Hirohito, held sway until the end of the 1980s. Incredibly, the NPO law is the first Japanese law in which the word "citizen" appears. LDP politicians and government bureaucrats had avoided the word, as it implies individuals with a strong sense of independence and a robust capacity for criticism.

Second, much of the blame must also be shaped by intellectuals and the media, as the world of Japan's NGOs and social movements was long dominated by a simplistic template of good socialism versus evil capitalism. They had little interest in citizen activities or NPOs that were not in socialist countries and did not recognize that the United States is a land of many NGOs–NPOs or that they thrive in Germany and other European countries.

Third, because the iron triangle of big business, politicians, and bureaucrats was so strong and political opportunities were closed to all but a select few, the public thought that the basic role of social movements was to criticize the errors of those in power – it had no idea that citizens' and community movements could organize and develop programs, or make policy proposals. Consequently, those movements had not progressed beyond the point of mounting protests against specific local issues, such as opposing environmental damage or the construction of dams and nuclear power plants. Before the enactment of the NPO law, they were merely voluntary associations without any legal status that had little apparent impact on the national level (Hasegawa 1995, 1999, 2004).

Key changes in NGOs, and progress toward their institutionalization

While the 1990s are often described in Japan as the "ten lost years," this decade actually saw much progress in the area of citizen movements and NGOs–NPOs. In fact, these organizations were the only ones left untainted by the scandals and corruption. At this point I will use the term "civil sector" to describe the nongovernmental–nonprofit sector comprised of citizen activities, NPO activities, social movements, and the like – as opposed to the "government sector" comprised of the legislative, administrative, and judicial functions on the national and local levels; and the "business sector," which is comprised of profit-making enterprises.[3] Five key changes have recently occurred in the civil sector.

First, the organizing of citizen activities proceeded rapidly in conjunction with the enactment of the NPO law in March 1998.

Second, through the use of citizen ombudsmen and information-disclosure procedures, citizens' movements pushed through administrative and fiscal reforms in local municipalities.

Third, citizens' movements also adopted local referenda as a common strategy. Local assemblies were reluctant to go along and tried to block them, but referenda were held in several localities on issues that had split local public opinion.

Fourth, while NGOs had conducted confrontational campaigns that only pointed out and criticized government wrongs, an increasing number of them now partnered with experts in order to propose alternative policies, and to seek collaboration with government, administrative authorities, and business to bring about desired policies. Many Japanese NGOs now also strive to be "policy entrepreneurs" (see Chapter 6).

And fifth, information technology and internationalization are making inroads in citizen activities and social movements, bringing full-blown exchanges with movements and NGOs–NPOs in other countries, and accelerating the policy-oriented transformation and institutionalization of citizen activities.

All these changes are both directly and indirectly connected with the gradual institutionalization of citizens' activities, NGO activities, and social movements.[4] "Institutionalization" here means two things:

- The national government, administrative authorities, and others now accept citizens' activities, NGOs–NPOs, and social movements as entities with real influence regarding certain issues. When seeking a better understanding of policies and their infusion into society, the government and administrative authorities now view the civil sector as a vital partner.
- Rather than using direct action and demonstrations to make their point, the civil sector employs ordinances, petitions, assembly deliberations, and elections, or it designs new institutions it can use. Furthermore, there is a greater presupposition that civil sector groups are themselves institutions.

I will now discuss these five changes in detail.

Organization of NPOs

While people began advocating in the first half of the 1990s that citizens' groups should be able to acquire corporate status, it took the 1995 Kobe earthquake to trigger widespread recognition of the necessity of citizen activities and their social mission. The Diet enacted the NPO law in March 1998, and it took effect in December.

According to data from the Cabinet Office website (the former Economic Planning Agency), as of October 2002 the government had received 9,427 applications for certification as specified nonprofit corporations, and granted certification to 8,679. This number exceeds predictions, and shows that a bit of an NPO boom is taking place: in the first year after the law took effect, the number of certified NPOs exceeded 1,000, in the second year it surpassed 3,000, in the third year is was over 5,000, and it looks as though it will exceed 9,000 in the fourth. During 2002 the number of certified organizations increased by about 300 per month. NPOs have clearly found a home in society and are forming a new "civil culture."

People have great expectations for NGOs. The work of scholars like Pestoff (1988) has made people around the world more aware of the increasing incidence of market and government failures. As noted earlier, the bursting of the economic bubble and the Kobe earthquake during the first half of the 1990s revealed how power of the government and business sectors had declined. But families, kinship groups, community organizations, and other such groups have also lost some of their power and unity. Government, markets, families, and communities do not function as well as they did before, and people are hoping that NGOs and NPOs will take up the slack where these other social institutions are now falling short.

All this is reflected in a change in the Japanese concept of "publicness" (Hasegawa 2000, 2004: 199). There was been a powerful tendency in Japan for the concept of *oyake* ("public" as opposed to "private") to converge on the nation-state. *Oyake* had little of the sense of the English word "public" as regards matters concerning the general public: it was thought that the job of defining and realizing the public interest was exclusively that of the government and administrative authorities. However, ordinary citizens are now realizing that they can take it upon themselves to define the public interest by forming groups to deal with the specific challenges that concern them, and citizen groups and NGOs–NPOs are beginning to put this into effect in various ways.

But as more people subscribe to this view of the public interest and of publicness characterized by self-help and mutual help, the challenge is to find the people to do the job as well as the resources needed to sustain the activities. Japan's NPOs face the problems of insufficient funding and a lack of human resources, especially people who can staff offices full time. Insufficient human resources are an especially acute problem, and a few very able persons tend to work at multiple NPOs.

The vast majority of NPOs (90 percent) obtain certification from a prefecture, but, if they have offices in two or more prefectures, they are certified by the Cabinet Office. This arrangement may encourage NPO activities that are integrated into their locales, but it also makes it hard for them to grow into huge national bodies like the (South) Korean Federation for Environmental Movement (KFEM) or the Taiwan Environmental Protection Union (TEPU).[5] Strictly speaking, there is no counterpart to these organizations in Japan. The activities of the well-known worldwide environmental organizations in Japan are more specific (e.g. nuclear issues, global warming, bird protection). Their membership size is usually small (less than 10,000), and their influence on national environmental policy is quite limited.

While NGOs and the social movement in the United States are very pragmatic, Japan's social and environmental movements have strong puritanical tendencies, which to some degree indicate their limited links to government and business. There is also danger that hard feelings will arise between new NPOs and certain old-type movements, as the former are enthusiastic about collaborating with the government and administrative authorities to try to increase their influence over policy, while the latter try to maintain their distance.

On the other hand, there is also danger that NGOs–NPOs and citizen activities could end up a cozy club lacking a critical perspective from within as well as constructive criticism from without, which could lead them to stagnate and forget their social mission. The emotional ties among members and the continued existence of the organization could become ends in themselves.

As more and more NGOs–NPOs actively seek project commissions from administrative authorities, they also run the serious risk of becoming the authorities' subcontractors. One question that arises out of this is how to put NGOs–NPOs and the administrative authorities on an equal footing. Commissioning projects and paying subsidies and other funds also involve the problem of how to create and guarantee principles of fair and transparent implementation. Another issue is that, while Japan's public services have been provided by administrative authorities in accordance with standardized criteria, the interregional disparities in their quality could be further exacerbated by the vigor of NGO–NPO activities in and around major cities and the stagnation in rural areas.

Citizen ombudsman activities and freedom of information

In terms of Japanese social movements bringing about major changes and improvements in local government administration, the biggest achievements in the 1990s were realized by citizen ombudsman activities. Citizen campaigns built around lawyers, tax accountants, and other professionals used lawsuits, audit demands, and information-disclosure procedures to expose illegal public expenditures by municipalities and local assemblies. They also made additional progress in information disclosure and promoted changes, including amending ordinances and rectifying public expenditures.

The use of ombudsman activities is in the spotlight as a new kind of social movement and NGO activity for several reasons.

First, ombudsmen used a variety of means to make administrative authorities yield documents, and then exposed the authorities' improprieties by uncovering their contradictions and absurdities. Japan's citizens' movements have always complained that the national and local governments disclosed very little information. Citizens have therefore used information-disclosure procedures and specialized analyses to reveal improprieties and to show how audit systems existed in name only. This is a new type of movement: NGO activity that confronts administrative authorities by subjecting concrete evidence to the scrutiny of experts, instead of just making demands or complaints, or setting forth opposing ideas.

Second, the National Citizens Ombudsman Liaison Council was formed in 1994, the year after the ombudsman system began. This shows that the movement realized the importance of establishing a nationwide network right from the outset. On 25 April 1995 the council demanded the disclosure of local governments' meal expenses nationwide. In due course it revealed that about 80 percent of the meal expenses in the administrative and finance sections of 40 prefectures and cabinet-designated cities, as well as in their Tokyo offices, had been spent on entertaining central government bureaucrats. In other words, these funds were spent by bureaucrats entertaining other bureaucrats.

Third, by means of information gathering through networks and discussions, the council created a baseline for assessing the extent of information disclosure and has released national rankings every year since 1997.[6] This is a concrete attempt by citizens at a competing policy assessment.

Fourth, thanks to these efforts, Miyagi prefecture (where this idea of national rankings originated) has been rated first among all Japan's prefectures in the overall ranking of information disclosure four times out of five, while Akita and Aomori prefectures, which ranked at the bottom in the first and second assessments, have been moving up the ladder. In these and other ways, the assessment has succeeded in advancing nationwide institutional reform. Not only has information disclosure improved, but so has the auditing system itself, and illegal public expenditures have been substantially reduced. Prefectures took the lead in information disclosure through their ordinances, while national legislation only became effective in April 2001. This is a typical example in which localities created institutions earlier than the national government.

The referendum strategy

On 4 August 1996 the town of Maki in Niigata prefecture held the nation's first ordinance-sanctioned referendum on whether to allow the construction of a nuclear power plant. With a turnout of 88.3 percent and 60.9 percent of those voting opposed, this referendum had a huge impact on other disputes around the country concerning nuclear power plants, US military bases, and industrial-waste disposal sites. The Maki campaign triggered movements seeking referenda throughout the country, and 12 referenda had been carried out by various munici-palities by the end of October 2002.

Despite the many instances in which petitions to create referendum ordinances have been rejected by local assemblies, seeking referenda has in recent years become a major social movement strategy. Getting petitions approved to pass referendum ordinances requires increasing the number of assembly members in favor of them. Maki originally only had one or two assembly members who were opposed to nuclear power, and it only became possible to pass the ordinance after the number of members opposed to or cautious about nuclear power increased to nearly half. It is therefore likely that attempts to populate local assemblies with citizen activists will increase throughout Japan.

Policy orientation and globalization

Many of Japan's movements are now oriented toward proposing alternative policies and collaborating with government and business, instead of merely confronting them. Citizens' movements and NGO activities can function as non-institutionalized countervailing forces that critically monitor the social rationality of the policy-making process and of the policies themselves. For many years Japan's single-party, bureaucrat-led, centralized planning system, which coordinated the interests of involved industries in advance of policy implementation, rendered the deliberations in assemblies and other bodies mere formalities. They hardly allowed those bodies to exercise adequate oversight. Citizens' movements and NGO activities, which have the capacity to think and act in new and flexible ways, are capable of "exemplary practice," and can play a major role, especially in local autonomy and in responding to policy challenges at the local level.

In Japan there are now instances of collaboration even on issues that breed confrontation, such as nuclear power and policy on power production and energy. For example, beginning in 1997 the Tokyo Electric Power Company and the citizens' organization Renewable Energy Promoting People's Forum collaborated for three years on expanding the use of photovoltaic power. Meanwhile, NGOs and NPOs have been major actors along with governments at major international conferences since the 1992 Earth Summit.

At one time, Europe's environmental movement was characterized by distancing itself from policy-making authorities and by its anti-establishment character – much more so than that of the United States. However, with the end of the Cold War, major changes also occurred in Europe. In global warming, renewable energy, and other fields, environmental NGOs–NPOs increasingly lead experimental initiatives that begin in smaller cities, spread throughout the country, then spill over into other countries, and eventually become EU policy. International environmental NGOs–NPOs with their primary focal points in Europe, such as the World Wide Fund for Nature, Greenpeace, and Friends of the Earth, are becoming more influential regarding global warming and other global environmental problems (Josselin and Wallace 2001; Keck and Sikkink 1998).

Because of linguistic barriers and physical distance, information from other countries used to be communicated to the civil sector or was "translated" and "interpreted" by the government, media, and researchers. However, advances in information technology have not only improved access to data and information, but enabled daily contact among people around the world. Civil sectors in different countries now exchange information with each other on an everyday basis.

NGOs now set their goals and plan their strategies with an awareness of international trends and linkages. In view of the strong policy orientation of Western NGOs and of NGOs in South Korea and Taiwan, which are closer to governments and researchers, it is therefore quite likely that, as Japan's NGOs grow and mature, they too will have a strong voice in matters of policy.

Notes

1 Greenpeace has no national office in South Korea or Taiwan. Greenpeace China, which is located in Hong Kong, was founded in 1998.
2 Minamata disease is a severe neurological disorder caused by mercury in the environment. The first cases appeared in 1956 in Minamata; another epidemic took place in 1965 in Niigata. It was Japan's first known manmade environmental disaster.
3 In the United States and Europe this sector is also called the "private nonprofit sector," "nonprofit cooperative sector," "joint sector," "social sector," and "social economy." The most common term in English is "nonprofit sector."
4 See Mitchell *et al.* (1992) for explorations of the benefits and detriments of institutionalization in the environmental movement, with the United States as an example.
5 Founded in 1993 KFEM, with 47 local branches and 85,000 members, is the biggest and the most influential NGO in South Korea, and is this country's largest

environmental organization (see Chapter 6). TEPU, with 11 local chapters and about 1,000 members, was founded in 1987 and is the leading environmental organization in Taiwan. It has a strong influence on the environmental policy of President Chen and a very close relationship with him and his party (see Chapter 3).

6   See the website of the National Citizens Ombudsman Liaison Council to see the changes in the overall rankings over the five years 1997–2001 (http://www.jkcc.gr.jp/rank/05_01.html, accessed 8 May 2001).

References

Broadbent, Jeffrey. *Environmental Politics in Japan: Networks of Power and Protest.* Cambridge: Cambridge University Press, 1998.

Hasegawa, Koichi. "A Comparative Study of Social Movements for a Post-Nuclear Energy Era in Japan and the United States." *International Journal of Japanese Sociology,* 4 (1995): 21–36.

——. "Global Climate Change and Japanese Nuclear Policy." *International Journal of Japanese Sociology,* 8 (1999): 183–97.

——. 2000. "Kyodo-sei to Kokyo-sei no Gendaiteki Iso" [The Sociological Aspects of Communality and Publicity]. *Japanese Sociological Review,* 50, 4 (2000): 436–50.

——. *Constructing Civil Society in Japan: Voices of Environmental Movements.* Melbourne: Trans Pacific Press, 2004.

Japan, Government of. Cabinet Office website: http://www5.cao.go.jp/98/c/19981217c-npojyuri.html.

Josselin, Daphne, and William Wallace, eds. *Non-State Actors in World Politics.* Basingstoke: Palgrave, 2001.

Keck, Margaret. E., and Kathryn Sikkink. *Activists beyond Borders: Advocacy Networks in International Politics.* Ithaca, NY: Cornell University Press, 1998.

Mitchell, Robert C., Angela G. Mertig, and Riley E. Dunlap. "Twenty Years of Environmental Mobilization: Trends among National Environmental Organizations." In *American Environmentalism: The U.S. Environmental Movement, 1970–1990,* edited by Riley E. Dunlap and Angela G. Mertig. Bristol, PA: Taylor & Francis, 1992, pp. 11–26.

8 The state, local associations, and alternate civilities in rural northern Vietnam

Hy V. Luong

In July 1998 I returned to Son Duong commune (population 4,823) in the northern Vietnamese province of Phu Tho. It was the first time I had been back in seven years, and I was startled to find that I had returned during a profound crisis in the relations between the local population and the commune's administration.[1] As just one example of the magnitude of this crisis, from 1993 to 1998 three Communist Party secretaries and four presidents of the People's Committee quickly succeeded one another, partly due to strong local pressure.

Relations between the local population and the commune administration reached the boiling point during my visit. Local families reportedly refused to pay not only irrigation fees but commune taxes. These arrears totaled US$18,000[2] for half a year. As a result of this politically rooted financial crisis, the commune's cumulative debt to the state irrigation authorities spiraled to approximately $15,000; peasants reported that the flow of irrigation water to the commune had significantly slowed, causing them considerable hardships during the rice cultivation season; and commune cadres had not received their salaries for six months. Furthermore, at a major public meeting during which the party's secretary reviewed commune activities in the first half of 1998, a villager reportedly asked this political leader, "Who elected you to a position of authority?"

Relations between the local population and the state seemed to have undergone a fundamental transformation since I first visited the commune in 1987, in parallel with an extensive proliferation of kinship- and communal-based local associations. Within the context of intricately tight local social networks, the local population had clearly attempted to exert considerable pressure on the state and party apparatuses, not simply through a subtle resistance (Kerkvliet 1995), but through open confrontation and occasionally adversarial public dialogues.

This proliferation of voluntary associations is not restricted to northern rural Vietnam. For at least a decade and a half, numerous registered and nonregistered associations have sprung up in both urban and rural communities and in different parts of the country. They have emerged both within and at the margin of the state's regulatory framework in response to a fundamental shift toward a market economy under stronger global influences, as well as to the contraction of the state's role in providing social, health, and educational services. In the northern countryside these associations have entered into an active dialogue with the state and have challenged local state apparatuses in numerous communes.

More importantly, in Vietnam, it is neither the bourgeois-dominated and urban-based associations nor the large disenfranchised landless class in the socio-economically polarized Mekong Delta in the South that has exerted the strongest pressure on the Vietnamese Marxist state. In fact, the strong focus on urban-based and bourgeois-dominated associations in the NGO literature (see Gray 1999 and Suzuki 2002; cf. Sidel 1995) has led to a highly skewed picture of the relation between the voluntary and Vietnamese state associations. To date, the strongest and most effective pressure on the state has come from the communal-, kinship-, and religious-based associations that constitute "alternate civilities" (Weller 1999) and which have proliferated in the northern, rural part of the country, where the bourgeoisie had not fully emerged after decades of collectivization. In the Vietnamese context, these historically shaped and regionally varied alternate civilities have provided a powerful basis for a dialogic relation with the state that is at least as powerful as civil society and class dynamics.

Voluntary associations and the post-colonial Vietnamese state: historical overview

In its first three decades of power beginning in 1954, and in the context of the war with the United States, the Marxist-Leninist state in North Vietnam sought to expand the economic and sociopolitical space under its control in two ways: through land reform and collectivization, and by establishing its own organizations or supporting others for the exclusive mobilization of specific social sectors for various purposes. While the 1957 law on associations affirmed people's right to establish associations, its requirement that they have a legitimate purpose and contribute to the construction of the "people's democratic regime" led by the Vietnamese Communist Party (VCP) did not leave much space for voluntary associations outside the state's political framework. The state-established or -supported organizations were responsible for mobilizing the population in their sectors for numerous campaigns, ranging from wartime mobilization to peacetime local security and crime control, population planning, and fundraising for local infrastructure projects (see also Diep Dinh Hoa 1995: 258–62).

The most prominent state-established mass organizations, all under the umbrella of the Fatherland Front (*Mat tran to quoc*, the national party-state's popular mobilization apparatus), were the Women's and the Youth Unions and the General Confederation of Labor. The Youth Union included as its elite component the more activist Communist Youth League through which many young party members were recruited. Unlike a number of other state-organized associations, these three mass organizations were found not only at the national and provincial levels, but also at the district and commune levels (in the case of the Women's and the Youth Unions) and at the enterprise level (in the case of the labor confederation). The Peasant Association, which played a leading role in the controversial land reform campaign of the mid-1950s, ceased to exist in 1958, as the newly established cooperatives with memberships encompassing most cultivators began playing a dominant role in rural northern Vietnam. It was resurrected in 1979, when the agricultural production and procurement system encountered numerous difficulties (Phan Xuan Son 2002: 97, 103).[3]

In 1988, the VCP and the state also established the Veterans Association to facilitate the mobilization of millions of former soldiers from the various wars between 1946 and 1989. Like the three other mass organizations, both the Peasant and the Veterans Associations were organized not only at the national and provincial levels, but also at the district and commune–ward levels. They joined the ranks of the Women's and the Youth Unions and the General Confederation of Labor as the major mass organizations of the Communist Party and the state. The national heads of all these organizations, including the Communist Youth League, have routinely been members of the VCP's Central Committee.[4]

In order to mobilize intellectuals, the VCP and the state-organized professional associations (e.g. the Historical Association, General Association of Medical and Pharmaceutical Studies, Writers Association, Musicians Association), which were grouped into either the Union of Science and Technology Associations or the Union of Cultural and Artistic Associations. In contrast to the five aforementioned mass organizations, these associations were organized only at the national and, in a number of cases, provincial levels. These two unions and some of their older member associations, such as the Vietnamese Historical Association and the Vietnamese Journalists Association, were also constituent units of the Fatherland Front.

Two other major types of organizations that emerged in the first three decades of Marxist-Leninist rule were religious associations, and the state-established Red Cross and international friendship associations. The state allowed one religious association at the national and provincial levels for each recognized religion (Catholicism, Buddhism, and Protestantism in the North). Informal religious groups centered on particular churches and pagodas were tolerated in a number of localities and only loosely connected, if at all, to national religious associations. The Red Cross and the international friendship associations were established to facilitate the state's international relation objectives.

In the three decades since the consolidation of Marxist power in North Vietnam, the Women's and the Youth Associations functioned as extensions of the state and VCP in Son Duong commune. In a modernist discourse, the Marxist party-state launched attacks on such "superstitious" practices as the worship of communal deities as well as various practices among elderly women. This undermined neighborhood organizations (*giap*) for communal deity worship and the Buddhist elderly women's group (see Luong 1992: 56–8). In the name of national and communal construction during wartime, the VCP and the state also collectivized land and advocated frugality through the simplification of rituals, which undermined the existence of patrilineages and of the system of mutual assistance at weddings and funerals, which was partly sustained through rotating-credit associations.

Many groups, such as patrilineage and same-school associations (*hoi dong mon*), ceased to exist. Among the local voluntary associations of the French colonial period, only the Buddhist elderly women's group and some rotating-credit groups continued to function in the shadow of the state-controlled space without any official recognition. Although weddings and funerals were greatly simplified in Son Duong and throughout North Vietnam (Luong 1994; Malarney 2002, 2003), which reduced the need for rotating-credit associations, villagers still informally maintained some of them in connection with building and renovating homes.

However, as the chanting of Buddhist sutras is an essential component of any funeral, it was no coincidence that from 1954 onwards the pagoda-based elderly women's group was the most resilient of the voluntary associations. Furthermore, the Buddhist pagoda, with its primarily otherworldly orientation, and the pagoda-based and strictly local elderly women's group, were not seen as a direct potential threat to party and state power. The resilience of the Buddhist elderly women's group was also facilitated by a very tight kinship network within the village, due to the high rates of community endogamy throughout northern rural Vietnam.[5] At any point, virtually all the grandmothers, mothers, aunts and sisters of the party and government leaders in Son Duong are members of the Buddhist elderly women's association.[6]

In the past decade and a half, both registered and nonregistered voluntary associations have proliferated in number and categories in Vietnam, and their funding sources have diversified to include a more significant contribution from domestic and international nonstate sources. These changes have taken place as the state contracts its role in both the economic and social arenas, as the market has expanded, and as global forces have begun playing a role in Vietnam's economy and society.

For example, in the economic domain in 1986, the state and VCP officially sanctioned private enterprises, including ones that are foreign owned, as specified in the foreign investment law of 1987. Cooperatives in agriculture, to the extent that they remain, have provided only selected services (e.g. irrigation and plowing) to cultivators, who either de facto own land, as in the southern third of Vietnam, or have long-term usufruct rights, as in northern Vietnam and along the central coast. The number of industrial cooperatives suffered a precipitous decline, from 32,034 in 1988 to 949 in 1998, while industrial state enterprises dropped from 3,092 to 1,821 in the same period. In contrast, the number of private domestic enterprises increased from 318 in 1988 to 5,714 in 1998; those with foreign capital increased from 1 to 830, and handicraft households went from 318,557 to 553,043 in the same period (Luong 2003a: 10–11).

The state sector, which played a major role mainly in manufacturing and selected services such as utilities, telecommunication and petroleum distribution, accounted for only 38–40 percent of the GDP for most of the 1990s (ibid.: 14–15). In the social, educational, and health domains, the state and the VCP have called for a greater role of nongovernmental organizations and households in funding these services, and have also allowed a small number of nonpublic schools, clinics, and private medical offices. In this context, health care has become a two-tiered system in which anything beyond the most cursory or basic diagnoses costs extra money.

Despite its official commitment to socialism, the Vietnamese state financed only 51 percent of the total educational expenditures and 16 percent of total health care expenditures in 1992–3, and 48 percent of the former and 21 percent of the latter in 1997–8 (World Bank 1995: 86, 99–100; Vietnam and International Donor Group 2000 II: 98–9, 128). As an example of the widening rural–urban gap (see Luong 2003b), a major illness or medical operation would cost the equivalent of one year's income for a relatively poor rural family, while a university education is beyond the financial means of the majority of rural households.

As the state has contracted its economic and social space under strong societal pressures and in an active dialogic relation with society (see Luong 2003a: 22–5; Kerkvliet 1995, 2003), registered and nonregistered domestic and international voluntary associations have proliferated. The number of nationally registered domestic associations increased from 124 in 1990 to over 200 in 2000; the number of locally registered associations (including mostly the numerous branches of those national associations in Hanoi, Ho Chi Minh City, and 59 other provinces) increased from over 300 in 1990 to over 1,400 in 2000 (Thang van Phuc *et al.* 2002: 44–5, 215–17). The number of international nongovernmental organizations also increased from fewer than ten with intensive Vietnam contacts in the late 1980s to almost 500 registered ones in 2000. Of these, approximately 350 had active programs and 157 had offices or workstations in Vietnam (Nguyen Kim Ha 2001: 13–14; Thang van Phuc *et al.* 2002: 174).

Of the over 200 nationally registered domestic associations in 2000, the largest group was composed of almost 100 business associations that were established mostly since the early 1990s and operated under the umbrella of the Vietnamese Chamber of Industry and Commerce. There were 55 professional associations, 45 within the Union of Science and Technology Associations and 10 in the Union of Literary and Artistic Associations. The state-established Vietnam Union of Friendship Organizations had over 40 nationally registered domestic members (Thang van Phuc *et al.* 2002: 55, 68, 74, 77). The rest of the nationally registered domestic organizations were social service and philanthropic organizations, sport and hobby associations, and religious associations.

Business associations, which numbered almost 100 at the national level in 1999 and operated under the umbrella of the Vietnamese Chamber of Industry and Commerce, have strongly sprung up in the past decade, as private enterprises have been sanctioned again. They range from the banking association in the service sector; ceramics, footwear, and garment and textile associations, and others in different industries; gardening, coffee, and sugarcane associations, and others in agriculture; to the intersectoral Union of Cooperatives, Council of Young Entrepreneurs, and more than a dozen expatriate business groups (Thang van Phuc *et al.* 2002: 74, 77, 87).

Among the friendship organizations under the umbrella of the state-funded Vietnam Union of Friendship Organizations (VUFO), the fastest growing group is the international nongovernmental organizations, which are coordinated by VUFO's People's Aid Coordinating Committee (PACCOM) and which, as previously mentioned, numbered almost 500 by 2000. The overwhelming majority of international NGOs work in the social, educational, and health service sectors, where many national associations and a number of provincial-level ones have been established since the early 1990s, especially in the South, in order to complement the operation of the state-established Red Cross. Among the major nationally registered ones are the Association of the Blind, Association for the Protection of the Handicapped and Orphans, Charity Association, and Study Encouragement Association (*hoi khuyen hoc*).

Many associations have also been formed and registered in Ho Chi Minh City. The most successful of these is the Association to Sponsor Poor Patients, which is headed by a former chairman of Ho Chi Minh City People's Committee, and which over six years raised over $2 million from firms and individuals to cover medical expenses for poor patients (*Sai Gon Giai Phong*, 19 November 2002). The remaining nationally registered associations, the group of hobby and sport associations, are mostly composed of recently established groups, including the Philately and Chess Associations, the Sport Association of the Handicapped, and the Union of Sport Cyclists and Motorcyclists.

With the major exception of business, friendship, and sport and hobby associations, all five mass organizations, the majority of nationally registered associations, and all the provincial affiliates of the Federation of Cultural and Artistic Associations have their own new periodicals or newspapers. The Writers Association and some others also have printing presses and publish books. Some national or major provincial associations even sponsor or manage private universities and schools as well as national competitions in their fields, while the Vietnamese Lawyers Association also has many legal consulting offices (Thang van Phuc *et al.* 2002: 57–60, 92–101).

While the state retains strong control of many registered associations, just as many provincially registered research centers and social service organizations have been formed in response to international funding opportunities, the roles of the state and of international nongovernmental organizations should not be overestimated in the recent proliferation of voluntary associations in Vietnam. International NGOs disbursed approximately $80 million a year in the second half of the 1990s (Nguyen Kim Ha 2001: 16; Thang van Phuc *et al.* 2002: 157), mainly for social, health, environmental, and educational causes. A recent survey of 115 charity, social service, and research organizations in Hanoi and Ho Chi Minh City (i.e. the organizations in the sample that are the most dependent on international funding) found that only a quarter considered international funding their most important source of finance.[7] In an interesting regional variation, approximately 22 percent of those organizations in Ho Chi Minh City considered domestic voluntary contributions their most important funding source, while only 2 percent of those in Hanoi did (Wischermann *et al.* 2000: 50).

For Hanoi organizations in this group, 54 percent considered the sale of services their most important source of funding, while only 17 percent of those in Ho Chi Minh City considered this their most important funding source (ibid.).[8] Despite the prestige of its name among international donors, even the state-established Red Cross society raised over 70 percent of its funds (close to $100 million) between

1990 and 1998 from domestic voluntary contributions (Thang van Phuc *et al.* 2002: 84).[9] Domestic charity donations seem to be more important in the southern part of Vietnam, mostly due to the South's stronger flow of overseas remittances, its large number of private firms, and its stronger tradition of voluntary social service and philanthropic associations dating back to the pre-1975 period (see also Sidel 1995: 294, 298–300). There is no empirical support yet for the suggestion that "international NGOs constitute the heart of the NGO sector and play a sustaining role in Vietnam's social development" (Suzuki 2002: 145) or that "the rate of NGO growth [in Vietnam] will be largely determined by international donors" (Gray 1999: 710).

While international funding played a fairly important role, the significant expansion of the private sector and the average 8 percent annual growth of the Vietnamese economy in the 1990s seem even more important in sustaining registered organizations' activities. They do so by creating a space for their entrepreneurial activities and by increasing the potential for donations with greater household incomes and firm revenues. Once the analysis is broadened to include nonregistered voluntary associations at the local level, the role of international funding becomes even less important, as these nonregistered associations rely almost exclusively on domestic donations for the reconstruction of temples and ancestral halls, the establishment of scholarship funds, and various local social services.[10]

I suggest that a more comprehensive analysis of Vietnamese voluntary associations that includes the nonregistered ones will reveal that the growth of voluntary associations in the past decade and a half is rooted not as much in international funding as in the dynamics of state–society relations. On one level, the proliferation of registered associations in Vietnam in the past decade and a half can be seen as rooted in the state's renovation (*doi moi*) policy of contracting economic and social space under state control. However, on another level, the state adopted this renovation policy in the context of a serious economic crisis, from the late 1970s to the late 1980s, that resulted from strong societal pressures in the form of producers' everyday resistance to the command economy.

More importantly, in the past decade and a half, the strongest societal pressure on the state has come not from urban-based registered associations but from northern rural communities, where nonregistered voluntary associations have proliferated within the context of intricately bound kinship and communal networks. These nonregistered associations range from patrilineages and same-village or -province associations (*hoi dong huong*, mainly in large cities), to same-military-service, same-age, alumni, temple, and rotating-credit associations, among many others.

Furthermore, as can be seen in what follows, it is the nonregistered associations and the local branches of some national associations, such as the Veterans Association, especially in the northern countryside, that have provided a powerful basis for dialogic relations between local communities and the state. In urban contexts, on the other hand, even the newly formed business associations that are not dependent on the state for funding and are primarily concerned with exerting influence on state policies and measures affecting members' businesses simply submit petitions and make suggestions to the government in nonadversarial relations.

The unfolding of public dramas

Son Duong

The public drama in Son Duong began unfolding on 13 December 1996, when the family members of many war dead (*liet si*) and invalids gathered outside the commune's revolutionary and war dead cemetery. Because they were denied access to the commune meeting hall, the villagers had chosen to meet in the village's other officially sacred space. The elderly president of the commune association of *gia dinh chinh sach* (policy-favored households) started the meeting by burning incense in commemoration of those "native sons who sacrificed their lives for the independence and welfare" of the country. The family members of the war dead and invalids were joined by many residents of the commune neighborhood, whose leader was a sister of one of the commune's war invalids. During the meeting, villagers reacted with indignation to what the leaders of a spontaneous, local anti-corruption movement had uncovered in the previous few days:

- A list of 83 "war dead and war invalid" households, signed by the president and the main tax official of Son Duong commune, had been submitted in 1996 to higher authorities for full or partial exemption from agricultural taxes, as required by the government's tax exemption decree. However, the list contained nine households not eligible for the tax exemption, while a number of eligible households on the list were granted no exemption or only a part of their exemption by the commune administration.
- Of those 83 households, the agricultural landholdings of 59 were artificially inflated without their knowledge in order to obtain higher exemptions, which, needless to say, were not passed on to them.

The leaders of the local anti-corruption campaign accused local officials of pocketing the difference between the higher province-granted exemptions and the actual exemptions received by village households, and 84 villagers signed a resolution that demanded the firing of the commune's president and main tax official, a full investigation by the commune administration, the termination of the employment of any cadres who were embezzling or were responsible for the loss of public funds, a critical examination of the involved Communist Party members by local party cells (*chi bo dang*), and the criminal prosecution of corrupt officials.

Subsequent investigations uncovered the embezzlement of 28 tons of paddy in 1994 and the second half of 1995 alone. In 1994, for example, the president of the People's Provincial Committee approved the tax exemption for 127 Son Duong households though the district list contained only 83 and the village administration exempted taxes for only 53. According to the two leaders of the anti-corruption movement in Son Duong, the amount of paddy embezzled from 1994 to 1996 came to 42 tons.

The corruption trial of officials in the provincial court on 15 November 1997 inflamed local opinions. Many villagers signed a petition to the Supreme Court alleging procedural irregularities in the trial and questioning the verdict. They accused police and judicial authorities of lacking respect for the local population. They also alleged the following irregularities:

- Villagers who discovered the embezzlement were not invited to attend the trial, and invitations to eight victim witnesses were "problematic": four of them had died, one had moved to southern Vietnam, one was an elderly invalid, one suffered from mental illness, and the last allegedly had very limited education and knowledge.
- The exclusion from judicial consideration of the embezzlement in the first half of 1995 and in 1996 because of an "incomplete investigation" by the police and the government inspectorate.
- The court's refusal to take into account the aggravating circumstances of the crime (i.e. local officials' corruption at the expense of war dead and invalid families) and its narrow use of legal guidelines for embezzled amounts in deciding on the sentence for the commune's former head tax official.
- Not prosecuting district tax officials.
- Not suspending Son Duong defendants at the trial from their Communist Party cells, as required by laws and regulations.
- Sentencing only the head tax official, though the corruption involved other commune and district officials.
- Violating the 1993 governmental stipulation of a 50 percent penalty on the embezzled amount by requiring only that the convicted official return the embezzled funds.

The leaders of the anti-corruption movement in Son Duong also garnered signatures for a request to the National Assembly, the president, and the prime minister of Vietnam for further investigation. The petitioners denounced various local administrations for illegally selling agricultural land, underdeclaring the cultivated surface in the commune in order to lower the commune's agricultural tax bill, embezzling irrigation fee payments, and not showing financial transparency.[11] The petitioners emphasized that, because distinct authorities had oppressed their local denouncers of corruption, they could not be trusted to investigate the charges in the petition; that a commune investigation committee should be established on the basis of an October 1997 resolution by members of the Commune People's Council; and that the appeal trial should be held in Son Duong for the education of villagers. This letter from Son Duong commune to the central government constituted only a small part of the massive local grievances received by the Vietnamese Cabinet. The central government received 105,110 letters in 1998 and 50,523 in the first half of 1999 (*Cong An Thanh Pho Ho Chi Minh*, 15 July 1999: 39).

As the local convicted official remained free in the commune into the summer of 1998, despite being sentenced to prison in November 1997, Son Duong villagers became convinced that provincial, district, and commune officials had tried to protect many accomplices at the commune and higher levels by treating the indicted man leniently in exchange for his agreement not to expose other corrupt officials in the case. Although the provincial police sent two investigators each day from the provincial capital to the commune for a thorough investigation, it did not mollify villagers, as the investigation had not yielded any concrete results by the summer of 1998.

The villagers then refused to pay anything to the commune administration, with the exception of agricultural taxes, which they had to pay by law. This caused the commune's irrigation fee arrears to balloon to about $15,000, which in turn reportedly led to the reduction of irrigation water to the commune during the summer of 1998 planting season. By the time of my visit in July 1998, the local population's public confrontation with the state and party apparatuses at the commune level and beyond showed no sign of abatement.

The 1997 Thai Binh provincial unrest

The public drama in Son Duong was far from an isolated crisis in rural northern Vietnam in the late 1990s. One year earlier, Thai Binh province in the lower Red River Delta witnessed widespread unrest culminating in violence and destruction in quite a few localities:

- In late June 1997, in An Ninh commune (Quynh Phu district) of Thai Binh, villagers smashed flowerpots, chinaware, and furniture in the commune's administrative building, which had recently been constructed and furnished at the cost of 800 million dong (almost $70,000). A bust of Ho Chi Minh was smashed in the pandemonium. Villagers also caused damage in the houses of eight village officials (including the party secretary, the commune president, and the land registration official).
- In Quynh Hoa commune in the same district, in the same period, the local population put 20 outside policemen under house arrest for five days.
- On 11 May 1997, in the district of Quynh Phu at large, where the communes of An Ninh and Quynh Hoa are located, about 2,000 peasants from 36 of the 38 communes in the district rode their bicycles to the district and provincial capitals. At the district capital, it was estimated that the gathering at one point increased to 10,000 people. When the district leadership activated the police, who used gas grenades, dogs, and three fire trucks to spray water on the demonstrators, violence broke out, and nine or ten policemen were wounded.

Vietnamese President Tran Duc Luong said in the winter of 1998 that, in many localities, party and local government apparatuses were paralyzed in June 1997 at the peak of the unrest, leading to a situation of "no government." One year later the provincial party secretary said that, of the 285 administrative units in the province, tension remained high in 30 communes and the situation remained quite complicated in 207 others (*Thoi Bao*, 25 June 1998: 75).

The unrest and violence in Thai Binh caught the national political leadership by surprise. Thai Binh province had been considered a cradle of the Vietnamese Communist Party. It was here in 1929 that the first cell of the Indochinese Communist Party (ICP) was formed, and where in 1930 the ICP-led uprising against the French colonial regime in the Red River Delta gained the greatest momentum.[12] During the French and American wars, Thai Binh sent a total of 400,000 soldiers to the front, where nearly 48,000 died and more than 30,000 returned as invalids. In Thai Binh province, Quynh Phu district was considered a model district, and in this district, the commune of An Ninh had been considered exemplary for decades by the provincial leadership.

In his public postmortem analysis of the Thai Binh unrest at the Thai Binh Provincial Party Congress, President Tran Duc Luong (1998) attributed the unrest to three sets of factors:

- Onerous local taxes, imposed without consultation on poor local populations in order to finance 577 billion dong ($48 million) of infrastructure projects (roads, schools, clinics, and electric power grids) in a 44-month period from January 1994 to July 1997.[13] Local infrastructure taxes amounted to 161 billion dong in this period, while district and provincial ones totaled 15 billion.
- Corruption and inefficiency in the use of local resources. In Thai Binh province, in 62 of the 152 investigated communes where investigation had been completed by early 1998, it was reported that the majority of local grievances were valid to various extents. More specifically, in a number of localities, the costs of construction and infrastructure projects had been inflated by 20–25 percent by corrupt officials and project bidders in alliance with one another. In some others, the 5 percent of the land reserved at the commune level for unanticipated allocation needs and more commonly rented for additional local government revenues had been sold or leased without the public's endorsement.
- Authorities' unresponsiveness to grievances and lack of attention to the discontent of the population (including the discontent of "revolutionary elders, veterans, retired cadres, and party members"). Local cadres had reportedly even challenged people to file grievances, while authorities did not act quickly in response to local grievances, and even protected commune officials and hid the truth from higher authorities.

President Tran Duc Luong's analysis suggests similarities between Thai Binh and Son Duong, in terms of local officials' corruption and authorities' unresponsiveness to local grievances. In response to the unrest in Thai Binh province and the potential for unrest in many other localities, the Vietnamese state formulated a policy of grassroots democracy in 1998. It requires local governments to obtain considerably greater input from local populations into local finances, to show greater financial transparency, and to strengthen the latter's direct or indirect inspection roles in financial affairs (Vietnam 1999).

Among the issues requiring direct discussion with local populations and their direct decisions through popular votes are infrastructure projects and social contributions, local custom regulations, and the establishment of inspection committees for those infrastructure projects (ibid.: 18–19). Land use planning, hamlet boundary demarcation, and compensation for appropriated land are among the issues that require consultations with local populations before commune people's committees or councils can make their decisions.

Local populations can now also play more prominent inspection roles regarding the activities of commune administrations, commune finances, land use, local grievances, corruption, and social assistance to war dead and invalids. This can be achieved through the commune people's councils, Fatherland Front, or state-sponsored mass organizations (the women's, peasant, youth, and veterans associations), and by attending people's council meetings or participating in local inspection committees (ibid.: 22–3).

The dynamics of agrarian unrest in northern Vietnam

The transformation of state–society relations

In the 1990s, the unrest in Thai Binh and the crisis in Son Duong and possibly many other localities were unparalleled for the open confrontation and challenge by local populations to party and state apparatuses. They have led to a major national policy change that has strengthened the voices of local populations in commune affairs and sanctioned lasting changes in state–society relations at the local level.

On one level, these developments lend further support to Kerkvliet's perspective (1995) that the Vietnamese state is "mass-regarding" and can be responsive to pressures from society. Kerkvliet argues that the pressures can be channeled through state-sanctioned participation in state-organized mass organizations, but that they are mostly in the domain of everyday politics, which involves "trying to live within or modify the prevailing contours as well as engaging in subtle, nonconfrontational everyday resistance to slip under or to undermine the system" (ibid.: 400).

On another level, in the rural Vietnamese landscape, the social pressures to which state policies have responded can take more confrontational forms and involve more than subtle everyday resistance. From a historical perspective, the closest equivalents to the crises in Thai Binh and Son Duong were the open resistance of many Mekong Delta cultivators to collectivization in the late 1970s and the peaceful demonstrations of a number of former landowners in many *Nam bo* (southern Vietnamese) district and provincial towns in the late 1980s regarding their land from the pre-collectivization period (Luong 1994). The latter chain of events, however, was less openly confrontational toward the state, while to my knowledge the former was less than a concerted collective action. If the crises in

Thai Binh and other localities such as Son Duong were unparalleled under a Marxist state, did they mark a fundamental change in state–society relations in the socialist era?[14] What led to those crises and to a possibly fundamental transformation of state–society relations in socialist Vietnam? To what extent has the official analysis captured the dynamics of northern rural crises?

The dynamics of agrarian unrest in northern Vietnam

I suggest that the three factors discussed in President Tran Duc Luong's official analysis (onerous local taxes, corruption, and unresponsive authorities) constitute important but not sufficient conditions for the outbreak of agrarian unrest in Vietnam in the 1990s. From a cross-regional and comparative perspective, local corruption was neither limited to the Red River Delta of Vietnam nor necessarily more serious there than in other parts of the country; there is no clear evidence that local authorities in Thai Binh were less responsive to grievances than authorities were elsewhere; and the annual local taxes of 20 kilograms of paddy per person in both Thai Binh and Son Duong were not particularly onerous, as the subsistence margin of Red River Delta peasants as a whole had significantly improved in the 1990s.

In the 1990s, Son Duong villagers generally experienced a significant improvement in their standards of living, as did most rural residents of the Red River Delta and other parts of the Vietnamese lowlands. On the basis of village statistics and my July 1998 interviews with a good number of Son Duong villagers about their various economic activities that summer, I estimate that the net per capita income in Son Duong increased from 450 kilograms of paddy in 1991 to 530 kilograms in 1998. This increase took place despite the decline in per capita net yield from agriculture from 400 kilograms of paddy to 320 kilograms in that period due to a 15 percent population growth.[15] The increase in the standard of living for the average Son Duong villager resulted partly from the diversification of income sources and partly from a significant rise in the official incomes of active and retired state employees. Most significant among the new income sources was the seasonal and temporary migration of up to a quarter of the local labor force for jobs elsewhere in the country.

Retired state employees also enjoyed a significant rise in income: my village host's pension for his 30 years of service in the armed forces increased from 5 kilograms of rice in 1987 to 150 kilograms in 1998. Active state employees, including those working at the Lam Thao chemical fertilizer factory nearby, earned about $80 a month, thanks to the high demand for fertilizers in connection with the country's agricultural export boom.[16] From a long-term perspective, the average per capita annual income of 530 kilograms of rice in 1998 had risen significantly from 220 kilograms in 1980.

Socioeconomic inequality within the commune seems to have been limited, at least in comparison to the Mekong Delta, since agricultural land was distributed in a relatively egalitarian way.[17] Of the 1,034 households in Son Duong in the summer of 1998, approximately 450 owned televisions, while few had had them seven years earlier. In the context of a notable rise in per capita incomes and living standards from 1980 to 1998, the 1998 commune taxes in Son Duong, averaging 20 kilograms of paddy per person or 3.8 percent of the average net income, cannot be considered too onerous.[18]

While comparable data are not available for Thai Binh province, the World Bank's living standard surveys in 1993 and 1998 indicate that in this five-year period living standards increased most dramatically in the Red River Delta. The percentage of the delta's population living in poverty declined by 34 percent (from 63 percent in 1993 to 29 percent in 1998), in comparison to a drop of 19 percent in the country as a whole (Vietnam and World Bank 1999: 4, 15).

It was also here that the poverty gap index, which measures the depth of poverty among poor households, was reduced by the largest margin (from 18.8 percent in 1993 to 5.7 percent in 1998) (ibid.: 16). Of the seven socioeconomic Vietnamese regions, the Red River Delta was also the only one where rural household expenditures grew by a higher percentage than those of urban ones between 1993 and 1998 (ibid.: 75). Even if commune taxes consumed on average a higher percentage of rural household expenditures in the delta than elsewhere (see note 17), there is no evidence that they were so onerous that they threatened the subsistence of local peasants (cf. Scott 1976). In fact, from an historical perspective, these peasants' livelihoods were considerably more precarious in 1978 than they were in 1998. In comparative terms, the 1998 poverty rate and poverty depth index were lower in the Red River Delta than in five of the six remaining regions.[19] Yet unrest there was unparalleled by anywhere else in the country.

How can we understand the major crisis in state–society relations in Son Duong commune and Thai Binh province and its absence in the Mekong Delta, which had a greater poverty depth and sharper stratification, given the knowledge that local taxation in the Red River Delta was not too onerous and that commune governments there were neither necessarily more corrupt nor necessarily less responsive to local populations?

I suggest that the crisis in state–society relations in rural northern Vietnam cannot be fully explained without closely examining the local sociocultural framework, in terms of both social fabric and ideological formation. Having been partly restructured by the dialogic relation among the voices of the Marxist state and the pre-revolutionary era of Vietnam, the local sociocultural framework in the northern lowlands was characterized by a strong discursive emphasis on relative equality and by the extensive proliferation of kinship, communal, and religious local associations reminiscent of colonial social structure.

Ideologies, alternate civilities, and the state

Since 1975, when Vietnam was reunified under a Marxist state, the strongest public pressures on the Vietnamese state have been exerted neither by urban-based and bourgeois-dominated voluntary organizations constitutive of a civil society nor by the disenfranchised and landless class who make up at least a quarter of the southern rural population, but by local populations in the northern part of the country. The latter have been bound by both an ideology of relative equality and proliferating associations based mainly on kinship, communal, and religious ties, constitutive of alternative civilities (Weller 1999). In the Vietnamese context, these historically shaped and regionally varied alternate civilities have provided a powerful basis for a dialogic relation with the state.

In terms of ideological formation, I suggest that the Marxist state's collectivistic and egalitarian ideology from 1954 to 1989 has strongly influenced local discourses and penetrated local consciousness throughout northern Vietnam. At the national level, for example, in the November 1998 debates in the Vietnamese National Assembly on land law amendments, the northern and central representatives voted against the liberalization of the land market in the lowlands – more specifically, against removal of the three-hectare-per-household restriction and lengthening usufruct rights to more than 20 years. In contrast, southern representatives and the southern press strongly favored land-market liberalization that would increase the inequality in landholdings for the sake of productive efficiency (*Sai Gon Giai Phong*, 14 November 1998: 1).[20]

In the local arena, the strong discursive emphasis on relative equality moved the land distribution policy in Son Duong over the years in this direction, despite the state's emphasis on rewarding efficient agricultural producers that began in 1988. For example, in 1988, as the state's directive 10 encouraged communes to allow more efficient producers to bid for more land, Son Duong's leadership planned to reserve the more fertile fields in the commune (which constituted 15 percent of the commune land) for bidding by more efficient producers. By 1994, under local social pressures, the 5 percent of land available for bidding was mainly ponds, not fertile fields.

However, in the local population, the egalitarian ideology did not seem to penetrate the consciousness of all Son Duong villagers to the same degree. It was the older members, who endured the austere and more egalitarian periods of the 1960s and the height of the US war, who were the leading voices for lesser inequality and in the anti-corruption movement in Son Duong. The veterans were especially emboldened, due to their wartime sacrifices at the front, to take leading roles in mobilizing Son Duong villagers in 1997–8. One of the two leading figures in the exposure of local corruption was the president of the Son Duong veterans association at the time of my second visit. The other was the sister of a veteran who suffered mentally from his war experiences.

I suggest that local ideological formation in the Mekong Delta of South Vietnam was not dominated by egalitarianism. This results not only from the official ideological differences between North and South Vietnam during the Cold War and the US war period, but also from historically rooted regional differences. Up to the early part of the twentieth century, Vietnamese living in the southern third of the country were living in a relatively new and fertile land with more spatial and socioeconomic mobility opportunities, and were less concerned about their own survival and fellow villagers' greater wealth. This historical condition has in turn rendered wealth accumulation less an issue for public debate in southern Vietnam both in the past and in the present era.

I further suggest that tight social networks within communal boundaries have facilitated the mobilization of local populations for collective action in Son Duong and other northern localities. Like virtually all other northern communes, Son Duong has witnessed a dramatic proliferation of associations, as state-domain boundaries have contracted through reductions in the state's control of land and other local assets as well as its subsidization of health and educational services. The local associations belong to two main categories with distinctive relations to local and national governments: mass organizations of the Marxist party-state and spontaneous local organizations.

Mass organizations of the Marxist party-state

As mentioned earlier, the peasant, veterans', women's, and youth associations are mass organizations of the Marxist party-state that are linked to the national Peasant and Veterans Associations and the Women's and Youth Unions. The heads of these associations in Son Duong receive monthly stipends from the local government. The most active are the women's association (in family planning mobilization campaigns) and the veterans' association (in organizing funeral ceremonies for members).

The *elderly association* in Son Duong, which has almost 600 members over the age of 49, is officially recognized by the local government and the Fatherland Front, but elderly associations in various localities are strictly local and have no national representation on the VCP's Central Committee. Son Duong's elderly association organizes regular gymnastic exercises and monthly meetings for poetry recitals; holds annual longevity celebrations for members who reach the lunar ages of 70, 80, and 90; and coordinates visits to seriously sick members and to the families of deceased ones. The association also owns a four-wheeled coffin carrier that it lends free of charge to the families of deceased members.

Spontaneous local associations

The membership of the religious-based *Buddhist elderly women's association (hoi chu ba)* overlaps significantly with the elderly association of Son Duong village. With approximately 370 members above the age of 49, in 1998 the Buddhist elderly women's association was one of the largest spontaneous associations in Son Duong. Age and date of membership determine seniority, which in turn determines the seating proximity to Buddha's altar (see also Luong 1993: 272, 284). The association holds well-attended bimonthly prayer sessions in the local pagoda on the first and fifteenth day of each lunar month, and it also organizes special ceremonies on Buddha's birthday, on Lost Soul Day (the fifteenth of the seventh lunar month), and on the anniversary of the last presiding nun's death in the 1970s. The association also offers free prayer services for any deceased villager. It is the only association not linked with the Marxist party-state that has existed since the French colonial period, through the ebb and flow of nongovernmental associational activities under the Marxist regime.

Kinship-based patrilineages have been re-created in the past decade, though their structure and function are unchanged from the pre-1945 period. The head of a patrilineage remains the most senior male of the most senior branch, even if he is much younger and of a junior generation in relation to the senior males in other branches of the patrilineage. The main functions of patrilineages remain organizing of the rites of solidarity (ancestor worship ceremonies and ancestral tomb maintenance); transmitting values; transmitting knowledge about kinship hierarchy and about members' wider socioeconomic roles, for kinship network mobilization; and facilitating mutual assistance among members. Since patrilineages no longer have corporate landholdings, annual celebrations require financial levies on members. The largest lineage in Son Duong, the Nguyen Dinh patrilineage, has reconstructed its ancestral hall. Although Son Duong's second largest lineage (over 1,000 members, who constitute approximately a quarter of the village population) did not yet have an ancestral hall at the time of my revisit to the village in 1998, it had its own written charter and scholarship funds. The representatives of all the households in this patrilineage (numbering 360 persons on average) attended its annual ancestral worship ceremony and banquet, while virtually all the members (about 90) of the small Kieu lineage attended their ancestral worship banquet.

Communal-based associations. While not directly defined in communal terms, all the members of any same-class alumni association (*hoi dong hoc*) come from Son Duong village, because all of them graduated in the same year from the village junior high school. Similarly, in Son Duong, the memberships of the policy-favored-household association (*hoi gia dinh chinh sach*), the numerous rotating-credit associations (*ho*), men's same-age associations (*hoi dong nien*), the retired teacher association (*hoi giao vien huu*), and the bonsai association do not extend beyond village boundaries.

In 1991, only the retired teacher association and three same-age associations had been formed, and these were only open to men above the age of 49; however, the number of communal-based associations had significantly increased by the time I revisited Son Duong in 1998. The members of most communal-based associations provide financial assistance to one another for major life-cycle rituals (e.g. weddings, funerals, longevity ceremonies) or members' major expenditures (e.g. major illness, constructing a house for a married son and his family). Rotating-credit associations, for example, specify the amount of paddy contribution that each member must make on the particular occasion. Other associations with relatively well-off members, such as the same-age and the bonsai associations, also require a membership fee of 50–100 kilograms of paddy to establish association funds that can be lent to members at low interest. The members of same-age or -class alumni associations also normally meet at least once a year for a feast.

The majority of spontaneous local organizations have been re-created on the basis of a pre-1945 social structure. The Buddhist elderly women's association has retained its structure and has functioned since the pre-revolutionary era. As discussed earlier, patrilineages have also remained unchanged in their structure and functions, despite the lack of corporate properties in the post-colonial period.

Similarly, among the communal-based associations, rotating-credit associations (*ho*) function in the same way that the *ho* of the French colonial period did: A member wishing to receive funds early offers a discount on the amount to be contributed by other members; alternatively, members contribute money, paddy, or labor on the occasion of major life-cycle ceremonies in fellow members' families (Luong 1992: 58–60).

Same-class alumni associations (*hoi dong hoc*) are also conceptually linked to the alumni associations (*hoi dong mon*) of the pre-revolutionary era, although the latter, whose membership includes all of the former students of a particular teacher over the years, focused more of its activities on honoring a teacher, while the modern *hoi dong hoc* is oriented more toward maintaining ties among students graduating in the same year from a particular school. Similarly, the retired teacher association bears some resemblance to the literati association (*hoi tu van*) of the pre-revolutionary era, although the latter included all educated men, retired or not, not simply retired teachers. In terms of function, the *hoi tu van* was an elite association whose main activity was worshipping Confucius, while the retired teacher association of the past decade is simply an occupation-based mutual aid society.

Among the new associational forms are the same-age associations among men (*hoi dong nien*), the same-military-service associations (*hoi dong ngu*), and the policy-favored-household associations (*hoi gia dinh chinh sach*). All but two of the spontaneous local associations are directly or indirectly communally based. The exceptions are the same-military-service associations, whose memberships are based on military service in the same divisions or branches of the armed forces and normally come from a cluster of neighboring villages or communes, and the same-class alumni associations of the senior high school in the district, whose members are natives of neighboring villages in the same district. All the spontaneous local associations in Son Duong are also voluntary, with organizers and leaders fully accountable to association members. The exception is patrilineages, which have ascribed memberships and a strong male orientation, to the disadvantage of women.

As virtually all Son Duong villagers relate to one another either consanguineally or affinely, due to the high rate of village endogamy over centuries, the spontaneous local associations in Son Duong have increased the multiplexity of social ties, intensified social networks, reinforced trust, and reduced transaction costs among villagers. As social networks have intensified, life-cycle rituals have also become more elaborate through the involvement of people in one's social network. In 1991, the banquets for brides and grooms in Son Duong may have included 120 and 180 guests respectively; by 1998, the average size of a wedding banquet had reportedly increased to at least 240 guests. If the groom or one of the parents worked at a nearby state factory, the number of guests might reach 600, because co-workers had to be invited. Death anniversary meals in Son Duong also increased in size from 20–30 guests in 1991 to 60–150 guests by 1998. This type of mutual assistance at life-cycle ceremonies both reflects the strength of relations and reinforces them further in the context of the state's contracting role.

The reproduction and reinforcement of social ties, partly through these events and partly through the formal structures of many associations that are reminiscent of those that were active in the pre-revolutionary era, have considerably tightened communal boundaries and social networks in Son Duong. When the policy-favored households and the veterans associations took a concerted action against corrupt commune cadres, they easily mobilized fellow villagers as relatives and as fellow members of many other voluntary associations. Similarly, in the anti-corruption movement in Thai Binh province, leaders reportedly exerted pressure on some reluctant fellow villagers by raising the question of who would help them at wedding and funeral time if they did not participate in the movement. I suggest that the proliferation of these local voluntary associations in highly endogamous villages throughout the Red River Delta in the past decade and a half has increased the potential for the mobilization of local populations for collective action in rural northern Vietnam.

In contrast, the much looser social networks in Vietnamese cities and more open southern villages are less conducive to concerted collective action. In southern villages, pagoda, communal-house, and church-centered religious organizations are among the most vibrant local associations. In a southern village, they range from the strictly local communal-deity-worship association (*ban hoi huong*) to Buddhist, Christian, and numerous Cao Daist organizations strongly tied to national religious hierarchies.[21] However, without corporate property, the communal-deity-worship association raises funds for its activities through levies on members, which means that many poor villagers cannot participate. Buddhist, Christian, and sectoral Cao Dai groups, while facilitating mutual assistance within each group (especially at funerals), do not link virtually all village households in the same way that Buddhist elderly women's associations in most northern villages do. Furthermore, the strong linkages of Buddhist, Christian, and Cao Dai religious groups in southern villages to national religious hierarchies that are closely monitored by party-state apparatuses for any sign of organized dissent render them more vulnerable to state crackdowns (see Luong 1994: 98–9).

Beyond religious-based associations in villages in the southern third of Vietnam, patrilineages tend to be quite weak, if they exist at all. Performing arts groups and sports teams tend to be small and are neither linked to crucial life-cycle events nor vital to households' mobility strategies (cf. Diep Dinh Hoa 1995: 264–9). Among nongovernmental associations in southern villages, only the numerous rotating-credit associations play a potentially important role in enhancing their members' ability to meet their various needs.[22]

Furthermore, given the low rates of community endogamy and generally loose kinship networks in southern rural communities, local nongovernmental associations neither render relations as multiplex nor increase trust to the same degree that they do in the north.[23] A similar situation exists in urban contexts, though there is a wider range of urban associational forms that cover particularistic same-village associations (*hoi dong huong*) in northern cities at one end, and the internationally linked Red Cross Association and professional and business associations at the other. I suggest that the intricate and crosscutting network of local associations in the context of a tight kinship network in northern villages, in contrast to those in cities and in the southern countryside, facilitates local mobilization for concerted action that can at times take the form of open confrontation with local administrative apparatuses.

Conclusion

From a theoretical perspective, the numerous local associations in the village of Son Duong and in other northern Vietnamese villages do not constitute a civil society as normally conceptualized in the Western social science literature, multivocal as this term "civil society" is, due to its embedding in different Western theoretical and ideological perspectives (Brook and Frolic 1997; Frolic 1997; Chamberlain 1993; Weller 1999: 14–16). Since these perspectives develop in relation to Western historical experiences, as pointed out by Madsen, for most of these theorists, "civil society consisted in the utilitarian, contractual relationships characteristic of a bourgeois society created by a modern market economy" (Madsen 1993: 188). In the broader meaning of the term, "civil society" refers to any institutionalized association relatively independent of the state and of such "traditional" ties as kinship and communal relations (ibid.: 189).

Because of the radically different historical trajectories of Vietnam and the West, civil society as conceived on the basis of Western historical experiences has not really emerged in rural northern Vietnam, since most communities here have not witnessed the emergence of a bourgeois class.[24] However, voluntary associations have proliferated, as the domain under state control has contracted in the past decade and a half. In Son Duong, only two of these new associations, the veterans and the elderly associations, receive some state support (cf. Frolic 1997); the rest are not even recognized by the state. While none of those new associations are political or would be tolerated as political in their orientation, the ties formed through them can be mobilized for collective action and for a concerted voice for better local governance (cf. Brook 1997: 41–2).

In the northern Vietnamese rural landscape, kinship-, religious-, and communal-based local associations can directly or indirectly serve as effective bases for the dialogic relations of local populations to party-state apparatuses. The collective actions in Son Duong village and in numerous localities in the northern province of Thai Binh and beyond have led to a major national policy change (the Grassroots Democracy Decree) that has strengthened the voices of local populations in community affairs, and sanctioned lasting changes in local state–society relations. Spontaneous local associations based on kinship, religious, and communal ties and constitutive of alternative civilities in rural northern Vietnam can serve as a strong foundation for mobilizing for collective action in the face of growing local socioeconomic inequality. They are at least as effective in strengthening the voices of local populations as bourgeois-dominated voluntary associations are in communities with a greater market penetration. These mostly spontaneous local associations in rural northern Vietnam have little to do with international funding or the state's regulatory framework for associations.

The focus on state-sanctioned, urban-based, and bourgeois-dominated voluntary associations in the literature on Vietnam and many other non-Western societies reflects analytical assumptions that are deeply grounded in Western historical experiences and in the dominant Western social theoretical framework on the state and civil society. I suggest that without considering alternate civilities and the differences between the historically shaped sociocultural frameworks of the Red River and the Mekong Deltas, we cannot fully explain the magnitude of the serious crisis in state–society relations in the northern Vietnamese rural landscape.

Notes

1 Son Duong is located about 90 kilometers north of Hanoi, in the heartland of the first Vietnamese kingdom. I first conducted field research there in 1987 and revisited the village in 1988 and 1991 (Luong 1992). Although Son Duong is technically in the northern midland province of Phu Tho, it is much closer to the Red River Delta of northern Vietnam and more similar to Red River Delta communes than to those in the northern highlands.

2 All amounts are in US dollars, unless otherwise indicated.

3 In the late 1970s, the command economy encountered a major crisis when cultivators and workers engaged in everyday resistance by foot dragging, moonlighting, paying greater attention to household economic activities, and refusing to sell agricultural products to the state at low state-procurement prices. Resistance was considerably stronger in the southern third of Vietnam, which had been well incorporated into the world capitalist system since the days of French colonialism (see Luong 1994, 2003a). In response to this crisis, the Vietnamese state sanctioned the household contract system in agriculture, which allowed agricultural households to keep surpluses above specified production targets on contracted land. Similarly, in the industrial sector, in 1981 the state allowed state enterprises to procure raw materials on the open market; to use surplus labor, materials, and equipment to produce beyond the state's specified targets; and to sell their products directly to other parties at mutually agreed prices.

4 While local peasant associations and trade unions pre-dated the VCP's establishment, the VCP established other associations such as the Youth and the Women's Associations and encouraged the establishment of peasant associations and trade unions in many localities in order to mobilize local populations for anti-colonial struggles. More specifically, from 1941 to 1954, the VCP, which played the leading role in the anti-French Vietminh front, created various "National Salvation" associations among youth, students, the elderly, and women (respectively named *doan thanh nien cuu quoc, hoi hoc sinh cuu quoc, hoi phu lao cuu quoc, hoi phu nu cuu quoc*), to mobilize various sectors of the Vietnamese population for its independence movement (Phan Xuan Son 2002: 86–92).

5 The community endogamy rates in the two northern villages where statistical data were collected in the 1990s are in the 50–70 percent range (Luong and Diep Dinh Hoa 2000: 57–9; Krowolski 2002).

6 The tight sociopolitical space for voluntary associations outside the framework of the Fatherland Front in the North stands in contrast to the numerous international nongovernmental organizations and domestic voluntary associations which were under the control of the Saigon government in the South, especially in the social, health, and religious domains and for mutual assistance, as in the case of Vietnamese patrilineages or same-origin associations (*hoi dong huong*). While for political purposes, the US-allied state in the South also established some organizations (e.g. the Solidary Women's Union under Madame Ngo Dinh Nhu), and supported many others (e.g. the

Unified Vietnamese Buddhist Sangha), a plurality of religious associations existed in South Vietnamese Buddhism and within the Cao Dai religion.

7   In the study by Wischermann *et al.* (2000), "international funding" means grants and donations from international organizations or governments.

8   The survey sample included 257 organizations chosen from over 700 provincially registered ones, analytically divided into four categories (state-established mass organizations; professional associations; business associations; and charity, social service, and research organizations). Only 10 percent of all the sampled associations in Hanoi considered international funding their most important source of finance, while 38 percent, 28 percent, and 8 percent respectively relied most heavily on state funding, the sale of services, and domestic donations. In Ho Chi Minh City, the corresponding figures were 14 percent (greatest reliance on international funding), 19 percent (state funding), 26 percent (sale of services), and 15 percent (domestic donations) (Wischermann *et al.* 2000: 50).

9   The Vietnamese Red Cross raised 78 percent of its voluntary donation funds from domestic sources in the 1990–8 period. If we include funding from state as well as nonstate sources, in my calculation, domestic donations amounted to 72 percent of all Red Cross funds (Thang van Phuc *et al.* 2002: 84).

10   Many local nonregistered associations receive donations from overseas Vietnamese. These contributions, however, are relatively few in number, although possibly larger in size than the majority of domestic donations. Data are not available on the relative importance of the overseas Vietnamese funding source.

11   Agricultural land was sold to finance the electrification of the commune, as the local population had to pay for the construction of an electric grid from a provincial road about 2 kilometers from Son Duong commune.

12   On a national level, the ICP-led agrarian unrest gained the greatest momentum in the provinces of Nghe An and Ha Tinh in northern central Vietnam.

13   Of those 577 billion dong, the central government contributed less than 7 percent, approximately 25 percent was raised directly through commune taxes on local populations, 42 percent was borrowed from various local sources, and 26 percent came from the sale of local land (Tran Duc Luong 1998).

14   The term "socialist era" is used here as an abbreviation to refer to what in the official Vietnamese literature has been called "the transitional period towards socialism" (*thoi ky qua do len chu nghia xa hoi*).

15   In 1998 the net annual agricultural incomes in Son Duong averaged 550,000 dong per person ($42).

16   Vietnamese rice exports increased from 1.6 million tons in 1990 to 3.6 million tons in 2001, while coffee exports rose dramatically from 76,000 tons to 910,000 tons in the same period (Luong 2003a: 14).

17   In the 1994 land allocation in Son Duong, 95 percent of the land of economic value was distributed to commune residents other than long-term state employees as follows: 540 square meters for each person in the active labor force (women aged 16–55, men aged 16–60); 240 square meters for each child below 16, and up to two children for each couple; and 72 square meters for each elderly person. The 194 households (18 percent of commune households) that still owed taxes to the commune at the time of land distribution received only 288 square meters for each active laborer – the rest was temporarily withheld until the tax arrears were settled. Most had not been settled by the summer of 1998, while a few others had been unable to pay taxes from 1994 onwards. The commune rented out the temporarily withheld land to supplement its revenues. The 5 percent of reserve land, which included many fishponds, was open for bidding by villagers.

18   The World Bank's living standard survey in 1998 indicates that commune taxes (including "voluntary contributions") averaged 4.8 percent of the expenditures of

Vietnamese rural households. They reached 6.6 percent of rural household expenditures in the Red River Delta, and dropped to 2.6 percent of those in the southeast region around Ho Chi Minh City (Vietnam and World Bank 1999: 97).

19 The poverty rate and poverty depth index in the Red River Delta were higher only than those in the southeast (provinces in the Ho Chi Minh City region).

20 As a legislative compromise, landholdings exceeding the holding limit before the November 1998 amendment are recognized to be legal, while new agricultural land exceeding the holding limit from 1998 onwards has to be rented from the state (*Sai Gon Giai Phong*, 17 November 1998).

21 The Cao Dai religious movement in southern Vietnam sprang up in the 1920s, under French colonialism, as a syncretic religious movement. Its pantheon includes Buddha, Confucius, Jesus, and even the French writer Victor Hugo. Over the decades, this movement has splintered into at least 12 sects (Luong and Diep Dinh Hoa 2000: 68–9; Werner 1981: 78). In the village of Khanh Hau in the Mekong Delta alone, Cao Daists belonged to four different sects at the time of my field research in 1992 (Luong 1994: 81, 98–9; Luong and Diep Dinh Hoa 2000: 68; cf. Hickey 1964: 66, 292–4).

22 In his ethnographies of two villages in the southern Dong Nai province (north of Ho Chi Minh City), the Vietnamese ethnologist Diep Dinh Hoa has also reported on funeral-assistance associations (Diep Dinh Hoa 1995: 266–8; Diep Dinh Hoa and Phan Dinh Dung 1998: 260–4). However, I have neither found them in the village of Khanh Hau in the Mekong Delta, nor seen any reference to them in the literature on the Mekong Delta south of Ho Chi Minh City.

23 For comparative purposes, the rate of commune endogamy in Khanh Hau, the only southern rural community where data have been systematically collected, is around 30 percent (Luong and Diep Dinh Hoa 2000: 57–9).

24 The main exceptions in the northern rural landscape are such communes as Ninh Hiep and Bat Trang, which have specialized in commerce and manufacturing for centuries and whose members have accumulated considerable wealth since Vietnam's shift to a market economy in the late 1980s (To Duy Hop 1997; Luong 1998).

References

Brook, Timothy. "Auto-organization in Chinese Society." In *Civil Society in China*, edited by T. Brook and B. Michael Frolic. Armonk, NY: M.E. Sharpe, 1997, pp. 19–45.

——, and B. Michael Frolic. "The Ambiguous Challenge of Civil Society." In *Civil Society in China*, edited T. Brook and B. Michael Frolic. Armonk, NY: M.E. Sharpe, 1997, pp. 3–16.

Chamberlain, Heath. "On the Search for Civil Society in China." *Modern China*, XIX (1993): 199–215.

Diep Dinh Hoa. *Lang Ben Go Xua va Nay* [The Village of Ben Go in the Past and Present]. Bien Hoa: Nha xuat ban Dong Nai, 1995.

——, and Phan Dinh Dung. *Lang Ben Ca Xua va Nay* [The Village of Ben Ca in the Past and the Present]. Bien Hoa: Nha xuat ban Dong Nai, 1998.

Frolic, B. Michael. "State-Led Civil Society." In *Civil Society in China*, edited by T. Brook and B. Michael Frolic. Armonk, NY: M.E. Sharpe, 1997, pp. 46–67.

Gray, Michael L. "Creating Civil Society? The Emergence of NGOs in Vietnam." *Development and Change*, XXX (1999): 693–713.

Hickey, Gerald. *Village in Vietnam*. New Haven, CT: Yale University Press, 1964.

Kerkvliet, Benedict. "Village–State Relations in Vietnam: The Effect of Everyday Politics on Decollectivization." *Journal of Asian Studies*, LIV (1995): 396–418.

——. "Authorities and the People: An Analysis of State–Society Relations in Vietnam." In

Postwar Vietnam: Dynamics of a Transforming Society, edited Hy V. Luong. Boulder, CO: Rowman & Littlefield, 2003, pp. 27–53.

Krowolski, Nellie. "Village Households in the Red River Delta: The Case of Ta Thanh Oai, On the Outskirts of the Capital City, Ha Noi." In *Gender, Household, State: Doi Moi in Viet Nam*, edited by Jayne Werner and Daniele Belanger. Ithaca, NY: Cornell University Southeast Asia Program, 2002, pp. 73–88.

Luong, Hy V. *Revolution in the Village: Tradition and Transformation in North Vietnam, 1925–88.* Honolulu: University of Hawaii Press, 1992.

———. "Economic Reform and the Intensification of Rituals in Two North Vietnamese Villages, 1980–1990." In *The Challenge of Reform in Indochina*, edited by Borje Llunggren. Cambridge, MA: Harvard Institute for International Development, 1993, pp. 259–92.

———. "The Marxist State and the Dialogic Re-Structuration of Culture in Northern Vietnam." In *Indochina: Social and Cultural Change*, by D. Elliott, H.V. Luong, B. Kiernan, and T. Mahoney. Keck Center for International and Strategic Studies, Claremont, CA: Claremont McKenna College, 1994, monograph No.7, pp. 79–117.

———. "Engendered Entrepreneurship: Ideologies and Political-Economic Transformation in a Northern Vietnamese Center of Ceramics Production." In *Market Cultures: Society and Morality in the New Asian Capitalism*, edited by R. Hefner. Boulder, CO: Westview, 1998, pp. 290–314.

———. "Post-war Vietnamese Society: An Overview of Transformational Dynamics." In *Postwar Vietnam: Dynamics of a Transforming Society*, edited by Hy V. Luong. Boulder, CO: Rowman & Littlefield, 2003a, pp. 1–25.

———. "Wealth, Power, and Inequality: Global Market, the State, and Local Sociocultural Dynamics." In *Postwar Vietnam: Dynamics of a Transforming Society*, edited by Hy V. Luong. Boulder, CO: Rowman & Littlefield, 2003b, pp. 81–106.

———, and Diep Dinh Hoa. "Bon cong dong nong thon va thanh thi Viet Nam: Canh quan kinh te, xa hoi, va van hoa" [Four Vietnamese Rural and Urban Communities: Economic, Social, and Cultural Landscapes]. In *Ngon tu, gioi, va nhom xa hoi* [Discourse, Gender, and Social Groups], edited by Hy V. Luong. Hanoi: Nha xuat ban Khoa hoc xa hoi, 2000, pp. 39–97.

Madsen, Richard. "The Public Sphere, Civil Society and Moral Community." In *Modern China*, XIX (1993): 183–98.

Malarney, Shaun Kingsley. *Culture, Ritual and Revolution in Vietnam*. London: Routledge Curzon, 2002.

———. "Return to the Past? The Dynamics of Contemporary Religious and Ritual Transformation." In *Postwar Vietnam: Dynamics of a Transforming Society*, edited by Hy V. Luong. Boulder, CO: Rowman & Littlefield, 2003, pp. 225–56.

Nguyen Kim Ha. "Lessons Learned from a Decade of Experience: A Strategic Analysis of INGO Methods and Activities in Vietnam 1990–1999." Report of the NGO Resource Centre of the Vietnam Union of Friendship Organizations, 2001.

Phan Xuan Son *et al. Cac doan the nhan dan voi viec bao dam dan chu o co so hien nay* [Mass Organizations to Guarantee Grassroots Democracy at Present]. Hanoi: Nha xuat ban Chinh tri quoc gia, 2002.

Scott, James. *The Moral Economy of the Peasant.* New Haven, CT: Yale University Press, 1976.

Sidel, Mark. "The Emergence of a Voluntary Sector and Philanthropy in Vietnam." In *Emerging Civil Society in the Asia Pacific Community*, edited by Tadashi Yamamoto. Singapore: Institute of Southeast Asian Studies, 1995, pp. 477–90.

Suzuki, Chizuko. "Vietnam: Control of NGOs by NGOs." In *The State and NGOs: Perspective from Asia*, edited by Shinichi Shigetomi. Singapore: Institute of Southeast Asian Studies, 2002, pp. 145–60.

Thang van Phuc *et al. Vai tro cua cac hoi trong doi moi va phat trien dat nuoc* [The Role of Associations in the Renovation and Development of the Country]. Hanoi: Nha xuat ban Chinh tri quoc gia, 2002.

To Duy Hop, ed. *Ninh Hiep: Truyen thong va phat trien* [Ninh Hiep: Tradition and Development]. Hanoi: Nha xuat ban Chinh tri quoc gia, 1997.

Tran Duc Luong. "Tu nhung viec xay ra o Thai Binh, Dang, nha nuoc va nhan dan ta rut duoc bai hoc quy gia" [From the Events in Thai Binh, the Party, the State, and People Have Drawn a Valuable Lesson], *Sai Gon Giai Phong*, 4 and 5 March, 1998, p. 5.

Vietnam. *Nhung van ban phap luat ve Dan Chu va quy dinh dam bao thuc hien* [Legal Documents on Democracy and Implementation Regulations]. Hanoi: Nha xuat ban Lao Dong, 1999.

Vietnam and International Donor Group. *Vietnam: Managing Public Resources Better*, 2 volumes. Hanoi: Vietnam Development Resource Center, 2000.

Vietnam and World Bank. *Attacking Poverty*. Hanoi: World Bank-Vietnam, 1999.

Weller, Robert P. *Alternate Civilities: Democracy and Culture in China and Taiwan*. Boulder, CO: Westview Press, 1999.

Werner, Jayne. *Peasant Politics and Religious Sectarianism: Peasant and Priest in the Cao Dai in Vietnam*. New Haven, CT: Yale University Southeast Asian Studies, 1981.

Wischermann, Joerg, Bui The Cuong, and Nguyen Quang Vinh. "Quan he giua cac to chuc xa hoi va co quan nha nuoc o Viet Nam – nhung ket qua chon loc cua mot cuoc khao sat thuc nghiem o Ha Noi va Thanh pho Ho Chi Minh" [The Relation between Social Organizations and State Agencies in Vietnam: Selected Results from an Empirical Study in Hanoi and Ho Chi Minh City]. Report at a workshop on nongovernmental organizations in Hanoi and Ho Chi Minh City, April 2000.

World Bank. *Vietnam: Poverty Assessment and Analysis*. Washington, DC: World Bank, 1995.

9 Nongovernmental organizations and democratic transition in Indonesia

Philip Eldridge

Introduction

President Suharto's resignation on 21 May 1998, after nearly 33 years in power, launched Indonesia on an uncertain path of democratic transition. Since then, major political and constitutional reforms have significantly enlarged the scope for association and mobilization across civil society. However, these political gains have been diminished by significant social and economic disruptions that cast doubt as to whether Indonesia will be able to achieve effective democratic consolidation,[1] or will again fall under military control or another form of authoritarian rule.

This chapter will explore NGO responses to the current environment of opportunity and uncertainty. The central focus will be the impact of political change on NGO–state relations, by integrating their domestic and external aspects. Overall, legacies from the Suharto era, which have shaped the outlook of key NGO players, still overshadow these relations, despite the emergence of many new groups. While NGOs have been promoting democratic agendas since 1998, powerholders' resistance has also intensified. These issues also have an impact on the conflicting discourses on globalization and Indonesian national sovereignty, as economic crisis has returned Indonesia to external dependence. Such conflict is not new, but it has been sharpened by the pace of political and economic change. These themes are illustrated by corruption, debt, urban poor groups, the environment, and human rights.

Another factor in this conflict is NGOs' continued dependence on foreign funds, due in part to their lack of energy in seeking alternatives, which is causing them to become targets of nationalist resentment. In addition, the large volumes of aid channeled through NGOs often increase their resources more rapidly than their capacities, while their high-profile links with international networks represent a potentially powerful ideological weapon in the government's hands, as the country's political and economic crises are widely blamed on the United States and other Western governments, as well as the International Monetary Fund (IMF) and the World Bank. Even the United Nations has come under suspicion since the loss of East Timor, which has triggered deep anxieties about Indonesia's territorial integrity.

NGOs are nevertheless very salient to Indonesia's democratization prospects. Very diverse NGOs and activists share core values of popular participation, self-reliance, and empowerment as vehicles for enhancing both quality of life and human dignity. While such values are imperfectly realized in practice, they are central in explaining NGOs' understanding of their goals and identity. For NGOs, "participation" transcends mere electoral participation and takes on the broader meaning of asserting rights for people's involvement in decisions affecting their daily lives. Achieving such ideals entails broad-based strategies for empowerment, also known as "capacity-building."

NGOs tend not to confront their diffuse understandings of democracy, which reflect ideological conflicts across Indonesian society, with liberal democracy opposed by assorted radical, nationalist, and Islamic alternatives. NGO democratic participatory core values intersect, but they by no means coincide with the principles of liberal democracy. Popular disillusionment with both globalization and processes of political reform has weakened the legitimacy of liberal ideology, presenting dilemmas for Indonesian NGOs, which are well aware of the importance of indigenizing their norms and practices.

Indonesian NGOs are broadly supportive of universal human rights values, but, apart from those that focus on civil and political rights and associated legal reforms, most are primarily concerned with social and economic outcomes. There is no ultimate contradiction here, as the weight of the United Nations human rights system is directed toward integrating these two streams of human rights under the rubric of "indivisibility and interdependence." In practice, Indonesian NGOs tend to select the concepts of democracy which best serve their socioeconomic agendas.

As in other developing countries, dominant economic growth models were strongly challenged in Indonesia during the 1970s and 1980s, including unequal distribution, top-down decision making, and cultural inappropriateness. Enhancing the capacities of disadvantaged groups for improving their situation emerged as a key response, but many activists labeled their microdevelopmental approaches "apolitical." Over time, a broader consensus has emerged that recognizes the political nature of NGO engagement with the state at every level. Forms of engagement include drawing on public resources at local levels, policy interchange, and vigorous advocacy programs.

Overall, continuity is evident in NGOs' central agenda of seeking means to improve the socioeconomic condition of those they seek to represent, which is compatible with participatory understandings of democracy relevant to Indonesian contexts. But their leading networks see this as impossible in the current environment, without deep engagement in macropolitical processes of all kinds.

Nongovernmental organizations in Indonesia: definitions, nature, and scope

The term "nongovernmental organization" embraces several legal and structural forms in the Indonesian context. Sakai (2002: 165–7) identifies problems in determining NGO numbers, citing estimates ranging from 7,000 (Hikam 1999: 9) to

12,000 (Riker 1998: 143–4) in the mid-1990s. The numbers registered with the Home Affairs Department support the lower figure, with 70 to 80 percent based at the village and subprovincial levels. A significant regional imbalance is evidenced by proportionately lower coverage in eastern Indonesia and Sumatra. NGO activities embrace developmental, advocacy and mobilization aspects, spanning agriculture, forestry, health, family planning, water and sanitation, gender issues, environmental issues, urban development, informal sector, children, credit unions and cooperatives, and labor and human rights.

Some understandings of the term "nongovernmental organization" embrace the full range of nonprofit societal organizations outside the sphere of government, politics, and business. Though logically consistent, such usage is too broad to have any operational value. Distinctions between governmental and nongovernmental spheres are, in any case, problematic in the Indonesian context, particularly at village and subvillage levels. Semiformal religious, women's, and cooperative groups spanning formal boundaries have long served local roles in fields such as water use, health extension work, and credit unions, tapping into government services where they are available. Many mainstream NGOs work directly with such groups.

NGOs' legitimacy and effectiveness are challenged by the presence of organizations initiated by or closely associated with government agencies, often described as "government-organized nongovernmental organizations" or "GONGOs" (Kothari 1988: 84–6). While the rationale for their activities is diminishing with the dismantling of the functional groups that were central to political control under Suharto's New Order regime, these structures retain residual local and regional strength. Emerging semiofficial, often criminalized vigilante and militia groups associated with party, religious, military, bureaucratic, and political interests represent a further threat to NGOs and social activists.

By the early 1980s, NGOs had convinced influential elements within the government of their potential contribution to social and developmental tasks. But following the advice of "friends at court," notably Professor Emil Salim, minister for population and environment, many became convinced that a change of name was desirable in order to avoid the dangers of "nongovernmental" being interpreted as meaning "anti-government." "Self-reliant community organization" was considered to have greater historical and cultural resonance and consequently gained currency (Eldridge 1995: 14–15, 47–9). Radical critics later used this terminological shift to accuse NGOs of supine accommodation to the state.

The issue of NGOs' relations with political parties, of little importance under Suharto, has yet to be adequately addressed in the emerging democratic context. Repression under the New Order generated demands for NGOs to undertake representative roles more typically performed by political parties, and such expectations continue to generate confusion. The prime tasks of parties in liberal democracies are to win elections and gain and hold governmental power by consolidating diffuse demands and aspirations into overall ideologies and programs. NGOs are not equipped for these tasks, and to the extent they pursue them, or become adjuncts of parties, they cease being nongovernmental, and their potential for mobilization and capacity-building may be weakened. An opposite but extreme response would be to withdraw from engagement with political parties – but this would ultimately lead to NGOs' alienation from the democratic process. As with their engagement with government agencies, NGO practice is likely to be more pragmatic than their rhetoric.

These choices are rendered less stark by the reality that the boundaries between what may be broadly described as the "social movement sector" and political parties are historically blurred in Indonesia. For example, mass organizations such as Muhammadijah and Nahdlatul Ulama combined religious education and welfare with sociopolitical mobilization during Indonesia's independence struggle. They formed political parties during the 1950s and combined educational and developmental work with quasi-party formations under Suharto. During the current democratic era, both political parties and base-level factionalism continue to multiply among Muslim groups.

Organizational structures and legal context

While it is important to contextualize NGOs within the broader social movement sector, relatively distinct forms of organization differentiate them. NGOs commonly pursue multiple objectives aimed at serving either designated reference groups or society at large. In principle at least, they operate as legal entities within the framework of internally determined rules, as either membership-based organizations or foundations.

Under Suharto, the foundation format was favored as a means of minimizing government control, while maximizing flexibility in determining objectives and internal structures (Eldridge 1995: 45–51). But the effect has been to distort processes of internal democracy to the extent that NGO foundations have been more successful in promoting participatory practice among base-level groups than within their own organizations. Such arrangements also tend to foster dependence, as they require NGOs to play ongoing intermediary roles. Registered member-based organizations, notably credit unions and cooperatives, initially used high-level contacts to negotiate a measure of operational autonomy. This enabled them to establish relatively democratic and accountable structures and expand their capacities to deal directly with local and subregional authorities (Eldridge 1995: 74–98).

"Forums" and "study groups" initiated by students and other activists have often proved short-lived, though many have shown a capacity for regeneration as part of broader social movements. Several leading NGO networks began as loose forums aimed at legal, environmental, or other social sector reforms. Federation processes obliged regularization of their arrangements to include both legally based and informally structured organizations.

Although NGOs have benefited from the general expansion of civil rights since 1998, the dismantling of formal controls over them has been relatively slow. The 1985 Social Organizations Law requires all "social organizations" to adopt the official ideology of Pancasila (five principles)[2] as their "sole foundation."

Law 2/1999 requires political parties to acknowledge Pancasila as the basis of the Indonesian state and not promulgate anything contrary to its principles, but it no longer obliges them to have it as their foundation. By extension, this law has been assumed to apply to civil society organizations, as well.

However, pending replacement of the 1985 law, NGOs remain formally subject to provisions that require the relevant authorities' approval before receiving foreign funds and that allow official intervention in internal management and programs. NGOs adapted flexibly to such rules under Suharto through accommodations with ministries and local authorities deemed friendly. They also successfully ignored 1990 Home Affairs Ministry guidelines for administrative relations with NGOs, on grounds that these lacked legal force.

While registering as foundations has provided NGOs with a simple and flexible legal framework for conducting their activities under conditions of political repression, these structures also provide a loose framework for many kinds of business and welfare arrangements, some of which are operated by powerful military and political leaders. Reform in this field is necessary for Indonesia's democratic transition. Resistance or stalling on the part of NGOs will not sit easily with their demands for transparency and accountability in other contexts, and would align them with powerful groups they publicly oppose.

In electoral democracies such as India, Malaysia, and Singapore, legislation regulating counterpart societies imposes serious constraints on grassroots action. By comparison, Indonesia's Draft Law on Foundations (Masindo Business Media Ltd. 2001) does not appear to go beyond norms of transparency, honest and effective management, and public accountability. The law will require foundations to harmonize their structures and processes to agree with objectives stated in their articles of association, avoid conflicts of interest, and clearly separate the property designated to achieve specific religious, social, or humane objectives from the founders' private property (article 1).

As in the countries cited above, the minister of justice and law, not the home minister, must approve a foundation's establishment deed (article 10), including articles of association, for which minimum information is specified in article 13. Approval must be notified within two months and rejection within three months. The reasons for rejection must be stated in writing and must refer to specific noncompliance with provisions of the law and associated regulations.

Articles 7 and 14, which require that a foundation's objectives and name not be contrary to public order, prevailing laws, and ethics, may open the door to wider intervention. The minister must also approve any new deed caused by a merger of foundations and receive a copy of the auditors' annual reports. Finally, the perception of NGO objectives as "social, religious, and humanitarian," implied in the general elucidation of the law, reflects a traditional mindset that could more openly constrain political NGOs.

Democratization and regime change

NGO evolution under Suharto

While Indonesian NGOs are often portrayed as playing major roles in democratic reform, historical reality is more complex. Some operated within the framework of New Order structures to achieve favorable local developmental outcomes; others acted as strong advocates for both political and economic human rights (Eldridge 1995). It was this latter segment of the NGO movement that, allied with students, intellectuals, journalists, workers, peasants, professionals, religious groups, and others, networked with foreign supporters to ultimately achieve a democratic breakthrough.

Rapid NGO expansion occurred during the 1970s, alongside the mobilization of students demanding democratic government, rule of law, accountability, a more socially just model of economic development, and an end to corruption. The destruction of the student movement in the early 1980s caused many activists to initiate NGOs as a means of forging links with grassroots groups. However, these tended to concentrate on socioeconomic development, and did not lead to broader social mobilization.

A new generation of students came to play key roles in the mobilization for democratic change in the late 1980s (Aspinall 1993), and the broader political critique they developed confronted NGOs' perceived retreat into local programs. Together with journalists, professionals, intellectuals, and religious groups, various student factions extended their outreach to farmers, landless peasants, laborers, women, minorities, and other marginalized groups. Concerns over civil and political rights, which were conventionally associated with the middle class, were popularized by linking them with issues that affected people's daily lives, such as land, wages, working conditions, the environment, violence against women, and corruption. Dialogue, joint advocacy, the activation of regional forums, and programs for paralegal and environmental impact training with local NGOs subsequently achieved a measure of convergence.

Competing democratic discourses

NGOs' understandings of democracy reflect their generational and social bases and are linked to broader ideological divisions. In an earlier work (Eldridge 1995: 20–4), I proposed that three broad traditions of democracy in Indonesia have influenced NGO theory and practice. These center on liberal democratic models of representative government, voluntary consensus ideals drawn from Pancasila ideology, and radical mass participatory mobilization.[3] Islamic groups pursue recognizably distinct discourses and styles of mobilization (Uhlin 1997: 63–83; Eldridge 1995: 177–82; Eldridge 2002: 125–9), but they traverse a broadly similar terrain.

Liberal democracy has attracted articulate advocates throughout the modern era and now dominates much of Indonesia's formal political discourse and institutions, but it has rarely enjoyed mass appeal or understanding. Support for liberal democracy has been concentrated among intellectuals, students, and the professional and middle classes, though popular support for it broadened with an emphasis on transparency and rights for organization struggles against the New Order. At the same time, focusing on outcomes can cause NGOs and other activists to downgrade the importance of constitutional processes (Huntington 1991) and heap scorn on accommodation and bargaining, which lie at the heart of liberal democratic politics (Crick 1992).

Such tendencies are illustrated by the International Forum for Indonesian Development's initiative in drawing together some 60 NGOs and networks to demand an independent commission to replace the People's Consultative Council's control of the constitutional amendment process (INFID 2002b). Bypassing Indonesia's parliament[4] in such a key process would be both undemocratic and, if every amendment were to become subject to popular vote, unworkable. However, this need not preclude establishing an expert advisory panel or collecting popular input through appropriate consultative structures. There is also merit in proposals to consider constitutional reform in a comprehensive rather than piecemeal fashion.

The International Forum for Indonesian Development cited frustration caused by "political horse-trading" and a deadlock of constitutional interpretation as reasons for demanding that all state institutions return their mandate to the people, a "snap election with a more democratic political modus [*sic*]," and legal changes requiring political parties to "comply with the principles of the people's sovereignty" (INFID 2001b). Taken literally, such demands entail replacing representative democracy with direct democracy.

In mid-2001, disappointed by parliament's treatment of a reforming president, some NGOs are reported to have supported President Wahid's attempt to avoid impeachment by declaring a state of emergency and suspending parliament (Schreiner 2001), a proposal the military had already rejected. If true, this would represent an extreme example of the low esteem in which leading NGO layers hold democratic constitutional processes.

Despite significant post-Suharto political and constitutional reforms formally favoring liberal democratic principles, praxis is strongly influenced by competing conservative and radical discourses which both enjoy significant mass appeal. Conservative discourse invokes harmony and consensus in the name of the Pancasila. Public life under the New Order was monopolized by functional groups that were tied to the state, which effectively negated freedom of association and organization. Despite distortions under Suharto, core values underlying Pancasila retain strong cultural resonance, particularly among the Javanese and Balinese, who constitute over 60 percent of Indonesia's population. During the New Order many NGOs were able to develop effective empowerment strategies by working among local groups within this framework.

Some Pancasila advocates attempted to appropriate liberal–democratic discourse during the late New Order years. Some reformers, notably Abdurrachman Wahid, president of Indonesia from 1999 to 2001, explored prospects for synthesis

(Eldridge 2002: 119–21). In any case, ideals of voluntary consensus are not unique to Indonesia, and are pursued by many community groups in Western as well as Asian societies.

Radical traditions of mass participation have enjoyed a strong revival since the late 1980s. This discourse, which centers strongly on "people's sovereignty" and "struggle," draws on the revolutionary experience of the immediate post-independence period (Anderson 1972). In theoretical terms, Gramsci's notions of ruling class hegemony (Bobbio 1979) are employed to reject liberal distinctions between state and civil society. Consequently, civil and political rights are seen as instrumental in transforming power structures rather than goals in their own right.

As issues of democratic participation lie at the heart of their identity, all major tendencies are represented among contemporary NGOs (Eldridge 2002: 121–5), reflecting divisions within as well as between them. Such labeling nevertheless represents a continuum of ideal types rather than rigid categories: in practice, elements of each are combined in many different ways according to context and organizational needs.

Political and constitutional change post-1998

Following Suharto's resignation the largely rubber stamp parliament elected and appointed under him was persuaded to democratize its composition and provide for genuine elections in which parties could form and operate freely. Forty-eight parties competed in the June 1999 elections, which were broadly judged as free and fair by most observers. Many more parties indicated their intention to compete in the 2004 election.

The quality of evolving political parties is of the greatest importance to consolidating Indonesian democracy and the legitimacy of its processes, which will thereby ensure real political choices for citizens. There is currently no obvious distinction between the parties that support and oppose the government in parliament, as all seek a share in the spoils of office.[5] Internal democracy and a capacity for policy development are also crucial in countering personality-based factionalism, as much for political parties as NGOs.

The transfers of power and resources to district administrations responsible to elected councils[6] offer NGOs new opportunities for promoting local participation. However, major issues remain unresolved, notably the future role of the military, which retains residual strength within Indonesia's territorial system of government, and the respective powers of parliament and the president. A constitutional amendment in August 2002 provided for direct popular election of the president which took place in 2004 (Moestafa and Kurniawan 2002).

Media freedom was greatly widened both by legislation and by President Wahid's abolition of the Ministry of Information (Eldridge 2002: 132–3). A minis-terial decree on 28 May 1998 acknowledged the right to form unions, abolishing the monopoly enjoyed by the government-controlled All-Indonesia Workers' Union (SPSI), but retaining reporting requirements.[7] Broader rights guaranteeing freedom of speech and association were entrenched in a new chapter XA, which greatly expanded article 28 of Indonesia's 1945 constitution in the form of a bill of rights (NDI 2000: 12–14, 24–6). But monitoring the implementation of these rights, which are linked to the reform of Indonesia's notoriously corrupt judicial body and the establishment of human rights tribunals, will constitute a major task for human rights NGOs in association with Indonesia's National Human Rights Commission, which was established in 1992. Human rights tribunals manifest serious conceptual and structural weaknesses, particularly regarding requirements for presidential and parliamentary approval in each instance and confusion over issues of retrospective judicial power (ICG 2001).

NGOs' engagement with the state

This section considers four high profile advocacy networks: the Indonesian Corruption Watch, Kontras (The Commission for Disappearances and Victims of Violence), the Urban Poor Consortium, and the Indonesian Environmental Network. The first two emerged from upheavals surrounding Suharto's fall in 1998. The Urban Poor Consortium, whose work is concentrated among informal-sector workers in Jakarta, represents a coalition of groups formed during the economic crisis that began in 1997 and more established groups operating in this field. The Indonesian Environmental Network was founded in 1980.

Both Indonesian Corruption Watch and the Urban Poor Consortium are issue focused, though their initial entry points have led them into more general political fields. Kontras has a broad human rights mandate, with a primary focus on violence and the misuse of power by the military. The Indonesian Environmental Network is a large and diverse umbrella body representing a loose association of NGOs, networks, and forums operating at national, regional, and local levels.

These organizations offer contrasting styles of operation. Indonesian Corruption Watch focuses on investigating and exposing misbehavior by public officers and demands punctilious adherence to legal and constitutional processes. The Urban Poor Consortium combines public advocacy, organization of support groups, and often violent street demonstrations. Kontras's approach stresses nonviolence and combines investigative research with public gatherings. The Indonesian Environmental Network embraces vigorous public advocacy, operational research, and community programs. Its stance toward the government is both cooperative and critical, because of both the diverse nature of its affiliated groups and its long engagement with the New Order state. Its advocacy and networking have been progressively extended into governance issues relating to transparency and corruption, which it considers crucial to environmental outcomes.

Indonesian Corruption Watch

Indonesian Corruption Watch (ICW),[8] established on 21 June 1998 at the height of the reform movement following Suharto's fall, represents the action arm of a coalition of civil society organizations' "pledge for a corruption-free Indonesia"

(INFID 1999). It reflects a new brand of coalition drawn from activists across a wide spectrum of backgrounds in human rights, legal aid, labor, environmental, and rural development NGOs.

ICW's mission statement stresses accountability, transparency, and democratic participation. Its aims include legal and constitutional reform and changing societal ethics through a strong popular movement. Detailed guidelines and strategies for pursuing investigations target legislators, electoral processes, the judiciary, and foreign-funded loan projects. The organization's code of ethics requires checks to ensure that every member has a clean record in relation to crime, corruption, human rights violations, and conflicts of financial interest. Members may not belong to political parties.

ICW assisted in the establishment of an anti-corruption commission, which was announced on 15 June 1999. Agitation against "corruption, collusion and nepotism" was widespread at that time, and the People's Deliberative Council had granted President Habibie a mandate to fight it the previous year.[9] An anti-corruption joint investigation team was established within the attorney general's department as an interim measure, and was headed by Professor Adi Andojo Soetjipto, a member of the ICW's board of ethics. While investigative agendas and processes are autonomous, the team's work is formally coordinated by the attorney general. The team claims to have encountered strong resistance from the Supreme Court during an investigation of three of its justices (Soetjipto *c.* 2000). After numerous seminars and training sessions, a Corruption Eradication Commission was finally established in December 2003.

In some respects, Indonesian Corruption Watch's aims appear both sufficiently all-embracing to justify their intervention on any front and too imprecise to allow evaluation of its own performance. However, the culture of impunity pervading Indonesian public life invites such broad-based challenges.

Kontras: the Commission for Disappearances and Victims of Violence

Kontras[10] was formed in March 1998 by a coalition of 12 pro-democracy NGOs, including the Independent Committee for Election Watch, the Alliance of Independent Journalists, the Foundation of Indonesia Legal Aid Institutions (YLBHI), and the Indonesian Islamic Student Movement. Kontras's formation was initially motivated by the unexplained disappearances of activists, which were blamed on military responses to demonstrations during Suharto's final year as president. It has subsequently embraced a broader human rights mission focused on eliminating state violence and reducing the military's political role. It participated in reporting on proposed national security legislation, which was subsequently withdrawn in the face of massive demonstrations (YLBHI 1999), and the role of security forces in interethnic conflict in Central Kalimantan (INFID 2001a).

On 13 March 2002, Kontras's Jakarta office was ransacked, files relating to cases in Aceh, Papua, Maluku, and Poso were removed, and the staff were severely beaten by thugs styling themselves the "Families of Cawang Victims 1998." This hitherto unknown group justified its attack by claiming it was in response to Kontras's unwillingness to take up the case of pro-military vigilantes killed in 1998 during clashes with pro-democracy student activists in the Cawang subdistrict of East Jakarta. Kontras claims that no family member of those killed had ever approached them (AHRC 2002).

The Urban Poor Consortium

The Urban Poor Consortium (UPC) emerged as an advocacy coalition dedicated to alleviating the impact of the economic crisis on the urban poor.[11] It took up the cause of defending informal-sector workers, such as pedicab drivers, sidewalk vendors and street musicians, against a "clean up" drive by Jakarta Governor Sutiyoso that threatened their livelihood. UPC claimed that over 8,500 pedicabs (*becak*) had been confiscated or destroyed by September 2001, while many families were forcibly evicted from their dwellings.

The coalition gained national media coverage in May 1999 with allegations that senior ministers and officials had channeled US$800 million of World Bank social safety net funds into pro-government party campaign funds. Credits for distribution to farmers and owners of small and medium enterprises were alleged to have been channeled through designated cooperatives. Recipients had to become party members or pledge support at the forthcoming election, but funds did not have to be repaid if the Golkar Party won (Hikam 1999). The government denied these charges, but Wardah Hafid, a UPC leader, nevertheless became a continuing target of violence and harassment.

Conflict came to a head after the consortium brought a successful class action lawsuit against the Jakarta administration, which was ordered to cease its evictions. On 28 March 2002, demonstrators against the governor's refusal to obey the court order were violently assaulted outside the office of the National Human Rights Commission by some 200 members of the Betawi Unity Forum. The organization claims it was established to help Betawi (native Jakartans) youths find jobs. Membership is estimated at around 7,000 mostly blue-collar workers, motorcycle taxi (*ojek*) drivers, and the unemployed. Leaders claimed that Jakarta locals were angry at "trouble-making outsiders," whose activities they saw as designed to attract foreign funds. Forum members were in turn accused of carrying weapons and being paid by Governor Sutiyoso (Tempo Interactive 2002).

Sutiyoso was Jakarta military commander during the bloody 27 July 1996 attack on the Indonesian Democratic Party's (PDI) headquarters that was aimed at unseating Megawati Sukarnoputri's leadership. Megawati, who became president in June 2001, subsequently threw her political support behind him. The Betawi Unity Forum claims it has no political affiliations, but its leader, H.A. Fadloli El Muhir, is Jakarta chapter chairman of the Indonesian Democratic Party of Struggle, which was formed by Megawati. The impunity Muhir enjoys is illustrated by reported comments that as "legal action takes time . . . we would favour beating up Wardah if she continues slandering us" (Junaidi and Nurbianto 2002).

Over 50 Indonesian NGOs and the Asian Human Rights Commission view these cases as part of a pattern of intimidation against human rights defenders and organizations that was tolerated and probably encouraged by various authorities, and as evidence of the growing involvement of vigilante and paramilitary groups in Indonesian politics. Both coalitions demanded the protection of human rights defenders and the investigation and prosecution of those responsible (AHRC 2002; INFID 2002a).

The Asian Coalition for Housing Rights (ACHR 2001), the Urban Poor Consortium's regional partner, further claimed that Jakarta authorities were employing criminal gangs to terrorize and divide the poor by means of ethnicity and religion, setting Betawi against non-Betawi, Muslims against Christians. A larger Betawi coalition subsequently joined with the Urban Poor Consortium and other groups in a mass mobilization against Sutiyoso (Nurbianto 2002) but failed to prevent his re-election as governor of Jakarta for another five-year term.

Such cases suggest a more general return to new forms of an earlier historical phenomenon of private, semicriminal gangs (*preman*) acting as intermediaries and enforcers on behalf of powerholders and those who aspire to power. This trend, increasingly apparent in the late Suharto years, is aggravated by Indonesia's protracted and disorderly democratic transition. If Indonesia follows the pattern of India and the Philippines, political parties as well as military, bureaucratic, and business elements may be expected to recruit their own paramilitary and vigilante groups, as is already occurring among politico-religious groups. Both human rights and the rule of law will be threatened if such trends take hold.

The Indonesian Environmental Network

In contrast to the single-mindedly adversarial role played by Indonesian Corruption Watch and the Urban Poor Consortium, the Indonesian Environmental Network (WALHI)[12] for the most part pursues a strategy of critical collaboration with state authorities. Founded in 1980, WALHI brings together several hundred diverse NGOs, nature lovers, and other groups that subscribe to its charter, which challenges the misuse of resources caused by an unjust and unsustainable development model. WALHI structures are built around national, regional, and local forums that retain operational autonomy. This arrangement provides flexibility for information exchange, training programs, and facilitating dialogue between society and government at each level.

In a pioneering attempt to persuade Indonesians to fund nonprofit activity outside religious educational and charity spheres, WALHI established a Friends of the Environment Fund in 1983 (Eldridge 1995: 52–3). Funds were raised from individual subscriptions, national and international organizations, and business companies considered legally and environmentally clean.

WALHI has linked environmental, social, and political change from its inception, seeing popular mobilization as essential for promoting transparency and sound ecological and resource management. However, the continuing entrenchment of the military at local and regional levels, which thwarts democratic change, negates this prospect.

WALHI member organizations have nevertheless cooperated with agencies and individuals within the government wherever common ground is found. Professor Emil Salim, minister for population and environment from 1978 to 1993, was a member of Friends of the Environment board of trustees. Salim, who enjoyed high esteem in economic and planning circles, was instrumental in establishing, through article 19 of the 1982 Environment Law,[13] the right of local community groups, including NGOs, to participate in environmental policy and planning processes (Eldridge 1995: 136–7). This law, amplified by Ministerial Regulation No.29 of 1986, laid the foundation for an extensive system of environmental impact analysis coordinated by a specially established national Environmental Impact Monitoring Board (Koesnadi 1987). Salim's advice that NGOs stress scientific rigor and tone down ideological rhetoric was only partially accepted.

WALHI's analysis linking Indonesia's debt burden and consequent adoption of economic liberalization strategies with pressures to accelerate logging and extraction of natural resources causes it to be active in networks that advocate external debt relief. Concern for transparency similarly brings it into coalition with anti-corruption networks – a consideration that also drives USAID, Asia, and Ford Foundation programs that promote participatory monitoring and advocacy by environmental groups. WALHI is thus torn between the necessity of constructive cooperation with the government and international agencies, and its strategic analysis, which is critical of both.

International coalitions

Three distinct trends are evident in international coalitions between Indonesian NGOs and outside international players. One points to cooperative change, another to sharp criticism, while various combinations of critical collaboration are found in between. NGO networks, which contain diverse, substantially autonomous organizations, can display all three tendencies. Similarly, there is not a simple alignment between foreigners and Indonesian NGOs against the Indonesian government, but rather a multifaceted interaction between the Indonesian government, local NGOs, foreign governments, and international NGOs and institutions.

While the roles and approaches of the International Monetary Fund and the World Bank are distinct from United Nations agencies, their charters require each to deal exclusively through governments. The World Bank and the UN have nevertheless set up strategies to include NGOs. Member governments of the Consultative Group for Indonesia, convened by the World Bank, cooperate within the framework of the United Nations Development Program and the World Bank Partnership for Governance Reform, which coordinates donor support in areas of judicial reform, decentralization, legislative strengthening, bureaucratic reform, and the strengthening of civil society. Individual governments nevertheless pursue their own philosophical, strategic, and sectoral emphases, which can diverge from the World Bank's more rigorously formulated blueprints. Moreover, the World Bank's targeted anti-poverty programs indicate a different emphasis in responding to the post-1997 economic crisis compared with the International Monetary Fund's more monetarist, neoliberal approach (Hill 1999; Severino 1998).

The United States Agency for International Development (USAID)

As an agency within the US State Department, USAID reflects broad US policy; however, its substantial administrative autonomy has allowed it to develop flexibility in developing local approaches. Rather than advocating large-scale foreign investment, USAID has supported institutional strengthening of a kind favorable to local small and medium enterprises. This could be seen as promoting neoliberal and related governance agendas. Nevertheless, democracy, pluralism, and responsive and accountable institutions rather than free markets represent core program objectives. Thus, USAID's post-Suharto strategies prioritize confronting sectarian and political violence, corruption and judicial performance, poverty, improving the environment and natural resources, economic management, and decentralization. Program areas[14] currently cover democratic reform, economic growth, decentralization, natural resources management, health and nutrition, and assistance to alleviate the impact of conflict and crisis. Gender equity and governance components span all programs.

Democratic reform programs include assisting official legislative, administrative, and judicial institutions and the civil society groups that monitor them and advocate alternatives. Advisors in key ministries assist the government of Indonesia in drafting laws and policies and implementing regulations for decentralization and national dissemination. USAID works with selected local governments to strengthen core governance processes relating to budgeting, financial management, and medium-term planning. It claims over 100,000 community meetings have been supported as part of a new approach being piloted in nine cities, with over 100 local NGOs assisting citizens to voice their priorities to elected local officials. Special focus is placed on water services in the hope of demonstrating the advantages of decentralization in a poorly managed sector.

The Asia and Ford Foundations

Both the Asia and Ford Foundations have operated as independent bodies in Indonesia since the Republic's early years. Their broad philosophies center on strengthening civic culture in a democratic direction. Programs have been developed eclectically, spanning several regime changes, working with both government and nongovernment institutions. Currently, there is a strong measure of convergence and, consequently, cooperation with USAID priorities and programs.

Asia Foundation programs encompass the reform of legal and private sector policies to create accountable government institutions and empower small and medium enterprises. The foundation's programs are also designed to address issues like local governance, human rights violations, religious and ethnic conflict, and women's participation in politics and government. The foundation has conducted long-term research programs relating to Islamic law and has supported research and public education promoting pluralist and tolerant approaches in fields such as law, gender issues, human rights, interfaith dialogue, and reconciliation (Asia Foundation 2000, 2001).

The Ford Foundation has provided similar support to Islamic groups in relation to women's reproductive health. Major programs focus on community forestry, sustainable agriculture, gender equity, local governance, and crisis mediation. Ford Indonesia also provides significant support to the arts and cultural and media development.

Despite much quality technical and sociocultural analysis, the institution-building and social-engineering strategies driving USAID and its partners' programs place the onus of change one-sidedly on domestic relative to external factors. By contrast, while many local NGOs participate in these programs, public commentary by major Indonesian NGO networks and their international counter-parts places greatest weight on macropolitical aspects and structural obstacles to achieving democratic reforms and sustainable development. Such analysis apportions equal responsibility between Indonesia, rich country governments, business, and international agencies. These themes will be explored with reference to networking around issues of the environment, debt, and anti-corruption.

Debt and corruption

The International Forum for Indonesian Development (INFID) succeeded the International NGO Forum on Indonesia, which was established in 1984–5. Its focus on monitoring and lobbying the World Bank-sponsored consortium of international donors supporting Indonesia[15] enabled it to become a powerful vehicle for criticizing both the conditionalities of official aid and Indonesia's overall development strategies. Strong international campaigns, notably in relation to forest and dam projects, brought the forum into serious collision with the Suharto government, which forced the withdrawal of Holland from the aid donors' consortium in 1992.

The organization's subsequent name change to the International Forum for Indonesian Development was partly intended to mollify the government, while clearer separation between Indonesian and overseas members was signaled by shifting the secretariat to Jakarta. Indonesian NGO policy stances are worked out prior to joint meetings, at which official statements are formulated on a consensus basis. Forum membership remains fluid. Participation varies between issues and conferences, based on a core of 40–50 Indonesian and 30–40 foreign organizations, mostly established NGOs and networks.

Forum advocacy stresses the assault on Indonesians' economic rights caused by corruption and debt. Development spending cuts following the economic crisis were estimated at almost a third, with social spending declining around 40 percent in real terms from 1995–6 levels. The number of poor people was estimated to increase to about 20 million, with about 1.3 million children dropping out of school (INFID 2000, 2001c). The major blame for Indonesia's ills was attributed to external agencies such as the World Bank, the International Monetary Fund, and Western governments.

As part of its campaign to include Indonesia in a debt moratorium for the world's poorest countries, INFID has urged exclusion of portions of its debt deemed odious by reason of corrupt interests involved in its acquisition. Mismanagement and poorly conceived programs have denied the Indonesian people ownership of the direction of their future development (INFID 1999, 2000, 2001c). Demands for a debt moratorium have so far been rejected by international donors, who have nevertheless maintained pressure to establish an anti-corruption commission.

In that context, anti-corruption advocacy has gained high-profile international support from Transparency International, which has 70 national chapters, though not yet in Indonesia. In September 1998, INFID, WALHI, Indonesian Corruption Watch, and Transparent Society Indonesia established the Anti-Corruption Forum as an informal counterpart. Transparency International's *Source Book on National Integrity Systems*, intended as a standard reference for reformers, has been translated into Indonesian. Innovative aspects include developing national action plans with civil society groups and integrity pacts, which Transparency International claims it has successfully applied in several countries (Rooke 1999).

The International Monetary Fund was widely blamed for the economic disruption caused by forcing the government to close 16 insolvent private banks without adequate preparation (Hill 1999: 51–2). The government was further forced to accept loans for their recapitalization at an annual interest rate of 12 percent (INFID 2001d). The International Forum for Indonesian Development pushed for Indonesia's inclusion in the Initiative for Heavily Indebted Poor Countries (HIPC), launched by the IMF and World Bank in 1996. Citing Bank Indonesia and international sources, Indonesia's public debt–GDP ratio was estimated at 100 percent plus a further 7 percent of private debt. The annual debt service ratio of 33 percent is deemed unsustainable by respected Indonesian and Western economists in a world trade environment in which Indonesia's total debt–export ratio has been estimated at 251.75 percent (INFID 2001d).

While advocacy by INFID and others does not yet appear to have won more than further debt rescheduling, in line with principles supported in orthodox financial circles, its powerful critique of international creditors serves to offset exclusive focus on Indonesian shortcomings, generate support from the international NGO community for economic relief, and at least partially mollify nationalist sensitivities. However, as part of its anti-corruption drive, INFID campaigns for immediate suspension of arms sales, training, and other support to the Indonesian military until it is brought under civilian control (INFID 1999).

In response to "leakage" of around 30 percent of disbursed funds from its social safety net adjustment loan program (World Bank 1999a), the World Bank called on NGOs to form a coalition similar to Indonesian Corruption Watch as part of an urgent strategy to protect these programs (Marshall 1998). The bank sought to link the second phase of this program with extensive consultation and government and civil society input.[16] But NGOs have been reluctant to participate in monitoring programs despite conditionalities attached to the disbursement of the second tranche of funds based on program performance, a transparent operation, and follow-through on complaint resolution. The Indonesian government's frustrations are reflected in attempts to set up its own social safety net programs (Haeruman 1999).

A Social Monitoring and Early Response Unit was established, which sought to establish participatory monitoring systems in three subdistricts of Bandung City and Lombok. These operated via representative forums drawn from the community, regional government, universities, media, and NGOs. The monitoring units employed a "multilayered problem-solving approach," working down to village and ward levels, and transmitting feedback back up the ladder (World Bank *c*. 1999b). The World Bank claims that the late arrival of several cases of rice, incompletely paid scholarship funds, and the misuse of public employment programs were corrected by these means. However, imposed program uniformity was reported across diverse locations.

Continuing skepticism toward World Bank participatory initiatives by high-profile NGOs could be viewed as automatic opposition on ideological grounds linked to the conviction that they alone are capable of mobilizing popular participation. In that sense, complaints of "tokenism" or "lack of consultation" can be seen as code for handing primary responsibility to NGOs. The World Bank in turn, though encouraging NGOs' input, warns that they must equally adhere to high standards of accountability, transparency, and democratic management structures. Moreover, they are not democratically elected and are as vulnerable as others to corruption (World Bank 2001).

NGO skepticism was reinforced by a strongly critical survey of the World Bank's poverty reduction strategy program (World Bank 2002) conducted by a coalition of international nongovernment organizations allied with the Jubilee Plus network (Jubilee South *et al.* 2001). Strengthening civil society, fighting corruption, and promoting environmental sustainability are all subcomponents of this program. While local World Bank representatives may prove flexible at the margins, the survey found guidelines that embraced non-negotiable, neoliberal agendas and prescriptions as preset in Washington. The overall effect is to strengthen leverage for imposing structural adjustment programs. Uniformity in approach across diverse communities further negates genuine participation and a sense of ownership. According to this view, stepped-up consultation with NGOs represents a public relations exercise designed to legitimize World Bank and International Monetary Fund activities.

Conclusion

The environment for engaging with the Indonesian state has changed dramatically since 1998, allowing NGOs vastly greater freedom of expression and association and social, cultural, and intellectual space. But important limitations remain, as they have yet to gain legal security specific to their roles. Along with other human rights defenders and civil society groups, NGO activists' security as citizens is still far from fully guaranteed. The challenges of political and economic reconstruction have yielded NGOs more opportunities and resources. But this attracts competition from new players, including state-sponsored NGOs, paramilitary formations, and criminal gangs. These both constrict the social space of independent NGOs and threaten the human rights of all Indonesians.

Responses to these opportunities and challenges can be characterized as marked by uncertainty. Such uncertainty extends beyond pragmatic ambivalence toward government agencies to the ideological and strategic domain, exposing confusion in NGOs' understandings of democracy and stance toward the political process. This appears to reflect a deeper crisis that NGOs have not yet confronted.

During the early and middle Suharto years, in a political climate of extreme repression, Indonesian NGOs demonstrated possibilities for grassroots organizations to gain a measure of self-management and internal democracy. Over time, they developed networking capacities sufficient for engaging in policy dialogue with relevant authorities. They also reached out to wider constituencies through public advocacy, which played a key role in placing new issues, such as the environment, public health, consumer rights, the status of women, and human rights, on the political agenda.

From the late 1980s, expectations and demands grew that NGOs would undertake a wider political role in pressing for democratic change. Although their partial response disappointed students and other activists, NGOs were substantially identified in the public mind with the ethos of the democracy movement and the demise of Suharto. However, their underlying and perhaps necessary ambivalence toward political processes, whether democratic or otherwise, remains unresolved. Whereas they could formerly enjoy the status of champions of democracy, the opening of new channels for expressing popular opinions and demands, especially through the formation of political parties, challenges that status.

Important tasks remain in monitoring corruption and illegal actions by state officials and promoting administrative and constitutional change – challenges that have been vigorously pursued by contemporary NGO networks. Here, Indonesian NGOs could usefully draw on the experiences of their counterparts in Thailand and the Philippines, where NGOs have successfully mobilized popular participation in processes of constitutional amendment, incorporating strong human rights directives (Eldridge 2002: 49–50, 54–6, 85–6). Parallel tasks remain in confronting ethnic and religious conflict and building a pluralist democratic culture, although both political parties and other civil society groups also legitimately expect to play a role in such matters.

NGOs' effectiveness can be weakened by a tendency to overplay their hand, as evidenced by moralistic pronouncements on democracy and political processes in general. In terms of the three models of democracy outlined earlier, they tend to combine liberal and radical participatory rhetoric in confusing ways. At the same time, although Pancasila ideology has fallen out of political favor, harmony and consensus approaches remain important to NGO praxis in a climate of social uncertainty and violence, particularly in rural areas.

In applying core NGO values of direct participation and empowerment, it appears that, while "rule of law" and procedural rectitude are strongly upheld in principle, liberal-style competitive values are abhorred, particularly in relation to electoral competition between parties. Ideals tend to be pursued with a disdain for politics reminiscent of what has been described in relation to certain Indian contexts as a tradition of "gentle anarchism," in which candidates for office are expected to pursue the "public good" as independents only, subject to recall by "the people" at any time (Ostergaard 1985).

Consideration of Indonesian NGOs' international links reveals two distinct discourses: the one that prevails among the International Monetary Fund, World Bank and USAID networks, and another among Indonesian and international NGO coalitions. Despite many practical meeting points, evidenced by cooperative programs and a common desire to check arbitrary and unaccountable exercise of power by the Indonesian military and bureaucrats, these two discourses are intrinsically opposed.

The first is an essentially optimistic blueprint that focuses on domestic aspects, identifying the necessary legal, administrative, economic, and social corrections. The second highlights external as well as domestic causes of Indonesia's woes; it places little credence on incremental reform and is pessimistic about achieving the desired overall structural change.

The priority for the Indonesian state, relatively sidelined by both these critiques, focuses on survival. To this end it counters both domestic and foreign protagonists with strong nationalist rhetoric, which also resonates with unattached streams of public opinion. But the state also draws resources from NGOs by participating in joint programs with both local and international organizations. Indonesian NGOs, which also assert their patriotism, offer important, albeit critical collaboration in battles with the International Monetary Fund, the World Bank, and Western governments over issues of debt, terms of aid, and trade. This partly balances their anti-government criticism on human rights, corruption, and environmental issues.

Indonesian NGOs' rhetorical bark can appear stronger than their bite, considering their extensive aid dependence and pragmatic collaboration with those they criticize. Yet this duality can be justified in terms of both base-level groups' overall welfare and their own survival. NGOs can consequently behave along lines similar to political parties, to the extent they maximize the vagueness of their messages in order to draw support from diffuse constituencies (Lissner 1976).

When judging Indonesian NGOs' effectiveness, it is important to avoid extremes of uncritical praise or wholesale dismissal. Although ideological discourse is commonly couched in terms of ultimate ends, most change is incremental and multicausal. Nevertheless, the current democratic transition provides a new context for understanding their inherent strengths and weaknesses. While diversity and pluralism in social composition and outreach plus creative networking enable them to transcend many sociocultural, administrative, and other barriers, they also create disunity in articulating goals and strategies. Local orientation, though a basic source of strength and legitimacy, limits capacity for national-level engagement to loose and complex networking coalitions. Finally, core participatory values, when effectively implemented, often conflict with goals of political change, as poor people are for the most part politically circumspect in pursuing their absolute priority of economic survival.

Hikam (1999) points out how Indonesian NGOs are able to challenge state legitimacy by bringing to light human rights abuses, political violence, and environmental destruction that would otherwise be concealed, but are unable to significantly change the unfavorable state–civil society power balance. Attacks on the Urban Poor Consortium and Kontras represent examples of "the empire striking back," putting NGOs generally on the defensive. According to Hikam, one reason for this has been public inaction, despite applause for NGO efforts. Curiously, both supporters and opponents share exaggerated fears or expectations of NGOs' political capacities. The changed international climate since 11 September 2001, with the United States again courting the Indonesian military as part of its "war on terrorism," also raises doubts about how far the international community will press the Indonesian government on human rights issues.

Finally, it is important to recognize continuities in the Indonesian NGO movement, including its considerable strengths during the Suharto period. Its survival and achievements during that time cannot be attributed solely to inconsistencies in state control (Sakai 2002). NGOs certainly took advantage of contradictions within the New Order state, but they also identified distinct niches, linking quality grassroots programs, policy dialogue, and public advocacy. Where these aspects become disconnected, NGOs' capacity to either serve the people or access resources will soon decline, leaving them marginalized in the eyes of society, government, and potential foreign supporters. Each new wave of NGOs cannot avoid learning this lesson anew.

Notes

1 Cf. Diamond 1999 for a comparative perspective on issues of democratic consolidation. This follows the earlier "transition" phase where he and most other observers would place Indonesia.
2 The five principles of Pancasila (belief in One Almighty God, national unity, humanitarianism, democracy, and social justice) were originally articulated by former President Sukarno in a speech on 1 June 1945 (Kahin 1952: 122–7).
3 Uhlin (1997: 84–154) offers a parallel though more elaborately subdivided categorization of democracy and associated human rights discourses, actors, and issues.
4 Parliament consists of the House of Representatives, which deals with budgets and routine legislation, and the People's Deliberative Council, which determines constitutional changes and, until recent amendments providing for popular election in 2004, has appointed the president and vice president. Military and police appointees were eliminated from the Parliament elected in 2004, balanced by increased provision for election of regional representatives.
5 An exception is the National Awakening Party, which has excluded itself from government in protest against the dismissal of its leader, former President Abdurrachman Wahid.
6 Under Laws 22 and 25 of 1999, the substance of which was later incorporated into chapter VI of the Constitution; cf. Habibie 1999 and NDI 2000.
7 Peraturan Menteri Tenaga Kerja Nomor PER-05/MEN/1998.

8 Website links via http://www.lsm.or.id/icw/.
9 TAP No XI/MPR/1998.
10 Website links via http://www.desaparecidos.org/kontras/.
11 Information for this section is drawn from the websites of the Urban Poor Consortium (http://www.urbanpoor.or.id/index_tpf1.htm) and the Asian Coalition for Housing Rights (http://www.achr.net/indonesia.htm).
12 Links via the WALHI website, http://www.walhi.or.id/.
13 Act of the Republic of Indonesia No.4 of 1982 concerning Basic Provision for the Management of the Living Environment.
14 Website links via http://www.usaid.gov/id/program-main.html.
15 Known until 1992 as the Inter-Governmental Group for Indonesia, when it became the Consultative Group for Indonesia.
16 Annex 5.
   http://www.worldbank.org/html/extdr/offrep/eap/projects/ssnal/annex5.pdf.

References

ACHR (Asian Coalition for Housing Rights). "Extract from the Finding Mission to Jakarta Indonesia." Manila. Update 28 November 2001. http://www.achr.net/indonesia.htm.
AHRC (Asian Human Rights Commission). "Attacks on Human Rights Defenders, Destruction of Property, Public Use of Weapons with Impunity." Hong Kong. Urgent Appeal Update, 20 March 2002.
   http://www.ahrchk.net/ua/mainfile.php/2002/219/.
Anderson, Benedict O'G. *Java in a Time of Revolution*. Ithaca, NY: Cornell University Press, 1972.
Asia Foundation. "Legal Reform in Indonesia." Washington, DC, August 2000. Program links via http://www.asiafoundation.org/programs/prog-asia-indo.html.
———. "Islam and Civil Society in Indonesia." Washington, DC, June 2001. Program links via http://www.asiafoundation.org/programs/prog-asia-indo.html.
Aspinall, E. "Student Dissent in Indonesia in the 1980s." Working Paper No. 79. Clayton, Melbourne: Monash University, 1993.
Bobbio, N. *Gramsci and Marxist Theory*. London: Routledge and Kegan Paul, 1979.
Crick, B. *In Defence of Politics*, 4th edn. Ringwood, Melbourne: Penguin Books, 1992.
Diamond, L. *Developing Democracy: Towards Consolidation*. Baltimore, MD and London: Johns Hopkins University Press.
Eldridge, P. *Non-Government Organisations and Democratic Participation in Indonesia*. Kuala Lumpur: Oxford University Press, 1995.
———. *The Politics of Human Rights in Southeast Asia*. London and New York: Routledge, 2002.
Habibie, B. "Accountability Speech by the President of the Republic of Indonesia before the General Session of The People's Consultative Assembly Jakarta, 14 October 1999." *Jakarta Post*, 15 October 1999.
Haeruman, H. "The Social Safety Net in Indonesia's Social and Economic Crisis." Washington, DC: World Bank, 1999.
   http://www.worldbank.org/eapsocial/meeting/haeruman.pdf.
Hikam, Muhammad. "The Role of NGOs in the Empowerment of Indonesian Civil Society: A Political Perspective." Jakarta: Paper prepared for the 12th INFID Conference Bali, 14–17 September, 1999.
Hill, H. *The Indonesian Economy in Crisis*. St. Leonards, Sydney: Allen & Unwin, 1999.
Huntington, S. *The Third Wave: Democratization in the Twentieth Century*. Norman, OK: University of Oklahoma Press, 1991.

ICG (International Crisis Group). "Indonesia: Impunity versus Accountability for Gross Human Rights Violations." Jakarta and Brussels: ICG Asian Report No.12, 2 February 2001. http://www.crisisweb.org.

INFID (International Forum for Indonesian Development). "Statement by the 12th INFID Conference, Bali, Indonesia, September 14–17, 1999." Jakarta, 1999. All INFID statements and reports online via http://www.infid.be.

——. "INFID Statement to the Consultative Group on Indonesia (CGI) and the Government of Indonesia – CGI Meeting, 1–2 February 2000, Jakarta." Jakarta and Brussels, 21 January.

——. "The Indonesian Government Must Resolutely and Properly Protect its Citizens." Jakarta and Brussels: Joint NGO Statement on the Sampit Tragedy, 1 March 2001a.

——. "Statement of the NGO Coalition on the Constitutional Stalemate and the Abuse of Power by State Institutions." Jakarta and Brussels, 22 July 2001b.

——. "Statement for the CGI meeting in Jakarta November 2001 – Indonesia's Debt Burden: When and How the Creditors are Accountable?" Jakarta and Brussels, 21 September 2001c.

——. "Reform the CGI, Cancel the New Order Debt, Reform the Military." INFID Statement on upcoming CGI Meeting 7–8 November 2001. Jakarta and Brussels, October 2001d.

——. "The Responsibility of the State to Guarantee the Safety and Integrity of Human Rights Defenders." Jakarta and Brussels, 3 April 2002a.

——. "NGO Coalition for a New Constitution on the Commission for Amendment of the 1945 Constitution." Jakarta and Brussels, April 2002b.

Jubilee South, Focus on the Global South, AWEPON, and the Centro de Estudios Internacionales, with the support of the World Council of Churches. "The World Bank and the PRSP: Flawed Thinking and Failing Experiences." Washington, DC: World Bank, 16 November 2001. http://www.worldbank.org/poverty/strategies/review/jsouth1.pdf.

Junaidi, A., and Nurbianto, B. "Mobs Signal Return of Political Thuggery." *Jakarta Post*, 1 April 2002. http://www.thejakartapost.com/detailheadlines.asp?fileid=20020401.@01&irec=0 1/4/02.

Kahin, G. *Nationalism and Revolution in Indonesia*. Ithaca, NY: Cornell University Press, 1952.

Koesnadi, H. *Environmental Legislation in Indonesia*. Yogyakarta: Gadjah Mada University Press, 1987.

Kothari, R. *State against Democracy: In Search of Humane Governance*. Delhi: Ajanta Publications, 1988.

Lissner, J. *The Politics of Altruism*. Geneva: Lutheran World Federation, 1976.

Marshall, K. "Combating Corruption in Indonesia – Aide-Memoire of the World Bank Team." Jakarta, 20 September 1998. http://www.worldbank.org/html/extdr/offrep/eap/corgov/amkm6.html.

Masindo Business Media Ltd. "Draft Law of Foundation (sic) (Rancangan Undang-Undang Yayasan)." In *Indonesian Associations and NGOs*, 2nd edn, VIII–XXXIV. Singapore and Jakarta, 2001.

Ministry of Home Affairs (Menteri Dalam Negeri). "Instruksi Menteri Dalam Negeri Nomor 8 Tahun1990 tentang Pembinaan Lembaga Swadaya Masyarakat." Jakarta, 1990.

Moestafa, Berni K., and Kurniawan, Hari. "Time, the Next Hurdle for 2004 General Election." *Jakarta Post*. 13 August 2002.

NDI (National Democratic Institute for International Affairs). "Road to Constitutional Reform: The 2000 MPR Annual Session." Jakarta and Washington, DC, October 2000. Online via http://www.ndi.org.

Nurbianto, Bambang. "Betawi Groups Plan Massive Rally to Thwart Sutiyoso's Re-election." *Jakarta Post*, 9 September 2002.

Ostergaard, G. *Non-violent Revolution in India: Sarvodaya, Vinobha Bhave and the Total Revolution of Jayaprakash Narayan.* New Delhi: Gandhi Peace Foundation, 1985.

Riker, James van. "The State, Institutional Pluralism, and Development from Below: The Changing Political Parameters of State–NGO Relations in Indonesia." Ithaca, NY: Cornell University. Ph.D. dissertation, 1998.

Rooke, P. "National Integrity, the Enemy of Corruption, Collusion and Nepotism: A Transparency International Perspective – Remarks by Peter Rooke, Member of the Board of Transparency International and Chief Executive of TI Australia, at 12th INFID Conference 'The Challenge for NGOs: The Role of Civil Society in Indonesia', Bali, 14–17 September 1999." Jakarta: INFID, 1999. Online via http://www.infid.be.

Sakai, Yumiko, ed. "Indonesia – Flexible NGOs vs. Inconsistent State Control." In *The State and NGOs: Perspective from Asia*, edited by Shinichi Shigetomi. Singapore: Institute of Southeast Asian Studies, 2002, pp. 161–77.

Schreiner, K. Brussels: INFID European Liaison Office, 23 July 2001. http://www.infid.be/jointstatement010722konstitusienbackground.html.

Severino, Jean-Michel. "Indonesia's Road to Recovery: Opening Statement to the Consultative Group for Indonesia by Vice President East Asia and the Pacific, The World Bank." Paris, 29 July 1998. http://www.worldbank.org/html/extdr/offrep/eap/jmssp072998.htm.

Soetjipto, Adi Andojo. "Fighting Corruption in Indonesia." Jakarta, *c.* 2000. http://www.fes.or.kr/Corruption/papers/Indonesien.htm.

Tempo Interactive. "FBR Desperately Seeking Wardah." Jakarta, 2002. No.30/II/2–8 April, 2002. http://www.tempointeraktif.com/majalah/eng/nat-3.html.

Uhlin, Anders. *Indonesia and the "Third Wave of Democratisation": The Indonesian Pro-Democracy Movement in a Changing World.* Richmond, Surrey, UK: Curzon, 1997.

World Bank. "Republic of Indonesia Social Safety Net Adjustment Loan (SSNAL)." ID-BB-63939. Jakarta, 1999a. http://www.worldbank.org/html/extdr/offrep/eap/projects/ssnal/ssnalexecsum.htm.

——. "Indonesia: Community-based Monitoring." Washington, DC, *c.* 1999b. Civic Engagement in Public Expenditure Management Case Studies. http://www.worldbank.org/participation/web/webfiles/cepemcase7.htm.

——. "Anti-Corruption: Civil Society Participation." 2001. http://www.worldbank.org/publicsector/anticorrupt/civilsociety.htm.

——. Poverty Reduction Strategy Papers (PRSP). Washington, DC, 2002. Online via http://www.worldbank.org/poverty/strategies/index.htm.

YLBHI (Foundation of Indonesian Legal Institutions). "The Military are 'Fishing in Troubled Waters' – Analysis on the Ordnance Planning for Safety and Security of the Nation." Jakarta, August 1999. http://www.desaparecidos.org/kontras/doc/fishing.html.

10 Constrained NGOs and arrested democratization in Singapore

Beng Huat Chua

Introduction

Domestic and international events in the 1990s, culminating in the 1997 Asian financial crisis, pushed all the capitalist countries in Southeast Asia into the process of political democratization. The exception is Singapore, where the hegemonic People's Action Party (PAP) still constitutes the single-party dominant government. Through a combination of overtly repressive measures, particularly in the early years of its ascendancy to power, and the ability to forge an ideological hegemony in terms of the pragmatics of economic development as nation-building, the PAP has never been seriously challenged since it took power in 1968.

However, even though the political structure has therefore remained largely unchanged over the last four decades, the society has changed radically as a result of the successful economic development. State–society relations have visibly improved since Lee Kuan Yew, the founding prime minister, stepped down in 1990 after holding office for more than 30 years. The second and current prime minister, Goh Chok Tong, promised a more consultative government as soon as he took office, and this promise has largely been kept. Individuals and groups who define their realities differently from the ruling regime have thus become more visible. In the process, some groups have gained greater discursive autonomy, even if the spaces to disseminate their views continue to be constrained by either the state-owned or the pro-government publicly listed media companies.

However, greater consultation in itself has not led and does not necessarily lead to social and political structural changes. On the contrary, it can contribute to further penetration of the state into the social body via a capillary mode of governance suggested by Foucault (1979: 26). Public opinion waxes and wanes on different issues, which can influence public policies, but structural political changes, including the sharing of power between different political parties, are unlikely in Singapore for the next 10–20 years.[1] This structural stability is grounded in a state ideology that, while not wholeheartedly embraced, nevertheless deeply resonates with the majority of the population.[2]

Peace and harmony as devices of social control

An ideology of survival is central to the PAP's entire ideological structure. It is a truism that every small nation faces the multidimensional question of its viability. However, Singapore is one of the few countries to have successfully transformed this into an explicit national ideology, making it the central rationalizing conceptual structure for the actions of private individuals, voluntary organizations, and the state itself. This transformation has been at least partly historically determined.

When Singapore separated from Malaysia in 1965, the immediate question facing its citizens and political leaders was how the newly independent island-nation could survive. The stark reality of a geographically tiny island without any natural resources made it relatively easy for the political leadership to transform the anxiety of survival into a national ideology. The leadership convinced itself that this is the central national concern at all times and has actively inscribed this as a central anxiety in citizens' minds and memories.

That this anxiety has indeed sunk deeply into the collective psyche is reflected in the commonsensical expression that hangs on the lips of Singaporeans, "Nobody owes us a free lunch," and by the fact that both the leaders and the led view economic success as the collective will to survive and thrive, without any apparent awareness of the historical contingencies of the new international division of labor, which from the 1960s till the early 1990s brought foreign capital investments not only to Singapore but to the other so-called dragon economies. Survival anxiety is the foundational idea for the PAP's ideological hegemony, in the strict Gramscian sense of moral leadership.[3]

Under this master ideological concept of survival, the political leadership deploys an entire constellation of ideological concepts and political practice, two of which are central: industrial peace and racial harmony. The political leadership, in collaboration with corporatist unionists, translated the intrinsic logic of global capitalist competition into an ideological constant of the necessity of "industrial peace" for the island-nation's economic survival. That "racial harmony" is central to social stability and order was only too obvious to all among Singapore's postcolonial multiracial population. That both concepts appear to be "naturally," "morally" good and desirable is central to their ideological efficacy, while embedding them in the PAP national ideology was again partly historically determined.

The political mobilization to decolonize Singapore immediately after World War II was led by communist-leaning intellectuals. Industrial actions and work stoppages, organized by trade unions with the support of other left-wing elements, such as Chinese-educated students, were the tactics of working-class political mobilization. English-educated emerging political leaders, such as Lee Kuan Yew and his British university-educated social democrat friends, were devoid of grassroots connections, which in 1954 forced them into an uneasy coalition with union leaders to establish the PAP. The party went on to win the first fully elected majority government in 1959. The inevitable split of the uneasy partnership took place in 1963, when the left-wing faction broke off to form the Barisan Socialis

(Socialist Front). The rest of the party retained the name PAP, and reinvented itself as a "moderate" and "pragmatic" government more interested in economic development as nation-building than ideological disputes.

For the PAP government, smashing the political left and its affiliated trade unions became the same act as establishing the requisite industrial peace for promoting economic development. Radical unions and Chinese student organizations were deregistered and their leaders jailed for allegedly legally proscribed communist activities, while pro-PAP government trade unions were established under the National Trades Union Congress. New legal structures for industrial relations, including the prohibition of strikes before compulsory arbitration, were legislated to constrain trade union activities. These repressive measures caused the Barisan Socialis to boycott parliament sittings, where it had a respectable one-third of the seats. It subsequently boycotted the 1968 general election altogether, which proved to be political suicide, as it opened the way for the PAP to capture absolute parliamentary power into the twenty-first century.

As for race relations, the colonial legacy of a multiracial population did not cohere as a "nation." The three visible racial groups of Chinese, Malays, and Indians, in numerically descending order, were each oriented towards the political struggles of their own homelands: the Communist–Kuomintang civil war in China, and the fight for independence from British colonial rule in both Peninsula Malaya and India. However, it should be noted that there was the beginning of a pan-Malayan movement among segments of the different races, united by the politics of decolonization. In 1964, race violence between Chinese and Malays broke out, leaving 23 dead and hundreds injured. This supposed tenuousness of racial coexistence has since been raised to the level of another central national anxiety. The population is constantly being reminded of the potential for racial violence, the better to use this imagined and imaginable disruption as a reason for government social and political interventions (Dayang 2001; Low 2001).

The PAP has always been a multiracial political party, and racial representation has been institutionalized in government through the establishment of the group representative constituency (GRC) in the electoral system.[4] GRCs are formed by grouping several constituencies together. During general elections, each contesting political party must field a team of candidates for the GRC with at least one non-Chinese member reflecting the 1:3 ratio of the non-Chinese to Chinese population. The team that garners the most aggregated votes wins all the contested seats in the GRC. One consequence of this parliamentary innovation is that the racial demographic reality is permanently translated directly into a parliamentary reality, producing an "elected" government with a permanent majority of Chinese representation.[5]

With every emergent issue in an increasingly complex economy and society, the government almost always veers back to the central theme of national survival and its constellation of component elements, which collectively constitute the discursive and practical space of politics and social control in Singapore. This space is highly elastic and extremely expansive. The need to maintain racial harmony and industrial peace can be and is constantly being expanded by the government into an undefined and generalized claim of the need to maintain "social order," which in turn allegedly requires a wide range of administrative interventions from controlling the media to policing everything from organizational activities to the public behavior of individuals. This last includes suing critics and other politicians for defaming and thus threatening to diminish the authority of PAP political leaders (Tay 2000: 176).

Put differently, "by repeatedly focusing anxiety on the fragility of the new nation, its ostensible vulnerability to every kind of exigency, the state's originating agency is periodically reinvoked and ratified, its access to wide-ranging instruments of power in the service of national protection continually consolidated" (Heng and Devan 1992: 343).

The past 40 years of Singapore's political history is strewn with incidents of the political repression of individuals and institutions in the name of maintaining social order: editors of Chinese newspapers have been jailed on grounds of "fanning" Chinese chauvinism, while an English-language newspaper was shut down on the grounds that its external financiers were using it to disrupt Singapore's political peace (Seow 1998). The Newspaper and Printing Presses Act empowers the government to shut down any press or publications by revoking its annual license. Young social workers who were trying to gain rights for Filipino domestic workers were detained without trial under the Internal Security Act for allegedly engaging in a "Marxist conspiracy" to overthrow the state (Haas 1989). The same act empowers the minister of home affairs to detain anyone, if he deems that person has acted in a manner prejudicial to the country's security or public order.

Licenses are required from the Public Entertainment Licensing Unit (PELU) of the police department for public entertainment – the Public Entertainment Act empowers the licensing officer, a member of the police force, to "place whatever restrictions on the venue and timing, number of speakers and use of amplification as he sees fit, so long as it is not an arbitrary decision, wholly without justification" (Tay 2000: 175). Certain artistic practices, such as forum theatre, in which the audience is asked to participate directly in the unfolding of the play, are banned on the grounds that they might incite civil disturbances, while plays have been banned on the grounds that they allegedly step on racial, religious, and other imagined or imaginable public sensitivities.[6]

By classifying public speech-making as public entertainment, the government subjects such activities to similar licensing requirements, on the grounds that it can threaten peace and social order, a move that violates the constitutionally protected rights to free speech.[7] The state reluctantly conceded to the establishment of a "free speech" corner in mid-2000, but anyone who wants to speak there must first register with the police station nearby, and no broadcasting instruments are permitted, despite the busy traffic din that surrounds the space and drowns out nonamplified voices. Furthermore, speeches about race and religious issues remain prohibited. It is little wonder, therefore, that two months after its opening the space fell silent.

The restrictive social and political space fashioned by the PAP is undoubtedly made bearable by the legendary economic success that has placed Singaporeans among the highest paid per capita population in the world; has spawned a substantial middle class of wage-earning professionals, civil servants, and managers employed by multinational corporations; and has greatly improved the material life of Singaporeans across the board. This very impressive economic growth, translated into an expansion of material life, is the reason why an overwhelming majority of Singaporeans continue to support the government.

The PAP in turn lives off and reinforces its ideological hegemony, arguing that Singapore's four decades of national economic growth are directly attributed to the exercise of the politically and socially repressive measures that have maintained industrial peace and social and political order. As I have pointed out elsewhere:

> Looking to the medium-term future: the rich will continue to enjoy an intentionally highly privatized life, well screened from public view; the present middle class will continue to strive to build a better material life for itself and its progeny; while the poor, having tasted some success in obtaining concessions from the government, will continue to use their votes to achieve further gains. None of these classes intends to bring about a radical restructuring, so long as the PAP government is able to keep the economy growing.
>
> (Chua and Tan 1999: 155)

This mass loyalty across class divisions, underpinned by an ideological framework, represents a tremendous inertia for political structural changes. Thus, contrary to the assumption of the causal linkage between the rise of the middle class and general political democratization,[8] Singapore shows that a middle class whose "good life" is dependent on government economic policies has very little interest in disrupting the political structure and stability that are delivering that good life, even when this stability is maintained by repressive measures.

Within this general political inertia, pockets of individuals continue to try to stretch the system in order to have more space for thoughts, expression, and practices, but without any apparent desire to overhaul the system. It is against this almost uncanny political stability that we must assess the development of civil society in an arena where economic globalization is embraced wholeheartedly in the interests of national survival.

To sum up the current context for civil society, in basic rights such as the rights of speech, association, and assembly, Singaporean law "is marked by a fairly large number of permissions and permits that need to be obtained before exercising these rights" (Tay 2000: 179), so much so that the government admits that the general impression of Singapore and Singaporeans has been "Anything not explicitly permitted, is proscribed." One of the consequences of this, which is itself a cost of maintaining absolute control of political power, is a generalized disenchantment and disinterest in public affairs among the population. This is reflected in the common observation that Singaporeans are apathetic when it comes to politics and public affairs.

If it is in fact apathy, it results from an awareness of the constraints of politics – and in this sense it is more an ennui that results from knowing that nothing is going to change in government routines than an apathy that reflects political ignorance. This generalized disinterest is reflected in the difficulties of convincing those who are already established in their professional careers to enter politics – even the PAP has difficulty recruiting fresh candidates at every general election, let alone the other by now moribund political parties, which are known locally as "opposition" parties, for having been in permanent, ineffective opposition since the island-nation's founding.

Local civil society development

Singaporeans' generalized disinterest in politics and public affairs has become a concern of the PAP leadership since the beginning of the 1990s. The leadership's rhetoric of the need to engage the citizenry in public affairs, especially the young, has become more urgent since 1991, when the then newly appointed cabinet minister of information and the arts, George Yeo, suggested that the large shade of the state had killed off much of the growth under it, and it was time to prune the tree. He called for more room for the development of the "civic society," a strategic choice of words that emphasizes civic duty, rather than "civil society," with its conventional understanding of freedom from the state.

This was followed by the push to increase public knowledge of the short history of the nation, with a multimillion-dollar exhibition and the publication of Lee Kuan Yew's memoirs. Then came the Singapore 21 Committee, which was convened in 1997–8 and led by younger MPs and selected high-profile individuals, with the aim of re-engineering the state-dominated public sphere by stressing "active citizenry."[9] This committee has generated few tangible results, but it has provided critics of the state with the ready ideological position of reminding the administrative apparatus of the government's promises for an active citizenry, whenever any part of the civil service appears to be out of line. After the November 2001 general election, the government convened a Remaking Singapore Committee, again with the younger members of the newly elected parliament, who promised to respect no sacred cows and to canvass public opinion from every Singaporean who wished to speak his or her mind.

However, the newly elected parliament did not sit until April 2002, five months after its election. At its first sitting, the ex-speaker of the House, Tan Soo Koon, blasted the government for the long delay at a time when serious economic and social issues were unfolding. During this period, Singapore was experiencing its worst economic recession since 1965, and issues of race had been brewing since the discovery of an Islamic fundamentalist group's plans to terrorize US expatriates in Singapore. He further wanted the ruling PAP to lift the rule that ruling-party MPs had to vote according to the party's desires, whatever their members' personal preferences, in order to allow for more free and frank statements from the party's own ranks in parliament – thus admitting that they do not always speak their minds. Finally, he chastised the government for not giving credit to groups and individuals who had made important contributions in terms of ideas and efforts in public affairs.

These criticisms, perhaps because they were made by someone who suffered in silence as the Speaker of the House for more than a decade, are both telling and ironic. All these attempts at opening-up began in the 1990s, and they all aimed at engaging the public, especially the young. The government will respond, it will even concede arguments made by others – but it holds all the initiatives for action and inaction on all fronts, because it holds absolute political power. Nor is there any sign that it is willing to share this power with other political parties or with other social groups in specific areas of public interest.

Not surprisingly, therefore, numerous laws and administrative practices that constrain the public sphere remain in place. In some instances, constraints have intensified, especially in view of the globalization of issues which transcend national boundaries, such as the environment, gender and sexuality, and labor and human rights, where connections between interested parties are enabled and mediated by new means and channels of communications. For example, as recently as 2001, legislation was passed to constrain civil society organizations by categorizing them as either "political" or "nonpolitical."

As is typical, the criteria distinguishing the two categories are very vague, which enables the authorities to make *ad hoc* rather than in-principle decisions, thus providing expansive policing powers to the state agencies. This vagueness of criteria makes it easier to impose tough *ad hoc* constraints in areas of public statements, public activities, and funding matters on allegedly political organizations (the same logic of vagueness can be seen in a discussion later in this chapter on the legal requirement for registering Internet websites). One explicit constraint is that "political organizations" are placed under strict funding regulations, where donations from foreign sources are disallowed and private contributions beyond a certain sum of money have to be registered. The consequence is not only a further restriction on the already very weak oppositional political parties, but the stifling of civil society organizations' activities.

The difficulty opposition parties have in fundraising was raised by the now retired veteran politician J.B. Jeyaratnam thus:

> Whilst the PAP have no problem at all in raising monies, the opposition parties face the almost insurmountable obstacle – the fear among our people to give any monies to an opposition party in case the government finds out and they are made to suffer. It is largely a fear self-imposed, but the PAP capitalizes on this *fear* and will not do anything to help people to rid themselves of this fear.
> (2000: 113, original emphasis)

One organization clearly illustrating the effects of the new regulations is the Think Center, founded in 1999, when it was registered as a business by its founder, James Gomez. He did this to avoid the relatively more arduous task of registering a civil society organization, which is subject to the much more restrictive jurisdiction of the Societies Act. The act requires a registered society to only serve the interests of its declared constituency of members, disallows any collaboration with other registered societies for common causes that are not within the specific purview of the organization's declared objectives, and disallows any political activities, which are designated as strictly the business of political parties.

The center's founder called himself an entrepreneur of politics; its business was presumably to provide political consultancy, a field with rather slim pickings in Singapore. The center collaborated with other organizations, including political parties, to organize public forums on various political issues, such as transparency in elections and limits on the rights of assembly and organization. Overall, it was able to navigate the minefields of Singapore's restricted political terrain with great agility, careening close to the edge of the law without ever breaking it.

One example of its highly attention-grabbing activities was the organizing of a mass rally, ostensibly to raise funds to help J.B. Jeyaratnam to raise the legal fees and damages he had to pay to some PAP MPs for defamation suits. The funds were to be raised from selling T-shirts and a book of Jeyaratnam's speeches (2000), but even at 50 Singapore dollars a copy there was no likelihood at all of coming up with the significant sum he needed. The objective of the rally was obviously something other than fundraising, and, during the process of organizing it, the press reported on every objection raised by various government authorities, from PELU, to the police security, to the license to sell the books, with Gomez very much quoted and photographed.

In Singapore's political aridity, the center was able to attract an inordinate amount of free media publicity through activities like the rally. It quickly became the talking point of all Singaporeans who read the daily newspaper, with one newspaper giving the founder the accolade of "Headline Grabber: When there's no news, he makes it" (*Today*, 3 April 2001). Of course it also drew the attention of the policing authorities, who were just waiting for an opportunity to rein the center in. So, when the parliament passed the categorization rules, the Think Center was designated a political organization, in spite of the fact that it was registered as a private business.

Soon after, Gomez resigned from the center's chairmanship to continue his employment with the German government-funded Friedrich Naumann Foundation, which moved its office to Bangkok. He subsequently joined the opposition Workers Party and returned to Singapore but failed to contest the November 2001 general election, because the documents for his team to stand in the election were misfiled and the team was disqualified. The center was never the same and is now a ghost of its past, occasionally sending out messages on the Internet, without attracting any further media attention.

The effect of the new categorization scheme even reached into the Internet, an avenue of alternative public space that has been commonly touted as an instrument of democratization because it might escape official censorship. In August 2001, a website called Sintercom, which had been running for five years, closed down. The public reason given by its founder was that he was "too tired to go on." This exhaustion referred not to the physical energy it took to maintain the site but to that induced by "the process of liaising with the Singapore Broadcasting Authority [SBA] over the material at the site" after the founder was asked to register it with the authority as a political site.

In compliance, he submitted Internet articles to the SBA for vetting and ruling, but received no clear response or no response at all. This was probably because the SBA does not have any clear idea of its own regarding what constitutes "political." The founder's final frustrated words were:

> I was thus put squarely in a position where I could be sued by the govern-ment at any moment for any of the content that someone in SBA may deem unacceptable. But I was not given any means by which I could prevent these lawsuits by removing any "offending" content. The only way was to practice extreme self-censorship. This ran against everything Sintercom stood for . . . the only honorable thing left to do was close it down.
>
> (*Straits Times*, 27 April 2002)

The SBA retorted that it does "not pre-censor objectionable material on the Net, but encourages industry self-regulation," without any qualm or apparent awareness of how this places people in a double bind. To individuals in civil society, the entire episode was the "collateral damage of an official policy that wants to make sure certain politically incendiary things don't get on the Net" (*Straits Times*, 27 April 2002). All these events took place within a country that as part of its strategy to globalize its tiny economy is among the most wired in the world.

This suggestion for self-regulation enables the relevant authorities to hide their hands, as each act of censorship is inevitably a political act that discloses and publicizes the state's repressive presence. Seeing this, some theatre companies, which have been given the same "freedom," choose to continue to send their scripts to the censors, so that the latter have to do their job and thus disclose themselves from behind the veil of "liberalization." Similarly, amendments in the Newspaper and Press Printing Act empower the incumbent minister of information and the arts to limit local circulation of international publications which "engage" in Singapore's domestic politics, leaving undefined what constitutes "engaging." In the interests of profit, many of these international publications have "resigned themselves to the special conditions of operating in Singapore after being in dispute over, and penalized for, their coverage" (Rodan 2000: 220).

This penchant to encourage self-censorship is locally conceptualized in terms of "out of bound markers," a term borrowed from the game of golf, which is favored by government cabinet ministers. The idea is that those who step out of bounds will be penalized either by strong public rebuke from the government or by being taken to court for defamation or other civil violations, where very significant financial compensation can be sought. The problem is that no one knows where and how these markers are delineated, leaving the government huge discretion as to when it can decide to take action against alleged violators. Indeed, it appears that the markers are in fact shifting goalposts, leaving individuals, groups, and institutions permanently guessing and vulnerable to negative official sanction.

Although the immediate consequence of the new categorization scheme was the eclipse of the Think Center and the Sintercom website, its general effect was to isolate civil society organizations in Singapore from international connections. But in a sense this is only a formalization of what was already common practice in Singapore's civil society. Most of the more established civil society organizations that directly engage the government in public debate, such as the Nature Society, an environmental group, and the Association of Women for Action and Research (AWARE), a women's interest group, have always been very careful to avoid foreign funding, because they are keenly aware that accepting same could return to haunt them. They have taken to heart lessons from past instances when newspapers were banned and individuals labeled "stooges of foreign interests" on account of their receiving foreign funds. It is significant to note that these organizations have not been reclassified as political organizations and their continued existence and effectiveness appear unaffected by the new regulations.[10]

The absence of global connections among civil society organizations is replicated at the regional level. This absence of regional connections is very significantly an effect of the agreement among members of the Association of Southeast Asian Nations (ASEAN) not to interfere in each other's domestic affairs. Thus, for example, the very serious annual environmental problem of forest burning in Indonesia, which covers Singapore and parts of Malaysia in a thick haze, has never attracted collaboration among the very active environmental groups in those three countries to contest the Indonesian state agencies. Instead, attempts to alleviate the problem were left to official negotiations between government agencies. Given the problematic political conditions in ASEAN member states, including the political legitimacy of some of the current regimes such as Myanmar with its military junta, the etiquette of international relations has had the effect of restricting civil society organizations from forming international connections.

However, in spite of a general atmosphere of constraint, some civil society organizations are given a greater degree of freedom than others. Among them are women's, environmental, and consumer-protection organizations. The issues raised by such organizations are unavoidably political: women's equality is a political issue in a society in which the government's ideology is openly patriarchal; in a land-scarce island-nation, environmental issues are invariably linked to issues of competition for land resources between social and economic developments and nature conservation; in a society where many of the service provisions are directly regulated by the state – public transportation, housing, and health – demands for consumer rights often turn into critiques of the public authorities and, indirectly, of government. For example, every price hike in the cost of public transportation becomes a controversy between consumers and the Public Transport Commission and invariably receives a large amount of debate and publicity in the local media.

Nevertheless, these organizations are not politically proscribed for two reasons. First, by keeping within the prescribed constraints for registered societies, they avoid state intervention: they champion only causes that are directly relevant to their constituencies and do not stray into direct criticism of formal political practices, structures, or individual politicians. Second, all these organizations claim to be operating for the public good. Gender equality is increasingly unavoidable, as women constitute up to half the labor force in a country that is severely short of labor. Being environmentally friendly is important to Singapore's national image as a "garden city"; indeed, it has been claimed that a green environment is one of its economic selling points in attracting foreign direct investments.

Furthermore Singapore's consumer association was in fact established by the government-friendly National Trades Union Congress as an institution to safeguard the interests of consumers, which obviously includes union members who may not have the means to protect themselves from unsavory retail and service providers. It is because of this claim to being in the public interest, rather than sectarian self-interest, that such civil society organizations are to a significant degree morally protected from repressive actions by the state.

The irrepressible Internet

Nevertheless, there are cracks in the system which defy the government's relentless effort at maintaining seamless control over public space. One such crack is, of course, the Internet. Whatever the shortcomings in arguments that promote the Internet as an instrument of democracy, it certainly has been useful for civil society activists in Singapore to create alternative spaces to local government-controlled and self-censoring media. One example is the transformation of the Sintercom website. After the founder shut it down and placed the archives in the public domain in August 2001, the site splintered and morphed into several different components, managed by different individuals.

In May 2002 it was reported that a website named New Sintercom was operating under an anonymous editor or editors, who "have also tried to take it beyond the reach of current laws by bringing it to parts of cyberspace that are difficult to police." In obvious parody to the founding strongman Prime Minister Lee Kuan Yew, the editor(s) has the pseudonym of Kee Luan Few. Maintaining anonymity goes against the conventional demand of local media, which will not publish anonymous letters in the forum pages. The Singapore Broadcasting Authority (SBA) has so far not asked the new site to register as a political site, as it did the old Sintercom, but noted that it would have to register if so asked. The SBA further suggested that "there is no need for anyone to go underground or hide behind the cloak of anonymity," which, in view of the government's past record of suppression of free speech, is sadly not a sentiment shared by the majority of Singaporeans. In obvious defiance of the law, the editor(s) responded that he would not register the site if requested to, and challenged the SBA to block the site if it so chose.

In addition to the New Sintercom, two other bits of the old site have been continued as newsgroups, which are not subject to SBA registration requirements, or as virtual notice boards that do not reside in any particular website and are, hence, hard to regulate by law. The editors of the two groups are known: SG-Daily is currently run by a researcher in the Institute of Policy Studies, a government-sponsored think tank, and the Singapore Forum is currently ran by a Singaporean student who is studying law in the United Kingdom. The New Sintercom has hyperlinks to these two notice boards, whose editors claim no knowledge of the New Sintercom editor(s).

Until the designation of specific sites as "political," the Singapore government, knowing full well that there is no fail-safe means of regulating the Internet, made a symbolic gesture of blocking known pornography sites. Then, given its obsessive need to control public discussions, it unavoidably added that regulations are needed to "maintain harmony and protect national security," which explains the demand that designated political sites be registered. The consequence of this, which is best put by the founder of the original Sintercom, is that the "SBA's policy of going after sites like Sintercom is not the conversion of such sites into ineffectual self-censoring ones, but that such sites will become anonymous and be hosted overseas."[11]

The internationalization of Islam and its disruptions

Significantly, it takes a distant event such as the destruction of the World Trade Center in New York City on 11 September 2001 to expose the cracks in an apparently seamlessly policed political space. Such disruptions are surprisingly close to the surface of social calm. All it takes is for a small segment of the population to take up linkages – whether material or ideological, such as trade or identity respectively – with individuals or collectives outside Singapore, to create social and political ripples within it. Thus the internationalization of Islam created a potential connection between Muslims in Singapore with others in the global Islamic community, which in turn opened up some spaces in the domestic public sphere.[12]

As noted above, Singapore is in the middle of a Malay–Muslim world. Beneath the surface of an official minimalist multiracialism of mutual tolerance with increasingly rigidifying racial boundaries, all three races had some dissatisfaction, each for their own reasons. However, because of a policy that suppresses open debate and discussion of race in an apparent desire to maintain harmony, sentiments of disaffection were left to simmer, glossed over by the mobilization of the population for economic nation-building.

Economic improvement had been broad based during the 30 years of rapid economic growth (1965–95). However, economic inequalities were also unavoidable, and the Malay–Muslim population remained relatively behind the Chinese and Indian communities. Here, the legacy of the colonial period proved to be more tenacious than perhaps expected. During the colonial period the Malays were favored with jobs in the lowest rank of the colonial administrative services, such as policeman, postman, and even the military. However, they were mainly viewed as rural folk who would continue to earn their living by agriculture. They were therefore provided only a rudimentary vernacular education in the Malay language that did not equip them to participate in the urban economy. Consequently, relative to the Chinese and the Indians, they were not nearly as well prepared to seize the opportunities that were made available by the rapid industrialization that took place in the first two decades after decolonization.

This historical legacy is slowly being redressed with common public education, and there is now a visible, emergent Malay middle class. The government balm to the persistent economic inequality along racial lines was to counsel each of the races not to compare themselves across racial lines but to take note of the fact that each community has made significant economic progress relative to its own past. One should not expect such a strategy to hold for long, as the inequalities were, and continue to be, all too apparent, and they intensified as the economy grew. Furthermore, in addition to this economic outcome, the Malay–Muslim community has other grievances.

The visible economic differences also tended to shade into the question of cultures. The global resurgence of Islam following the Iranian revolution at the end of the 1970s did not leave the Singapore Islamic community untouched: local Malay–Muslims began to take their religion much more seriously as reflected in overt appearance and behaviors. For example, beginning with the younger and better-educated individuals who were attuned to the globalization of Islam, Muslim women began to wear headdresses and loose-fitting outfits, forgoing the body-conscious sarong and *kebaya*, which are still commonly found through Southeast Asia. Injunctions about food are also taken more seriously, beyond just the taboo of eating pork: food items are divided into *halal* and *haram*, and only the former is acceptable. Enrollment has also increased in Muslim religious schools, the *Madrasahs*, where religious instruction has primacy over learning other subjects. The net effect of all these very visible symbolic practices has been increased social distance between Muslims and non-Muslims, rigidifying the racial boundaries.

The government began to express concern that religious school graduates, who generally fare poorly in the national examinations at primary and secondary levels, would be unemployable in the increasingly complex and knowledge-based economy. This in turn raised concerns among the Muslim community regarding possible government intervention in the religious schools, especially after it instituted a ten-year compulsory education for all children in early 2000. The religious schools agreed to incorporate the primary and secondary curricula of the national education system into their own teaching programs, alongside the religious instruction, but how the demands of the different curricula can be merged remains a question to be worked out by each school.

Perhaps the most significant dissatisfaction among Malay–Muslim Singaporeans is the issue of national service. Singapore has a conscripted armed force, and in principle all male Singapore citizens have to perform a minimum of two years of service in the armed forces. However, Malay youth were not called upon to serve in the first 15 years of the institution of national service, and it was not until the mid-1980s that their presence in the armed forces became noticeable, including in the officer ranks. The government admits publicly to this blatant discrimination. Its reason is that it did not want to put Malay–Muslims into a possible moral dilemma of having to choose to aim their weapons either at their compatriots or at their distant kin or fellow Muslims, should Singapore go to war with its Muslim neighbors. Geopolitics has placed the national loyalty of the Malay–Muslim Singaporean in a bind, some would say in doubt. The PAP government apparently does not expect to confront any military or imperialist ambitions on the part of the

People's Republic of China, which, while geographically farther away, is ethnically similar to the majority of Singaporeans.

Meanwhile, an emergent Malay–Muslim middle class with tertiary-educated professionals began to voice concerns about the economic state of their community. In the early 1980s, the PAP Malay MPs established a central council, Mendaki, with the aim of improving the educational achievements of Malay children, who were lagging behind Chinese and Indian children in schools. In the early 1990s, a group of Malay–Muslim professionals established the Association of Muslim Professionals (AMP), to provide an alternative voice and leadership to those of the Malay MPs, who, having to serve the PAP, the government, and thus the larger Singapore society, apparently have not adequately served the Malay community itself. AMP proposed in turn an alternative collective leadership structure that would be constituted of leaders from Malay–Muslim organizations that are independent of the government. This idea, first mooted at AMP's inaugural conference, was raised again in 2000, but was summarily dismissed by the government on the grounds that a collective structure would be racially divisive, because the Chinese and Indian communities would want to establish their own respective leadership structures.

Then came September 11. A group of young Muslims seized on this event to vent their dissatisfaction with the conditions of the Malays in Singapore. The president of Fateha (The Beginning, being the first chapter of the Koran) stated in the organization's website that Osama bin Laden represented Muslim interests better than the local MPs. This caused a huge public outcry, and political leaders, from the prime minister to parliamentary backbenchers and Malay community organizations, descended on the organization in a frenzy of public condemnation. Within a few days, the president of Fateha had resigned and the rest of the executive committee distanced themselves from his statements. Social and political isolation was immediate and effective.

The Singapore government, which is friendly to the United States, condemned the attacks. However, it is mindful of the fact that it is in a region where the largest Muslim community in the world is to be found, and it clearly distinguishes the larger community of Muslims from the extremists responsible for the bombings. Then, in late 2001, the plans of a cell of alleged al Qaeda members to harm US citizens in Singapore were discovered. Fifteen members of the cell were immediately detained under the Internal Security Act, which empowers the minister of home affairs to detain anyone without trial on grounds of suspicion of damaging national security; two members were released shortly thereafter; the rest remain in detention. This came as a shock not only to the Malay–Muslim community but also to the rest of the country, which has been complacent, even self-congratulatory, about the apparent racial harmony of the past 40 years.

Amidst the public trauma of the discovery of the cell, four Malay parents staged an act of civil disobedience, a rare event in Singapore. The parents decided to send their daughters to their respective schools wearing headdresses, in contravention of the school uniform rule. After two weeks of failed negotiations, the girls were suspended from the schools with the fate of their education left unresolved. In the meantime, the parents declined the Malaysian education authority's offer to take the students into Malaysian schools. The prime minister has suggested that the parents could take the government to court and challenge the school uniform rule, in view of the constitutional guarantee of freedom for religious beliefs. This has yet to come to pass.

These series of events within the Malay–Muslim community show that in spite of all the regulations and legislation to keep development of global social tendencies and organizations out of the domestic sphere – including the Religious Harmony Act which empowers the government to control proselytizing by "errant" religious speakers – serious slippages do seep into Singapore's social and cultural spaces. Furthermore, the potential for these ideas and organizations to be transformed into political issues is equally significant. The penetration of Islam, instead of other global civil society organizations or ideologies, is arguably aided by two factors. First, to the community of believers, religion occupies a much higher symbolic register than any worldly issue. Religion also occupies a much higher moral plane than any worldly morality, including that of the incumbent government.

Second, as mentioned earlier, Islam is the majority religion in the archipelagic Southeast Asia region, a fact that impresses on all the governments in the region, including Malaysia, Indonesia, the Philippines, Thailand, and of course Singapore, to deal very carefully with any issue regarding Islamic beliefs, practices, and organizations, lest it result in regional violence or other modes of disruption. This regional view of Islam was reaffirmed by the discovery of close links between the different alleged al Qaeda cells in Indonesia, Malaysia, and the Philippines, so much so that these nations have agreed on cooperative strategies for dealing with Islamic terrorist networks that operate across their national boundaries.

The future: a "new" nationalism?

The events following the September 11 bombings not only pressed the Muslim community into a defensive position vis-à-vis the other racial communities but forced the government to rethink its idea of multiracialism, which until then emphasized race as the essential division among the population that could potentially rupture into racial riots and violence. Drawing on past incidents of race violence, racial divisions have been used as a basis for state policing and intervention at the racial and religious boundaries. The population has been exhorted to be tolerant of each other's cultural and religious practices, particularly since 85 percent of Singaporeans live as neighbors in high-rise public housing estates, whose racial compositions are regulated by a quota system roughly proportionate to their respective proportion in the total population.

Faced with the threat that the racial divisions may indeed become entrenched and tear the country apart, the government did an about-turn in its race relations practices and began actively promoting interracial understanding as a necessary condition for containing any future "extremism." It immediately instructed grassroots organizations to organize intercommunity confidence circles to encourage cultural education across racial boundaries.

Community celebrations organized by these organizations used to have segregated dinner tables, where Muslims who do not eat pork and others who do sat at different tables. Now they are told to share tables, though each person will still abide by his or her own food preferences. Mosques and Chinese and Indian temples have been asked to open their doors and invite believers of other faiths to witness their respective rituals and ceremonies. Fortuitously, the first Muslim religious event after the series of publicly aired issues mentioned above was the ritual sacrifice at mosques to mark the end of the period of the Haj. Many Chinese Singaporeans witnessed for the first time the throat-slashing slaughter of the sacrificial lamb at the mosques.

In addition, race-based self-help organizations are being asked or volunteering to provide their services, particularly remedial classes for all needy students, regardless of race. This reverses the government's stubborn stance against previous criticisms that these race-based self-help organizations were disadvantages to minority groups (Ishak 1994).

Everywhere one turns, the government, individuals, and civil society organizations have been publicly displaying their desire to grow the common space they share with each other. At the beginning of the twenty-first century, Singapore appears to be waking up to the need for developing an ideological nationalism and not just maintaining a growth economy that will keep the population relatively materially satisfied and happy in its privatized racial cultures. In this new move towards nationalism, one of the necessary discursive and political institution-building ideas may be a civil definition of citizenship-based citizens' rights, regardless of race, religion, and language, as inscribed in the national pledge that every student in primary and secondary school has to recite during assembly. Indeed, this push to develop a greater common space contains within it the potential to encourage Singaporeans to insist that the government pay up on the pledge of a citizenship of rights and, hence, of greater political democratization.

Conclusion

With its economy intact, Singapore has not had to face the political transformations that have taken place in many of the Asian countries affected by the 1997 Asian financial crisis. The legitimacy of the PAP as the island-nation's dominant power remains intact. As one of the more successful corporatist governments, the PAP government has always depended on some forms of civil society participation to further its claim as "custodian" of the nation's interests and its legitimate hold on power. But the conditions for civil society organizations and activities continue to be highly circumscribed: within a generalized political culture of censorship and discouragement, if not overt repression, stringent legal requirements are imposed on all civil society organizations, especially those categorized as political organizations. Nevertheless, beneath the seemingly unchanged political structure, civil society activities have been expanding.

The level of constraints that civil society organizations face differs from one sphere of activity to another. For example, the more conventional ones, such as women's, environmental, and consumer groups, are given substantial space not only in the media but also in direct involvement with government practices and plans. For example, the Nature Society was involved in the development of a national green plan. These organizations are seen as working directly in the interest of the greater social good, even if they have criticized some government policies and actions. But those that are directly critical of the PAP's political practices are given shorter leashes.

Furthermore, to prevent civil society activities from achieving aggregated effects beyond a single organization's concerns and coalescing into a social movement, civil society organizations are legally constrained to stay within their declared constituencies and causes and are prohibited from sympathetically supporting each other's causes or sharing resources. Connections with international organizations are also seriously discouraged. All organizations are well aware of this and closely monitor themselves to avoid any connections, especially financial, from outside the country, lest they run the risk of being hastily deregistered by the state authorities. The only vector of globalization that is actively encouraged is the economic one.

Under these conditions, two types of civil society pose difficulties for state control. First and most obvious are Internet organizations that can escape the state's clutches by operating in cyberspace. Websites can be located anywhere, operated with great freedom under the relative protection of anonymity, and they are increasingly defying the strictures of political control. Furthermore, the PAP government appears to be responding to the issues raised on the Internet, if for no other reason than to "set the record straight" rather than letting "rumors" become truth by circulation.

The second group of organizations that pose problems for state control is those organized around officially recognized group-identity markers, such as race and religion. In many instances, the government has used these ascribed groups to carry out various welfare activities that it is either unable or unwilling to be directly involved in, such as providing additional welfare assistance to targeted individuals and households.

Furthermore, Singapore's local context has now been significantly influenced by the internationalization of Islam. Organized along a race–religion axis, the Malay–Muslim community has thrown up various civil society organizations with volunteer memberships, but they are based on an exclusive, ascribed status, combining "traditional" status with modern organizational structures and agendas. Among them are underground organizations that have transnational connections with other ideologically similarly disposed Islamic groups in Southeast Asia and beyond. The rise of these organizations has severely disrupted Singapore's complacent "racial harmony" of minimal racial tolerance for each other and may become a determining cause in the changing, future direction of its race relations and public policies.

Notes

1 I have on different occasions stated and restated this arrested development thesis (1994, 1997, and 2001) and have not yet been proven wrong by events in Singapore.
2 The absence of impact of an expanded civil society participation and voice in public affairs on the political structural change of a single-party dominant state can also be seen in the case of the People's Republic of China; see Chapters 2 and 5.
3 Chan Heng Chee, a local political scientist, analyzed the politics of survival (1971) soon after independence. On survival and the ideological hegemony of the PAP, see Chua (1995).
4 This is in contrast to Malaysia, where each of the same three components of the multiracial population is represented by its own racially exclusive political party. The three parties in turn constitute the major partners in the ruling coalition government.
5 The GRC arrangement also increases the difficulties for other political parties, which are already having difficulties finding desirable candidates who are acceptable to an increasingly educated and demanding electorate. The other political parties, which are generally funded from their personal pockets, also have difficulties funding their campaigns, including the hefty deposit of 13,000 Singapore dollars per candidate introduced in the 2001 general election.
6 In October 2000, a play that depicts family violence against women in Indian Muslim families was banned by the PELU because of objections from an all-male Indian Islamic organization and the central authority of Muslim religious organizations. For details see the extensive discussion in *Forum on Contemporary Arts and Society* (2001).
7 This regulation has been used against the secretary-general of the Singapore Democratic Party, Dr. Chee Soon Juan, who so far has been jailed three times for "providing public entertainment without a license" when he tried to give public speeches, after having been denied a license to speak at a designated time and public space.
8 For discussions on the possible linkage between the development of the middle class and democratization in Asia, see Rodan (1996: 1–13).
9 For details on Singapore 21, see the website: www. Singapore 21.org.sg.
10 For details on AWARE, the Nature Society, and some other civil society organizations, see Rodan (1996).
11 All the quotes in this section are drawn from the *Straits Times*, 8 May 2002.
12 Indeed, one could easily imagine similar processes at work among the Chinese population, as in the attempt by some Chinese to develop the idea and substance of a greater cultural China among the international Chinese diasporas (Tu 1991), and its local resonance inside Singapore in terms of the government-sponsored attempt to develop a Confucian value system among Singaporean Chinese.

References

Chan, Heng Chee. *Singapore: The Politics of Survival*. Singapore: Oxford University Press, 1971.
Chua, Beng Huat. "Arrested Development: Democratization in Singapore," *Third World Quarterly* 15, 4 (1994): 655–68.
——. *Communitarian Ideology and Democracy in Singapore*. London: Routledge, 1995.
——. "Still Awaiting New Initiatives: Democratization in Singapore," *Asian Studies Review* 21, 2–3 (1997): 120–33.
——. "Non-transformative Politics: Civil Society in Singapore." Paper presented at the Conference on Civil Society in Asia, Griffith University, Brisbane, Queensland, Australia, 10–12 July 2001.

——, and Joo Ean Tan. "Singapore: Where the New Middle Class Sets the Standard." In *Culture and Privilege in Capitalist Asia*, edited by Michael Pinches. London: Routledge, 1999, pp. 137–58.

Dayang Istiaisyah Hussin. "Textual Construction of a Nation: The Use of Merger and Separation." *Asian Journal of Social Science* 29, 1 (2001): 401–30.

Forum on Contemporary Arts and Society. The Necessary Stage. Singapore, 2001, pp. 173–210.

Foucault, Michel. *Discipline and Punish: The Birth of the Prison*. New York: Vintage, 1979.

Haas, Michael. "The Politics of Singapore in the 1980s." *Journal of Contemporary Asia* 19, 1 (1989): 48–76.

Heng, Geraldine, and Janadas Devan. "State Fatherhood: Politics of Nationalism, Sexuality and Race in Singapore." In *Nationalisms and Sexualities*, edited by A. Parker, M. Russo, D. Sommer and P. Yaegar. New York: Routledge, 1992.

Ishak, Lily Zubaidah Rahim. "The Paradox of Ethnic-based Self-help Groups." In *Debating Singapore: Reflective Essays*, edited by Derek Da Cunha. Singapore: Institute of Southeast Asian Studies, 1994, pp. 46–50.

Jeyaratnam, J.B. *Make it Right for Singapore: Speeches in Parliament 1997–1999*. Singapore: Jeya Publishers, 2000.

Low, Adeline Hwee Cheng. "The Past in the Present: Memories of the 1964 'Racial Riots' in Singapore," *Asian Journal of Social Science*, 29, 1 (2001): 431–56.

Rodan, Garry. "State–Society Relations and Political Opposition in Singapore." In *Political Opposition in Industrializing Asia*, edited by Garry Rodan. London: Routledge, 1996, pp. 95–127.

——. "Asian Crisis, Transparency and the International Media in Singapore," *Pacific Review*, 13, 2 (2000): 217–42.

Seow, Francis. *The Media Enthralled: Singapore Revisited*. Boulder, CO: Lynne Rienner, 1998.

Tay, Simon S.C. "Civil Society and the Law in Singapore: Three Dimensions for Change in the 21st Century." In *State–Society Relations in Singapore*, edited by Gillian Koh and Ooi Giok Ling. Singapore: Oxford University Press, 2000, pp. 170–89.

Tu, Wei-ming. "Cultural China: The Periphery as the Center," *Daedalus*, 120 (1991): 1–32.

Index

Note: page numbers in *italics* indicate tables or charts.

academic and research groups, 25, 47, 48, *49, 70, 86*
Academy of Chinese Culture, 81
accountability, 11, 151
activist groups, 87–88. *See also* protest groups
advocacy groups. *See also specific organizations*: China, 29–30, 37; Hong Kong, 69, *70*, 71, 89; Indonesia, 156, 158–59, 162; international support, 1; South Korea, 97, 107; Taiwan, 45, 47–52, 54, 86, *86*, 87
Africa, 17
age-related associations, 139
agriculture, 127, 134–36
Akihito, 114
Alliance of Taiwan Aborigines, 54
All-Indonesia Workers' Union (SPSI), 155
al Qaeda, 185
alternate civilities, 124, 136–42
alumni associations, 81, 139, 140
ancestral halls, 139
Anheier, Helmut, 12
animal advocacy, 55
Animal Protection Law, 55
An Ninh commune, 132–34
Anti-Corruption Forum, 163
Anti-Nuclear Alliance, 55
Asia Foundation, 34, 35, 160, 161–62
Asian Coalition for Housing Rights, 159
Asian financial crisis, 186
Asian Human Rights Charter, 54
Asian Human Rights Commission, 159
Asian Indigenous Peoples' Parliament (AIPP), 54
Asian-Pacific Public Affairs Forum (APPAF), 52–53

Association for Handicapped Youth, 31
Association for the Protection of the Handicapped and Orphans, 128
Association of Muslim Professionals (AMP), 184
Association of Southeast Asian Nations (ASEAN), 180
Association of the Blind, 128
Association of Women for Action and Research (AWARE), 180
Association to Sponsor Poor Patients, 128
Aum Shinrikyo, 114
authoritarianism: Hong Kong, 58, 73; impact on social organizations, 8–10; Indonesia, 148; South Korea, 97, 98–99; and state-society split, 7, 17; Taiwan, 42–45, 56, 84, 85, 91
autonomy of NGOs: China, 28, 30–34, 82–84; and funding issues, 6; Hong Kong, 58–59, 72; Indonesia, 151, 165; Singapore, 171, 180; Taiwan, 47–52, 56, 87

Barber, Benjamin, 12
Barisan Socialis (Socialist Front), 172–73
Basic Law, 71, 73, 88
Beijing, China, 20
Beijing Environment and Development Institute, 36
Beijing Philharmonic Orchestra Foundation, 27
Beijing Red Maple Women's Counseling Service Center, 35
Betawi Unity Forum, 158–59
Bill of Rights Ordinance (1991), 88
bonsai associations, 139

Boys and Girls Clubs Association, 61
breathing exercise groups (*qigong* groups),
    28, 81–82
bridging function of NGOs, 69
Buddha Light Mountain, 53
Buddhism, 10, 85, 87–88, 125–26, 141
Buddhist Association of the Republic of
    China, 87–88
Buddhist Compassion Relief Merit
    Society, 53
Buddhist elderly women's groups, 125–26,
    138, 139
budgets of NGOs, 49
Bureau of Industry and Commerce, 31
business-organized NGOs (BONGOs), 3,
    15, 25, 69, *70*, 127, 129–30. *See also*
    chaebols

Cao Dai, 141, 145n. 21
capitalism, 113, 116
case studies of NGOs, 102–6
categorizing NGOs. *See* types of social
    organizations
Catholicism, 61, 71, 125
censorship, 178–79, 181–82
Central Committee of the Chinese League
    of the CCP, 27
central governance, 116, 120
centripetal and centrifugal governance, 96
chaebols, 15, 103–5
charitable groups, 48, *49*, 56, 60, 61, 63,
    128
Charity Association, 128
Chee Soon Juan, 188n. 7
Chen Shui-bian, 121–22n. 5
Chess Association, 128
Chiang Ching-kuo, 43
Children Playground Association, 61
China. *See* People's Republic of China
    (PRC)
China Association for the Cooperation of
    International NGOs, 35
China Civil Affairs Statistical Yearbook, 25
China Disabled Persons Association, 92n.
    14
China Foundation for the Handicapped,
    27
China Qigong Scientific Research Society,
    81–82
China Youth Development Foundation,
    27, 35
China Youth League, 92n. 14
China Zhenhua Foundation, 27

Chinese Association for American Studies
    (CAAS), 36
Chinese Children's Fund (CCF), 53
Chinese Communist Party (CCP), 21
Chinese ethnic populations, 60, 188n. 12
Christian Children's Fund, 43, 53
Christianity, 30, 63, 141
Chun Doo-Whan, 99–100, 105
Chung Wah Wui Koon, 60
citizen ombudsmen, 116, 119–20
Citizens' Coalition for Economic Justice
    (CCEJ), 102–3, 106, *107*
citizens' groups, 99–101, 111, 116, 120–21
citizenship, 12, 186
City District Officer Scheme, 64
civic engagement, 32, 34, 38
CIVICUS Second World Assembly, 53
Civil Affairs Department, 28
civil rights, 153, 175
civil society. *See specific types of groups*
civil society organizations (CSOs), 3
class issues, 22, 101, 103, 112, 124, 155
Cold War, 95, 113–14, 121, 137
collaboration, 121, 160
collective action, 64–65
collectivism, 137
colonialism: decolonization, 59, 65, 67–68,
    172; and Hong Kong, 15, 16, 58,
    61–65, 67, 72, 77, 88, 89, 90; and legal
    environment of NGOs, 78; and South
    Korea, 98; and state-society split, 6–7;
    and Taipei, 77; and Vietnam, 124–30,
    143n. 3
Commercial Code (CC), 105
Commission for Disappearances and
    Victims of Violence (Kontras), 156,
    157–58
communal groups, 2, 123, 125, 129,
    136–37, 139–42
Commune People's Council, 131
communications, 12, 69, 121, 177. *See also*
    information technology; media
communism, 21, 86. *See also specific groups*
Communist Party, 80, 111, 125, 130, 133
Communist Youth League, 124–25
Community Chest, 63
community service. *See* social and
    community service groups
Confucian tradition, 6, 98, 140, 188n. 12
conservation, 26. *See also* environmental
    issues and groups
consultative democracy, 64–65
Consultative Group for Indonesia, 160

consumer groups, 9, 86–87, 180–81, 187
Consumer Protection Foundation, 88
control of NGOs. *See* restrictions on civil
  society
cooperation, 50, 69, 126, 151, 160, 166
co-opting of NGOs: Hong Kong, 59, 62,
  67, 69, 72, 89; Singapore, 171; South
  Korea, 101
corporate NGOs, 45, 110, 115. *See also*
  business-organized NGOs (BONGOs)
corporatism: China, 25, 30, 37, 79, 80,
  81–82, 91; and democratic transitions,
  11; and globalization, 14; Singapore,
  186; South Korea, 99; and state-society
  split, 17; Taiwan, 42, 56, 85–86, 87–88
corruption: China, 32; Indonesia, 156–57,
  158, 162–64, 165; Japan, 115, 116,
  119–20; South Korea, 105, 106;
  Vietnam, 130–32, 133, 135, 141
Corruption Eradication Commission, 157
Council of Young Entrepreneurs, 127
credit unions, 151. *See also* rotating-credit
  associations
cultural groups, 26, 43, 48, *49*, 73
cultural issues, 34, 185–86
Cultural Revolution, 6, 21, 29, 63, 79, 91

Dacom, 104
Daewoo Corporation, 104
danwei (work units), 21
Daoist Association, 85
Davos meetings, 1
debt, 166
decline of NGOs, 81
decolonization, 59, 65, 67–68, 172
defining civil society groups, 2–3, 24–27,
  96, 116, 142, 149–51
democracy and democratization:
  background of subject countries, 8;
  causality issue, 2, 10, 87; China, 24, 37;
  consultative democracy, 64–65;
  grassroots democracy, 133–34; Hong
  Kong, 66, 72, 88; Indonesia, 148–49,
  151–56, 161–62, 165; and the Internet,
  181–82; NGOs' role in, 5, 77, 91;
  pro-democracy demonstrations, 89;
  Singapore, 171, 178; and social capital,
  1–2; South Korea, 95, 97–99, 101, 107;
  Taiwan, 15, 44–45, 47, 50, 84, 87;
  transitions, 10–11
Democratic Progressive Party, 44
demonstrations. *See* protests and
  demonstrations

Deng Xiaoping, 20
Department of Social Affairs, 42
development of NGOs, 56, 59–68, 97,
  115–21
Dharma Drum Mountain, 53
Diep Dinh Hoa, 145n. 22
disaster relief, 78, 110, 114, 117
discrimination, 183
District Watch Committee, 60
diversity, regional, 14–17
donations. *See* funding for NGOs
Draft Law on Foundations, 152
dragon economies, 172
dualism in NGO development, 69
dual supervision, 25–26

Earth Summit, 1, 121
East Asian Deliberation on in Permanent,
  53
East Asian Women's Forum, 55
Eastern Europe, 1, 113
East Timor, 148
Ebert Foundation, 34
Echon Electric Company, 104
economic environment of NGOs: and
  Asian financial crisis, 171; bubble
  economy, 115, 117–18; China, 20–22,
  23; debt, 162–64; and environmental
  issues, 111, 112; and ethnicity issues,
  182–83; and future prospects, 186–87;
  Hong Kong, 68; Indonesia, 148–49,
  158, 162–64, 176; and Islam, 182;
  Japan, 113; market economy, 123; oil
  shocks, 112; reforms, 80; Singapore,
  171, 174–75; South Korea, 98–99;
  Taiwan, 44; and taxation, 135;
  unemployment, 23; Vietnam, 129,
  135–36
economic groups, 47, 86, *86*
Eden Social Welfare Foundation, 54
education and educational groups, 48, *49*,
  78, 125, 127, 139–40, 184–86
elderly associations, 125–26, 138, 139
elections, 65–68, 71, 93n. 16, 99, 155,
  167n. 4, 176
electronic media, 5
El Muhir, H. A. Fadloli, 158
Employment Ordinance, 64
The End of the Nation State (Ohmae), 12
endowments, 45, 46, 85
environmental groups and issues: and
  authoritarianism, 9; and democratic
  transitions, 10; illegal groups, 29;

Indonesia, 159–60, 167; Japan,
110–12, 115, 118, 121, 121n. 2, 121n.
5; and NGO funding, 85–87;
Singapore, 180–81, 187; Taiwan, 52,
55
Environmental Impact Monitoring Board,
160
Environmental Investigation Agency, 55
Environmental Law, 160
ethnicity. *See* race and ethnicity
Europe, 2, 116
Executive Council, 72
Executive Yuan, 46

Fagushan, 53
Falun Gong movement, 13, 25, 30, 36, 37,
81–82
famine relief associations, 78
Fateh, 184
Fatherland Front, 124–25, 134, 138, 143n.
6
Federation of Cultural and Artistic
Associations, 128
Female Migrant Workers' Association, 30
finances of NGOs. *See* funding for NGOs
First National Conference on the
Management of Social Organizations,
22
Fisherman's Service Center, 54
Foguangshan, 53
Ford Foundation, 34–36, 160–62
foreign funding, 17, 20, 35–38, 148, 152,
166, 172
Foundation for the Development of
China's Youth, 92n. 14
foundations, 24, 27, 43, 45–46, 48–49,
151–52. *See also specific organizations*
free speech, 174–76
Friedrich Naumann Foundation, 178
friendship groups, 30, 37, 47, *49*, 81, 86,
86
Friends of Nature (FON), 26, 31, 81, 88
Friends of the Earth, 121
Friends of the Environment Fund, 159
functions of NGOs, *49*, 51–52, 83, 96,
160. *See also* methods employed by
NGOs
funding for NGOs: amounts of, 35; and
autonomy, 6; cases compared, 82;
donations, 30–34, 48–49, 88; foreign,
17, 20, 35–38, 148, 152, 166, 172; and
globalization, 34; governmental, 89;
international, 17, 128–29; Japan, 119;

membership fees, 139; Singapore, 177,
180; sources listed, *33*; South Korea,
101–2; Taiwan, 45–46, 85; and
taxation, 92n. 14, 135; uses of, 35–36;
Vietnam, 126, 141, 144n. 8, 144n. 9,
144n. 10, 144n. 13
funerals, 125–26

Gansu province, 76
Garden of Hope Foundation, 55
General Confederation of Labor, 124–25
geopolitics, 183–84
Germany, 116
Giddens, Anthony, 12
Global Fund for Women, 35
globalization: cases compared, 90; China,
20, 34–37; and colonialism, 15; global
civil society, 185; Hong Kong, 79;
impact on civil society, 12–14;
Indonesia, 149; and Islam, 182–85;
Japan, 117; and policy advocacy,
120–21; Singapore, 175, 177, 178–79;
South Korea, 95, 106; Taiwan, 52–54,
56; Vietnam, 123, 126
Global Village Environmental Cultural
Institute of Beijing (GECIB), 27, 35
Goh Chok Tong, 171
Golker Party, 158
Gomez, James, 177–78
government-organized nongovernmental
organizations (GONGOs), 3, 26, 150
Gramsci, Antonio, 155
Grassroots Democracy Decree, 142
Great Britain, 5, 15, 58, 59
Great Leap Forward, 91
Green Consumers' Foundation, 55
Green Earth Volunteers (GEV), 29
Green Frontline, 55
Greenpeace, 110, 121, 121n. 1
growth and proliferation of NGOs: cases
compared, 79, 90, 93n. 18; China, 80;
Indonesia, 153; Japan, 117; South
Korea, 95–97; Vietnam, 126
Guangzhou, China, 26, *33*, 77–84, 89–90,
93n. 18
Guangzhou Handicapped Youth
Association, 26–27
Guo Jianmei, 28

Habibie, Bacharuddin Jusuf, 157
Hafid, Wardah, 158
Haixong Qiu, 83
Hakka culture, 43

Hall, Peter Dobkin, 6
handicapped persons, 26–27
Hanoi, 128–29
health-care, 126, 127
Heisei period, 114
hierarchy of NGOs, 2, 60
Hikam, Mohammad, 167
Hinduism, 6
Hirohito, 113–14, 116
hobby groups, 128
Ho Chi Minh City, 128–29
Hokosawa, Morihiro, 114
Home Affairs Department, 150
Home Affairs Ministry, 152
Homemakers' Union and Foundation, 55
Hong Kong, 58–74; and China, 7;
    Chinese population, 60; and
    colonialism, 15–16, 72; contemporary
    groups, 68–71; democratization, 11;
    demonstrations, 9; and globalization,
    79; growth of NGOs in, 93n. 18;
    historical background, 58–59, 59–68;
    legal environment of NGOs, 76, 78;
    NGO development in, 88–90;
    participatory modes of NGOs in, *70*;
    relationship with Taiwan, 54; return to
    Chinese authority, 65; study of NGOs
    in, 4, 77; support for Chinese NGOs,
    35, 38; and zero-sum approach, 6
Hong Kong Anti-TB and Thoracic
    Association, 63
Hong Kong Christian Service, 61
Hong Kong Council of Social Service, 61
Hong Kong Family Welfare Society, 63
Hong Kong Professional Teachers' Union,
    65
Hope Workers' Center, 54
House of Representatives (Indonesia),
    167n. 4
Humane Society, 55
human rights, 12, 54, 76, 149, 156–58,
    167

ideological frameworks, 136–42, 143
illegal organizations, 29
immigration. *See* migrant labor
Imperial Constitution, 111
income of NGOs. *See* funding for NGOs
independence movements, 5–6, 36, 86,
    143n. 4
India, 152
indigenous populations, 29, 54, 158–59
indirect rule, 89

Indochinese Communist Party (ICP), 133
Indonesia, 148–67; background of NGOs,
    148–49; debt and corruption, 162–64;
    definition of NGOs, 149–51;
    democratization, 2, 10, 153–56;
    demonstrations, 9, 11; and foreign
    NGO funding, 36; and globalization,
    14; international coalitions, 160–62;
    and Islam, 16, 185; legal context of
    NGOs, 151–52; NGO/state
    engagement, 156–60; prospect for
    NGOs, 164–67; social movements, 10
Indonesian Corruption Watch, 156–57,
    163
Indonesian Democratic Party of Struggle,
    158
Indonesian Democratic Party (PDI),
    158–59
Indonesian Environmental Network, 156,
    159
Industrial and Commercial Bureau, 35
industrialization, 63, 98–99, 111
influence of NGOs, 47–52
informal sector, 9, 16, 91
information disclosure, 119–20
information technology, 12, 117, 121, 177
Initiative for Heavily Indebted Poor
    Countries (HIPC), 163
Institute of Environment and
    Development, 36
Institute of Policy Studies, 181
institutionalization of NGOs, 4, 116–17
interest groups, 64–65, 89
intermediate organizations, 28–29, 77–78
Internal Security Act, 174, 184
International Campaign to Ban
    Landmines, 54
International Covenant on Civil and
    Political Rights, 88
International Economic and Technology
    Exchange Center, 35
International Forum for Indonesian
    Development (INFID), 154, 162–63
International Forum on Sex Worker
    Rights and Sex Industrial Policy, 55
International Monetary Fund (IMF),
    12–13, 14, 148, 160–61, 163, 166
International NGO Forum on Indonesia,
    162
international nongovernmental
    organizations (INGOs): described, 3;
    funding sources, 38; and globalization,
    12, 13; Indonesia, 160–62, 166; Japan,

121; Singapore, 179–80; South
Korea, 95; Vietnam, 127, 128–29,
144n. 8
Internet, 178–79, 181–82, 187
Iranian Revolution, 183
iron triangle, 115, 116
Islam: in Indonesia, 16, 153, 162;
mobilizing potential, 10; and
oppositional politics, 6; in Singapore, 4,
176, 182–85, 187, 188n. 6

Japan, 110–21; civil protest, 5; and
colonialism, 77, 78, 98; control of social
sector, 15–16; and democracy, 2, 8;
and globalization, 14; historical
background, 111–15; NGO
development in, 110, 115–21;
Sino-Japanese War, 62–63; social
movements, 10–11, 113; and
state-society split, 7
Japan Foundation, 34
Japan New Party, 114
Jeyaratnam, J. B., 177–78
Jihad vs. McWorld (Barber), 12
Jubilee Plus, 164
judicial systems, 156
Junior Chambers of Commerce (JC
International), 43

kaifong, 58, 59–60, 62
Kim Dae Jung, 101
Kim Young Sam, 99, 100–101, 106
Kin-man Chan, 83
kinship groups, 2, 123–24, 126, 129,
136–37, 139, 142
Kiwanis, 43
Kobe earthquake, 110, 114, 117–18
Kontras, 156, 157–58, 167
Korea. *See* South Korea
Korea First Bank, 103
Korean Federation for Environmental
Movement (KFEM), 118, 121n. 5
Korea Securities Exchange, 105
Kuomintang (KMT), 42, 44, 52, 56,
84–85, 87

labor groups, 9, 52, 61–62, 72, 78, 88,
98–99
land reform, 124, 134, 137, 144n. 17,
145n. 20
Latin America, 17
lawsuits, 103–5, 158. *See also* legal
environment of NGOs

Law to Promote Specified Non-Profit
Activities (NPO law), 110
Leadership for Environment and
Development, 36
leadership of NGOs, 5
Lee Kuan Yew, 171, 172, 176, 181
Lee Teng-hui, 43
legal environment of NGOs: cases
compared, 76; China, 3, 8, 76; and
colonialism, 15, 78; Hong Kong,
88–90; illegal groups, 29; Indonesia,
151–52, 155–56, 158; Japan, 110,
114–15, 116; Singapore, 173, 177–78;
South Korea, 103–5; and state
boundaries, 3; Taiwan, 46–47, 84–85
Legislative Yuan, 44
leisure time, 23
Liang Congjie, 26
Liberal Democratic Party (LDP), 2, 113,
115, 116
liberalism, 37, 90, 149, 153–54
liberalization, 20–22, 43–45, 95, 178–79
Liberal Party, 71
Life Conservationist Association, 55
life-cycle ceremonies, 140–41, 145n. 22
lineage groups, 4, 81, 125, 139–41
Lingnan Foundation, 34
Lin Junyi, 93n. 16
Lions Club, 43
Listed Company Regulations (LCR), 105
local governance: Hong Kong, 63–65;
Japan, 112; local civil society, 1, 9–10,
127, 138–42, 166, 176–81;
ombudsmen, 119–20; Taiwan, 50;
Vietnam, 130–36, 138, 142
Lok Sin Tong, 60
longevity of NGOs, 68, *100*
lost decade, 110, 116
Lu, Annette, 93n. 16
Luce, 34
Luoshan Civic Center, 27

MacArthur Foundation, 34
Madrasahs, 183
Maki, Japan, 120
Malay-Muslim populations, 182–85
Malaysia: control of social sector, 16; and
Islam, 185; legal environment of
NGOs, 152; and proxy NGOs, 9; racial
makeup, 188n. 4; Singapore's
separation from, 172; and state-society
split, 7
Male Migrant Workers' Association, 30

Management Method of Foundations, 24, 27
Man Mo Temple, 59–60
Mao Tse-tung, 21
marginalized groups, 10
martial law, 85, 91
Marxism, 22, 124, 136–37, 138
mass nonenterprise units, 27
Matthews, Jessica, 90
McDonald's, 12
media, 62, 155, 171, 174, 178, 181
Mekong Delta, 124, 136, 137
membership-centered associations, 45–46, 48–49, 85–86, 102, 110, 139
merchants' associations, 61
methods employed by NGOs, 103, *104*, *107*, 119–20
middle-class: China, 22, 32; Hong Kong, 71; Indonesia, 153; Singapore, 175, 182, 184; South Korea, 98–99; Taiwan, 43, 56
Migrant Forum, 54
migrant labor, 12, 30, 54, 58, 62–63, 135
Migrant Workers' Concern Desk, 54
militant movements, 99–100
military coups, 105
military service, 140–41, 183
Minamata disease, 111, 121n. 2
Ministry of Civil Affairs, 81
Ministry of Finance and Economy, 105
Ministry of Information, 155
Ministry of Interior Affairs, 85
minjung groups, 9, 99–100, 103
Minority Shareholders' Rights Movement, 103–5
Mishima, Japan, 111
missionaries, 61
Miyagi, Japan, 120
mobilization, 62, 64–69, 71, 73, 138
modernization, 4, 97. *See also* globalization
monitoring role of NGOs, 51
Muhammadijah, 151
multinational corporations, 13
Murayama, Tomiichi, 114
mutual assistance, 141. *See also* rotating-credit associations
Myanmar, 180

Nahdlatul Ulama, 151
Nakasone, Yasuhiro, 114
Nam Pak Hong Guild, 60
National Assembly (South Korea), 106
National Assembly (Vietnam), 131

National Citizen Ombudsman Liaison Council, 119–20
National Human Rights Commission, 156, 158
nationalism, 148, 166, 185–86
Nationalist Party, 84, 86
National People's Congress (NPC), 22, 88
National Salvation associations, 143n. 4
National Science Foundation, 27
National Social Science Fund, 27, 32
National Trades Union Congress, 173, 181
Nature Society, 180, 187
negotiated governance, 7–8, 17, 96–98, 98–102, 102–6, 107
neighborhood groups, 59–60, 62, *70*, 125
neoliberalism, 76–77, 79
networks, 140
New Economy and Globalization programs, 106
New Frontier Party, 114
"new knowledge class," 45
New National Comprehensive Development Plan, 111
New Order regime, 150, 153–55, 167
New Party Sakigake, 114
newsgroups, 181
New Sintercom, 181
Newspaper and Printing Presses Act, 174, 179
NGO Forum on Women, 76
Niigata, Japan, 121n. 2
nonprofit organizations (NPOs): China, 24, 27, 30; Japan, 115–19, 121n. 3; South Korea, 101; Taiwan, 85
nuclear power, 112, 120, 121
Numazu, Japan, 111
number of NGOs. *See also* growth and proliferation of NGOs: China, 24–25, 37, 80; Indonesia, 149–50; source materials, 77; South Korea, *100*; Taiwan, 47

oil shocks, 112
ombudsmen, 116, 119–20
opposition movements, 5
organization of NGOs, 68–69, 117–19
organized crime, 88
Oxfam, 34, 35
oyake concept, 118

Pancasila ideology, 11, 151–55, 165

parallel society, 21
Park Chun Hee, 99, 105
Parliament (Indonesia), 167n. 4
participation of NGOs, 23, *70*
Partnership for Governance Reform, 160
patrilineage associations, 125, 139–41
patronized groups, 28, 29, 37
Patten, Chris, 67
peasant associations, 124, 138, 143n. 4
People First Party (PFP), 52
People for Ethical Treatment of Animals
  (PETA), 55
People's Action Party (PAP), 171, 172–76,
  176–81, 183–84, 186–87
People's Aid Coordinating Committee
  (PACCOM), 127–28
People's Consultative Council, 154
People's Deliberative Council, 157,
  167n. 4
People's Republic of China (PRC), 20–38;
  Constitution, 80; control of social
  sector, 16; Cultural Revolution, 6, 21,
  29, 63, 79, 91; democratization, 10;
  ethnic groups, 184; and globalization,
  14, 34–37; growth of NGOs, 87,
  93n. 18; and Hong Kong, 7, 73, 89;
  legal environment of NGOs, 3, 8, 76;
  NGO funding and autonomy, 30–34;
  political changes, 2; prospects for
  NGOs, 37–38; provinces compared,
  79–84; and proxy NGOs, 9; reforms
  and transition, 20–22; Republican
  period, 78; role of NGOs, 22–24;
  Sino-Japanese War, 62–63; sovereignty
  issues, 13; study of NGOs in, 15, 77;
  Taiwan-China relationship, 53–54, 56,
  91; types of NGOs, 24–27; unregistered
  groups, 28–30
People's Solidarity for Participatory
  Democracy (PSPD), 102–3, *104*
philanthropic organizations, 43, 46, 62–63.
  See also charitable groups
Philately Association, 128
Philippines, 165, 185
Phu Tho province, 123
pilgrimage associations, 78
Pink Collar Solidarity, 55
place-of-origin associations, 61, 78, 81
Po Leung Kuk, 60, 62
policy advocacy, 96–97, 103, 105, 107,
  117, 119–21
policy-favored household associations, 139,
  140–41

political actions of NGOs, *104*, *107*
political environment of NGOs: and
  colonialism, 15; Hong Kong, 69–71,
  70; Indonesia, 153, 155–56, 167;
  oppositional politics, 5; Taiwan, 44–45;
  Vietnam, 123
political parties. *See also specific parties*:
  Hong Kong, 68, 88; Indonesia,
  150–52, 155, 157; Japan, 114;
  Singapore, 176, 178, 188n. 4, 188n. 5,
  188n. 7
pollution, 121n. 2. *See also* environmental
  issues and groups
post-totalitarianism, 22
poverty, 13–14, 63, 136, 145n. 19, 158–59,
  164
press, 62
pressure groups, 64–65, 66, 69
private enterprise associations, 31
Private Entrepreneurs Association, 83
privatization, 5, 21–22, 76, 126
procedural democracy, 2
professional groups, 25, 47, 48, *49*, 86, *86*,
  125
Project Hope Foundation, 27, 35, 92n. 14
prostitution, 55
Protestantism, 61, 125
protest groups, *49*, 52, 59, 113
protests and demonstrations: agrarian
  unrest, 134–36; civil protest, 5; and
  corruption, 130–32; and democratic
  transitions, 11; Hong Kong, 62–65, 67,
  71–73, 89; Japan, 117; Singapore, 173;
  South Korea, 103; Taiwan, 44;
  Vietnam, 132–34
Provisional Legislative Council, 88–89
Provisional Method for Registration of
  Social Organizations, 24–25
Provisional Regulation on the Registration
  and Management of Mass
  Nonenterprise Units, 24
proxy NGOs, 9, 11
Public Entertainment Act, 174
Public Entertainment Licensing Unit
  (PELU), 174, 178, 188n. 6
Public Transportation Commission, 180
Putnam, Robert, 1–2, 4

qigong groups (breathing exercise groups),
  28, 81–82
Qing Dynasty, 77
quasi-NGOs (QUANGOs), 3
Quynh Hoa commune, 132–34

race and ethnicity, 60, 159, 165, 172–76, 182–87, 188n. 4, 188n. 12
Reagan, Ronald, 5
Real Name Financial Transaction and Protection of Confidentiality Act, 106
Real Name Financial Transaction and Secrecy Act, 106
Real Name Transaction Proposal, 103, 105–6
Real Name Transaction System, 106
Recruit company, 115
Red Cross, 78, 125, 128–29, 141, 144n. 9
Red River Delta, 136, 141, 143n. 1, 145n. 19
referenda, 116, 120
reformism, 86, 103–5, 116, 149, 152, 154, 162
refugees, 62–63
regional diversity, 14–17
regional groups, 30, 62
regionalization, 52–54, 56
registration of NGOs, *26*, *33*, 81, 85, 88–89, 92n. 13, 129
regulation of NGOs, restrictions on civil society
Regulation on the Registration and Management of Social Organizations, 24–25
relevancy of NGOs, 102
religion and religious groups. *See also specific religions*: China, 26, 29–30, 37, 78, 81; conflicts with states, 187; Hong Kong, 61, 63, *70*, 71; Indonesia, 16, 153, 162; mobilizing potential, 10; religious conflicts, 165, 174, 182–85, 185–86; religious international NGOs (RINGOs), 3; Singapore, 4, 176, 182–85, 187, 188n. 6; South Korea, 101; Taiwan, 47, 85, *86*; Vietnam, 124–25, 136–37, 141–42
Religious Harmony Act, 185
Remaking Singapore Committee, 176
Renewable Energy Promoting People's Forum, 121
renovation policy, 129
repression of NGOs, 141, 150, 165, 174, 179
research organizations, 128
restrictions on civil society. *See also* legal environment of NGOs: China, 24; and corporatism, 81–82; financial controls, 31; Japan, 118; Singapore, 186–87;

supervision, 37, 46, 81, 88; Taiwan, 42, 46–47; Vietnam, 123
Rio Summit, 1
Rockefeller Brothers Fund, 34
Rockefeller Foundation, 34–36
Roh Tae Woo, 99, 100, 106
roles of NGOs, *49*, 51–52, 83, 96, 160. *See also* methods employed by NGOs
Rotary Club, 43
rotating-credit associations, 125–26, 139–40, 141
Royal Society for Prevention of Cruelty to Animals Australia, 55

Salamon, Lester, 3
Salim, Emil, 150, 160
Salvation Army, 61
Samsung, 104
Sanhe Hui, 88
Sarvodaya, 6
Save the Children Fund, 35
scandals. *See* corruption
second economy, 21, 22
Securities and Exchange Act (SEC), 105
Securities Related Class Action Act, 105
Security Transaction Act, 105
Sedition Law, 89
self-help groups, *49*, 186
September 11 attacks, 182, 184, 185
service-oriented groups, 45
sex industry, 55
SG-Daily, 181
shareholder's rights, 104
share-holding associations, 77–78
Shepherd's Foundation, 55
Shimizu, Japan, 111
Shizuoka, Japan, 111
Showa period, 113
Singapore, 171–87; authoritarianism, 8–9; background, 171; control of social sector, 16; democratization, 2, 11; and foreign NGO funding, 36; and globalization, 14; and the Internet, 181–82; and Islam, 4, 10, 16, 182–85; legal environment of NGOs, 152; local civil society, 176–81; new nationalism, 185–86; prospects for NGOs, 186–87; social controls, 172–76; and state-society relationship, 7
Singapore Broadcasting Authority (SBA), 178–79, 181
Singapore 21 Committee, 176
Singapore Democratic Party, 188n. 7

Singapore Forum, 181
Sino-Japanese War, 62–63
Sintercom, 5, 178–79, 181
size of NGOs, *48*, 68, 118, 121n. 5
social and community service groups: and
   authoritarianism, 8–10; China, 22–23,
   24; and democratic transitions, 10–11;
   disaster relief, 78, 110, 114, 117;
   Hong Kong, 61, 63–67, 69, *70*, 72;
   Indonesia, 150–51; international
   support, 1; Japan, 111; and political
   transitions, 4; Taiwan, 43, 44–45, 47,
   48, *49*, 51; Vietnam, 123, 126, 128;
   welfare groups, 21, 47, 48, *49*, 63–64,
   86
social capital, 1–2, 4, 5, 23, 38, 140–41
social conflicts, 73
Social Democratic Party, 111
Social Development Bureau, 27
social entrepreneurship, 102–6
socialism, 15, 22, 116, 127, 144n. 14
Social Monitoring and Early Response
   Unit, 164
Social Organizations Law, 151–52
Social Service Centre of the Churches, 61
social welfare, 21, 52, 56, 87, 110
Societies Act, 177–78
Societies Office, 88
Societies Ordinance, 60, 88–89
Society for Chinese Culture Study, 29
Society for Community Organization, 65
Society for the Protection of Women and
   Girls, 60
Soetjipto, Adi Andojo, 157
Solidarity Front of Women Workers, 55
Son Duong commune, 123, 125, 130–32,
   134–36, 137–38, 142, 143n. 1
Sourcebook on National Integrity Systems, 163
South Korea, 95–107; civil protest, 5;
   control of social sector, 15–16;
   corporatism, 8; democracy in, 2, 10,
   15; demonstrations, 9; and
   globalization, 14; growth of NGOs in,
   95–97; negotiated governance, 98–102;
   NGO case studies, 102–6; policy
   impact of NGOs, 110; prospects for
   NGOs, 107; scope of study, 3; social
   movements, 10–11, 113; and
   state-society split, 7, 17; status of
   NGOs, 121
sovereignty, 12–13, 88–90, 148, 155
Soviet Union, 113
Special Administrative Region of the

People's Republic of China (SAR)
   government, 65–68, 69, 71–73
sponsorship of NGOs, 101–2, 119. *See also*
   funding for NGOs
spontaneous local associations, 138–42
Sport Association of the Handicapped, 128
sports groups, 26, 73, 128
Sri Lanka, 6
St. James Settlement, 63
staff of NGOs, 50, 101, 102–3
state support for NGOs, 30–34, 124.
   See also funding for NGOs;
   government-organized
   nongovernmental organizations
   (GONGOs)
strikes, 61, 62, 87
structure of NGOs, 11, 60
student movements, 67, 153, 173
Study Encouragement Association, 128
Suharto: environment for NGOs under,
   150–51, 151–52, 159, 165, 167; final
   year in office, 157; and international
   NGOs, 162; resignation, 148, 155;
   social ties under, 16
Sukarnoputri, Megawati, 158
Sumatra, 150
Supreme Court (Indonesia), 157
surname associations, 78
sustainable development, 159, 162. *See also*
   environmental groups and issues
Sutiyoso, 158, 159

Taipei, Taiwan, 77–79, 84–88, 90
Taipei Alliance of Licensed Prostitutes
   (TALP), 55
Taipei Women Rescue Foundation, 55
Taiwan, 42–56; authoritarian rule, 42–45;
   characterizing NGOs in, 47–52;
   control of social sector, 15–16;
   corporatism, 8; current state of NGOs,
   45–47; and decolonization, 91;
   democracy in, 2, 10, 15; DPP
   government, 52; and globalization, 14,
   52–55; growth of NGOs, 79, 93n. 18;
   historical development, 42; legal
   environment of NGOs, 3, 76; NGO
   development in, 84–88; policy impact
   of NGOs, 110; and proxy NGOs, 9;
   social movements, 10, 113; and
   state-society split, 7, 17; status of
   NGOs, 121; study of NGOs in, 77;
   Taiwan-China relationship, 53–54, 56
Taiwan Association for Human Rights, 54

Taiwan Environmental Protection Union
(TEPU), 55, 118, 121–22n. 5
Taiwan Grassroots Women Workers'
Center, 54
Taiwan National Committee to End
Child-Prostitution in Asian Tourism,
55
Takeshita, Noboru, 115
Tan Soo Koon, 176
taxation: Hong Kong, 88; and NGO
funding, 92n. 14; South Korea, 101,
103, 106; Taiwan, 46, 85–86;
Vietnam, 123, 130–32, 133, 135–36,
144–45n. 18
temple associations, 85
terrorism, 114, 167, 176, 182, 184–85
Thai Binh province, 132–34, 134–36,
141–42
Thailand, 12, 165, 185
Thatcher, Margaret, 5
Think Center, 177–78, 179
Third East Asian Fundraising Workshop,
53
third sector, 23, 97, 101
Tiananmen Square, 24, 67, 81
Tiandi Hui, 88
Tibet independence movement, 36
Time for Environment (program), 27
Tokyo Electric Power Company, 121
tongs, 60–61
totalitarianism, 20–22, 23, 79. *See also*
authoritarianism
trade unions, 61, 62, 143n. 4, 173
traditional organizations, 29
Tran Duc Luong, 132, 133, 135
transaction costs, 140
Transparency International, 163
Transparent Society Indonesia, 163
triad societies, 88
trust, 32, 38, 140
Tung Chee-hwa, 71
Tung Wah, 60, 62
Turner Foundation, 35
Tusk Force, 55
types of social organizations: cases
compared, *86*; China, 24–27, *26*, 83;
Hong Kong, 73; listed, 3; Taiwan,
45–47, *47*
Tz'u-Chi foundation, 53

underground organizations, 30
unemployment, 23
Union of Cooperatives, 127

Union of Cultural and Artistic
Associations, 125
Union of Literary and Artistic
Associations, 127
Union of Science and Technology
Associations, 125
Union of Scientific and Technological
Associations, 127
Union of Sport Cyclists and Motorcyclists,
128
unions. *See also specific organizations*:
China, 30; Hong Kong, 64; labor
unions, 72, 78, 88, 99; Singapore,
172; trade unions, 61, 62, 143n. 4,
173
United Kingdom, 5, 15, 58, 59
United Nations Development Programme
(UNDP), 35, 76
United Nations Earth Summit, 1
United Nations Fourth World Conference
on Women, 76
United Nations (UN), 12–13, 43, 148–49,
160
United Nations Women's Conference
(Beijing), 1
United States: and environmental issues,
121; Indonesia's relationship with, 148;
Japanese perceptions of, 113, 116; and
NGO autonomy, 6; pragmatism, 118;
and privatization, 5; Singapore's
relationship with, 184; war on
terrorism, 167
United States Agency for International
Development (USAID), 1, 76, 160,
161, 166
United States Department of State, 161
unregistered groups, 28–30
Urban Council, 64
Urban Poor Consortium, 156, 158–59,
167
Urban Renewal Authority, 71
US-Japan Security Treaty, 111

veterans associations, 125, 129, 137, 138
Vietnam, 123–43; agrarian unrest,
134–36; alternate civilities, 136–42;
control of social sector, 16; corruption,
9–10; democratization, 10; and
globalization, 14; historical
background, 124–30; political changes,
2; public conflicts, 130–34; scope of
NGO study, 3, 4; voluntary association
development, 123–24

Vietnamese Chamber of Industry and Commerce, 127
Vietnamese Communist Party (VCP), 124–25, 143n. 4
Vietnamese Historical Association, 125
Vietnamese Journalists Association, 125
Vietnamese Lawyers Association, 128
Vietnamese National Assembly, 137
Vietnam Union of Friendship Organizations (VUFO), 127
violence, 11, 132, 158
voluntary associations: and communal ties, 4; Hong Kong, 72; Indonesia, 153; South Korea, 102; Taiwan, 69; Vietnam, 124–30

Wahana Lingkungan Hidup Indonesia (WALHI), 163
Wahid, Abdurrachman, 154–55
Wanghai Online, 88
wealth equity issues: China, 22; and globalization, 13–14; Japan, 113; and NGO establishment, 5; Singapore, 175; South Korea, 103, 106; Taiwan, 47; Vietnam, 135–37, 142
weddings, 125–26
welfare groups, 21, 47, 48, *49*, 63–64, *86*. *See also* social and community service groups
welfare states, 113
western influence on NGOs, 6, 38, 43, 163, 166
Westphalia system, 90
Women Awakening Foundation, 55

Women's Federation, 78
women's issues and groups, 9, 55, 87, 162, 180, 187, 188n. 6
Women's Legal Studies and Service Center, 28
Women's Union, 124, 125, 138
Workers Party, 178
work units, 21
World Bank: inclusion of NGOs, 1; and Indonesia, 148, 163–64; living standard surveys, 136, 144–45n. 18; monitors of, 162; and political corruption, 158; reliance on NGOs, 76–77, 90, 160–61, 166
World Forum on Capital Cities, 55
World Society for Protection of Animals, 55
World Trade Organization (WTO), 12–13, 80, 95
World Vision, 35, 43, 53
World War II, 113
World Wide Fund for Nature, 121
World Wildlife Fund, 35, 90
Writers Association, 128

Xiamen, China, 77, 78, 79–84, 89–90, 93n. 18

Yeo, George, 176
Young Men's Christian Association (YMCA), 27, 53, 61, 78
youth groups, 32, 113
Youth Union, 124, 125, 138

Zhu Rongji, 22

For Product Safety Concerns and Information please contact our EU
representative GPSR@taylorandfrancis.com
Taylor & Francis Verlag GmbH, Kaufingerstraße 24, 80331 München, Germany

www.ingramcontent.com/pod-product-compliance
Lightning Source LLC
Chambersburg PA
CBHW072132270326
41931CB00010B/1733